Rolling Out New Products Across International Markets

Also by George M. Chryssochoidis

INTERNATIONALISATION STRATEGIES (*co-editor*)

Rolling Out New Products Across International Markets

Causes of Delays

George M. Chryssochoidis

First published 2004 by
PALGRAVE MACMILLAN
Houndmills, Basingstoke, Hampshire RG21 6XS and
175 Fifth Avenue, New York, N.Y. 10010
Companies and representatives throughout the world

PALGRAVE MACMILLAN is the global academic imprint of the Palgrave
Macmillan division of St. Martin's Press, LLC and of Palgrave Macmillan Ltd.
Macmillan® is a registered trademark in the United States, United Kingdom
and other countries. Palgrave is a registered trademark in the European
Union and other countries.

ISBN 0–333–79464–8

This book is printed on paper suitable for recycling and made from fully
managed and sustained forest sources.

A catalogue record for this book is available from the British Library.

Library of Congress Cataloging-in-Publication Data
Chryssochoidis, George.
    Rolling out new products across international markets : causes of
delays / by George M. Chryssochoidis.
        p.   cm.
    Includes bibliographical references and index.
    ISBN 0–333–79464–8
    1. New products—Management—Mathematical models.   2. Time to market
(New products)—Mathematical models.   3. Product management—
Mathematical models.   4. Export marketing—Mathematical models.   I. Title.
    HF5415.153.C47 2003
    658.8'48—dc21   2003043144

10   9   8   7   6   5   4   3   2   1
13   12   11   10   09   08   07   06   05   04

Printed and bound in Great Britain by
Antony Rowe Ltd, Chippenham and Eastbourne

Contents

List of Figures

List of Tables

Acknowledgements

I would like to acknowledge many people and institutions for their support. I am grateful to all those executives who refined my thinking during the development of this research and spared their time to share their experiences with me. In relation to this, it is important to mention that some 6 years have passed since data collection, so some company practices that might have been considered confidential at the time may now be publicised. However, specific company details that may be considered strictly confidential have been omitted.

I am also grateful to the University of Wales, Cardiff Business School, for financial support for travelling and many colleagues for their valuable encouragement. I would also like to thank the participants of the following conferences where parts of this project were presented: Workshop on New Product Development, UMIST, 1994; EMAC Conference, 1994 and EMAC Doctoral Workshop, 1995; MEG Conferences, 1995 and 1996; and 3rd and 5th International New Product Development Conference, 1996 and 1998. Many respected academics provided invaluable comments during the evolution of this project, including Professors D. Diamantopoulos, J. Ettlie, A. Johne, G. Gemünden, K. Grønhaug, G. Lilien, K. Peattie, J. Saunders and Dr C. Strong.

I am also grateful to Professor Veronica Wong, who has been *unparalleled* as a supervisor for my PhD thesis from which the present book draws most of its content. Many thanks to Veronica for all her support, patience, effort and time.

On a personal note, I am grateful to Christopher, Georges and Micheline, who have helped me during long periods, and my mother: I am not sure if I will ever be able to return even a small part of her affection and support. Last but not least, I would like to thank Olga for so much during so many years. There is simply no way to express my gratitude to her. Let me, though, dedicate this to Minas and Nectaria: after all, I haven't asked them if they want to go out for a walk with their dad for a long time.

GEORGE M. CHRYSSOCHOIDIS

The author and publishers are grateful to the following for permission to reproduce copyright material: *International Marketing Review* for a figure in Wong, Veronica (2002) 'Antecedents of International New Product Rollout Timeliness', *International Marketing Review*, vol. 19, no. 2, pp. 120–32; and *Academy of Management Review* for two figures in Brown, Shona L. and Eisenhardt, Kathleen M. (1995) 'Product Development: Past Research, Present Findings, and Future Directions', *Academy of Management Review*, vol. 20, pp. 343–78.

Summary

The problem of delays in product rollout becomes more unwieldy for new products that are being launched across many countries. This concern arises when firms operate in rapid technological change and high internationalisation business environments.

This study aims to form an empirically based body of knowledge about rollout of new products across international markets, to build strong theory and to provide insights for better practice. The study focuses on both static and dynamic aspects of the management of new product rollout across international markets. The investigation considers an extensive set of variables describing the company's external and internal environment, as well as the company's action across borders. It attempts more precisely to identify:

- whether timeliness in new product rollout relates to new product success;
- whether companies roll out new products across their international markets simultaneously or sequentially; and
- the factors that lead to delay in rollout schedules and their interaction.

A six-phase research methodology was designed and implemented. These phases were: (1) a review of literature across several streams of research; (2) a pilot telephone interview study; (3) exploratory interviews in six companies and a preliminary cross-case analysis; (4) the refinement of methodological and theoretical framework issues; (5) an additional series of research interviews in 24 more companies; and (6) a second cross-case analysis. These were followed by the formulation of a model and the estimation of the magnitude of direct, indirect and total effects of each factor upon rollout timeliness. The main findings were:

- Timely rolled-out projects were far more successful than delayed rolled-out projects.
- Sequential new product rollouts were more frequent than simultaneous ones. Delays were consistently featured in the cases of sequential new product rollouts.

The main factors that lead to delay in rollout schedules were: insufficiency of marketing and technological resources, poor internal communications between the HQ and the country markets, lack of synergies in product handling by the sales force in both the HQ and the country markets, lack of synergies in customer familiarity with the product, lack of proficiency in the new product development process, and a deficient product.

Finally, the area and the findings of the project have been revisited about 5 years since its completion in an attempt to shed light on those issues that have retained significance over the years, considering the developments of current research, and those that have not. Chapter 7 explains these issues.

Cases of specific company new product projects are described in the Appendix. The names of the companies and some information have been disguised.

1
An Overview

1.1 Introduction

This chapter provides an overview of the present research. It discusses first the area under investigation and the status of the relevant theory. The problem under investigation and the research objectives are then described, together with a summary of the structure of this book.

1.2 Rolling out new products across international markets

The environment in which organisations operate is becoming increasingly dynamic and international. And it is to be expected that 'the more change there is in the firm's environment, the greater the need to develop the product mix constantly, so as it matches the environment' (Hart, 1988, p. 1). Consequently, it is likely that organisations will constantly have to seek the appropriate development and rollout of new products for international markets. Many researchers have devoted their attention to the study of new product development (Montoya-Weiss and Calantone, 1994; Brown and Eisenhardt, 1995) or diffusion of new products (Mahajan and Peterson, 1985; Sultan *et al.*, 1990) in a domestic market context. Although it is still important to examine new product activities in domestic markets it is critical to investigate new product rollout in a multi-country context. There is strong evidence that competition is becoming more international or global in an increasing number of sectors (Porter, 1986; Kobrin, 1991) and it is crucial to penetrate overseas countries in quick succession with new products to pre-empt competition. Oackley (1996) showed that there is a significant association between greater new product commercial successes and more ambitious and speedier overseas launches.

The timely completion of the new product rollouts across international markets is becoming, in this respect, a fundamental source of competitive advantage for an organisation. Researchers have surprisingly neglected the timeliness in the new product rollout activity across either domestic or international contexts leading to an incomplete understanding of the design and implementation of product policy (see Craig and Hart, 1992; Douglas and Craig, 1992). Some previous attention has been paid to new product development in multinational enterprises (Ronkainen, 1983) or modelling the international new product diffusion but little effort has been made to understand the causes of delays/timeliness of the overall rollout exercise. This may be due to the fact that new product development and product commercialisation can be considered to be a single process. However, these two activities are not necessarily the same and have different aims. It is reasonable to suppose that the purpose of the new product development process is to create or build a new product (Hart, 1996). Conversely, the purpose of the product commercialisation process is to make the product available for sale across the company's target markets (Mascarenhas, 1992a,b). At the same time, the diffusion of an innovation is defined as the process by which that innovation is communicated through certain channels over time among the members of a social system (Rogers, 1983). These are different issues and have to be considered as such. The issue of timeliness in rolling out a new product has, however, received scant attention, and discussion is still in its infancy. As such much remains to be done. This book intends to contribute to the knowledge of timeliness in new product rollout and to stimulate others to undertake additional research in this under-investigated crucial area.

1.3   Present status of theory

Douglas and Craig (1992) identified the subject of the present study as an area requiring urgent attention:

> In the case of product decisions, more in-depth examination of new product development in a global context – issues such as whether and when to develop products for global rather than national markets, as well as when and how to transfer products and brands from one country to another, and to develop appropriate positioning

strategies, need further study. Examination of factors influencing the composition of the international product portfolio, and the nature of product lines in each country, for example, similarity of target segments and product markets, the nature of competition and existence of potential economies of scope, is another area which merits greater attention (p. 308).

Several works have focused on issues such as the product's international life cycle (Vernon, 1966), multinational product planning (Keegan, 1969), the country-of-origin image (Samiee, 1994), product transfers across countries (Davidson and Harrigan, 1977; Hill and Still, 1984), the customisation of marketing (Walters and Toyne, 1989; Szymanski *et al.*, 1993; Cavusgil and Zou, 1994), as well as the characteristics of export performers (Madsen, 1987; Miesenbock, 1988; Aaby and Slater, 1989; Chetty and Hamilton, 1993).

Also, writers acknowledge that companies need to rapidly make their products available for sale in several countries to keep in line with the rapid pace of change in the business environment (Olson *et al.*, 1995; Oackley, 1996). Nonetheless, research efforts seem to have stopped short of examining the theoretical and practical dimensions of new product rollout. It is of concern that there is a considerable lack of understanding of the variables that might be relevant to the issue of timeliness in new product rollout. The importance of delays and the causes of these delays also remain unknown.

1.4   This study

This study constitutes an extensive empirical investigation of decision-making in the rollout of new products across international markets with particular reference to delays in the rollout schedule. The study:

- obtains an evaluation of the various factors from senior managers that lead to delays;
- formulates a causal model and determines the indirect, direct and total effects of each factor upon the others and rollout timeliness; and
- results in normative recommendations on the subject of new product rollout across international markets.

It is important to investigate if there are delays in new product rollout in cross-border activities. If they exist, it is also important to examine how they influence new product success, the factors that lead to delay and the similarity of these factors across organisations and technology settings. Variations in internal and external elements and the circumstances in which organisations operate may permit the development of in-depth knowledge on this subject. The study provides new empirical work into how manufacturing companies roll out their new products across several country markets and relevant issues.

1.5 Problem statement

The ultimate problem under study in this empirical investigation is how to improve the performance of new product rollout across international markets. The assumption made is that a theory of timely cross-border new product rollout will enable improved product decisions to be made and will improve the success rate of the new product launches across international markets. The general problem under study is:

'How can manufacturing companies active in international markets achieve the timely rollout of new products?'

1.6 Research objectives

The overall objective of this research is to gain an understanding of the nature of causes of delays when rolling out new products across international markets, the interaction between these causes, and the effects upon new product success. Subsidiary objectives are:

- to determine if timely rolled-out new products are more successful than delayed rolled-out new products;
- to acquire information with respect to the time schedules adopted by companies in rolling out new products across international markets (this research focuses on the European operations of international firms only and omits detailed investigation of operations in other countries), and whether both simultaneous and sequential rollouts are used by companies;
- to study if there is a link between product technology and sequential rollout and sequential rollout and rollout delays;
- to obtain a picture of the length of these delays;
- to understand the causes of these delays; and
- to explore the interaction between these causes of delays.

1.7 Research questions

The main research questions (RQs) are as follows:

- RQ1 Is rollout timeliness related to new product success?
- RQ2 Do firms roll out their new products across international markets simultaneously or sequentially?
  This question looks more precisely at two different aspects:
  - (RQ2a) Is there a link between the nature of product technology and sequential rollout?
  - (RQ2b) Is there a link between sequential rollout and delays?

- RQ3 What factors lead to rollout delay?
- RQ4 What is the interaction between these factors and their direct and indirect effects upon rollout delay?

1.8 Dimensions of this study and the structure of this book

Given the absence of previous empirical research on the timeliness of new product rollout across international markets, this research is exploratory in nature. A six-phase research methodology was designed and implemented. It consisted of: (1) a review of literature across several streams of research in both the domestic and international business fields; (2) a pilot telephone interview study; (3) exploratory interviews in six companies and a preliminary cross-case analysis; (4) the refinement of methodological and theoretical framework issues; (5) an additional series of interviews in 24 more companies; and (6) a second cross-case analysis. These are followed by the construction of a model and the estimation of the magnitude of direct, indirect and total effects of each factor upon rollout timeliness. The decomposition of effects provides important insights into these factors that lead to delays in the rollout of new products across international markets. The sampled population in this investigation belongs to the manufacturing sector. The author sought organisations of different sizes and different nationalities of ownership in the wider electronics industry. The organisation of this book is as follows:

- Chapter 1 overviews the project and clarifies the research questions and objectives.
- Chapter 2 discusses the importance of the product variable and rollout timeliness. This is followed by a review of pertinent literature and the development of an initial conceptual framework.

- Chapter 3 explains the methodology of the present study.
- Chapter 4 presents the cross-case analysis of the investigated cases.
- Chapter 5 answers the research questions and expands on the formulation of a model that explains the interaction between the factors leading to rollout delays. This is followed by the measurement of the interrelationships among these factors and their effects upon rollout delays.
- Chapter 6 concludes with a discussion of the key contributions made by this study, limitations of the present project and areas for future research.

2
Literature Review

2.1 Introduction

The discussion first focuses on the importance of the product variable for organisational survival and the current shift of attention to time as the source of competitive advantage. Advantages of timely new product rollout are presented alongside the repercussions of delays in rollout schedules (section 2.2). This is followed by a literature review and consideration of the insights previous research provides to the present project (section 2.3). The chapter concludes with the construction of a conceptual framework based upon these insights.

2.2 The product variable and timeliness

2.2.1 The significance of the product variable

The product is the *raison d'être* of the company, its *sine qua non* (this section is drawn from Avlonitis, 1980). All business activity revolves around the product. While many factors contribute towards the outcome of organisational activities, the right product in the right place and at the right time plays a decisive role in long-runing company success. All marketing strategy and tactics revolve around the product because it is the basic tool with which organisations bargain for revenue (Buskirk, 1966, p. 227). As Borden (1963) postulates:

> Generally, no single functional area, has so much bearing on the sales and profit opportunities present and future, as that of having products that meet the desires of consumer groups and yield margins that permit a satisfactory profit (p. 252).

Products stimulate growth in the firm and constitute responses to competition and changing environments. Products also reflect the creativity of management and organisational innovativeness (Hisrich and Peters, 1991, pp. 7–8).

Much of the literature in economics up to 1930 omits discussion of the product variable. Under the assumption of demand and supply homogeneity, the basis for competition is the price. This assumption – partially valid in the eighteenth and nineteenth centuries by virtue of companies' orientation towards mass-produced products – became non-sustainable by the beginning of the twentieth century. Concurrent revolutions in production, communications and transportation, and industry structure have changed the basis of competition. In the early 1930s, Chamberlin (1933) asserted that managers combined advantageous prices, advertising and product aspects for the sale of their products. Chamberlin's assertion had a tremendous impact in the sense that the assumption of homogeneous products was abandoned. Nonetheless, the admission of the importance of product as a variable came only in the early 1950s when aspects like product quality were recognised to affect product differentiation (Brems, 1951, p. 12).

It is this product differentiation and the development of the concept of differential advantage (Clark, 1954, pp. 326–8) that constitute a fundamental platform of much of today's competition. Chamberlin considers that buyer preferences for one product variety over another lead to non-entry into an exchange (Chamberlin, 1957, p. 56). This creates an imbalance between sellers in so far as their activities and individual products must match customer preferences. These buyer preferences reflect a variation in needs and wants, and they allow competitors to pursue a policy of differential advantage in general and product differentiation in particular. Sellers need to adjust the product and the elements surrounding its sales according to the requirements of each market segment. However, the sellers have to readjust their approach and offering constantly to sustain differential advantage because of constant changes in these buyer preferences.

In the 1950s and 1960s, it was easy for managers to experience growth of sales in markets because of an environment of economic stability, affluence and increased customer consumption. International competition and the rate of technological change were still mild, national growth curves were moving upwards every year, and national markets were well protected against competition from other nations. But in the 1970s, the rules changed. The marketing environment deteriorated sharply. The oil crises, long periods of recession, decreased income, rocketing change in technology, the formation of economic trade blocs and the globalisation of competition changed marketing practice for good.

The transition from steady growth to unstable economic conditions during the early 1970s brought substantial changes in the industrial systems and with them increased attention on the product variable. It was then that the product started to become a primary weapon and a marketing variable of fundamental importance for organisational survival (Wentz *et al.*, 1973). Since then, rapidly changing economic conditions established firmly the role of the product variable at a prominent position. Product innovations by competitors have, for instance, become pivotal in disrupting market equilibrium (Littler, 1994, pp. 293–300). Advances in business strategy have also highlighted the contestability of markets due to the non-exclusivity of sustainable advantage and the rapid imitation of innovative products by competitors at a fraction of cost (Ghemawat, 1979, p. 27). In parallel, failure costs increased. Research on the outcomes of R&D programmes in a variety of industrial sectors suggested a 'success' rate between 12 and 20 per cent (Mansfield *et al.*, 1972), with only one in seven products actually launched achieving commercial success (Booz *et al.*, 1982).

The emergence of the 'borderless world' forced companies to reconsider and elaborate their strategies (Bartlett and Ghoshal, 1987a, pp. 7–8). It also created a new set of challenges for organisations, in which global management of products and the cohesion between strategic and product decisions became instrumental for survival (Ohmae, 1991). This is because corporate and business strategy decisions are reflected and embedded in product decisions. For instance, Ansoff's (1958), Drucker's (1963) and Abell's (1980) work, on the appropriate ways to identify which business an organisation is in, is largely based on the type and scope of its products and markets. Within the framework of a broader business strategy, setting of pertinent business objectives would provide adequate guidance for concrete product operations and plans.

2.2.2 Time as a source of competitive advantage

Profit seeking or maximisation of profit seemed once to be the single business objective. Such a normative objective was the doctrine of traditional economists. Yet, even prominent economists such as Papandreou (1952), Williamson (1963), Baumol (1965), and Gabowski and Mueller (1972) have argued that several economic objectives are necessary for the survival of an organisation, including high levels of sales growth, market share and profit. Achievement of these objectives was understood to indicate a well-performing organisation. However, such accomplishments may have become increasingly difficult to achieve in the recent years. This has happened for several reasons, including the substantial changes in the wider business environment. Ansoff and McDonnell (1990) shows that economic and environmental turbulence has substantially risen over recent years. Doyle (1994) mentions the major changes that continue to affect marketing and strategy. These are: fashionisation; the creation of micromarkets; rising customer expectations; requirements for improved service and products; product commoditisation; erosion of brands; increase in constraints imposed by government; politics and society; rapid technology change; increasing competitive rivalry; and globalisation.

The influence of these changes upon company action is important and will intensify more in the years to come (Doyle, 1994). For instance, technological advancements are no longer isolated within individual countries, but transcend national boundaries and change the competitive scene across the globe. Events such as European integration facilitate the rapid diffusion of technology through the abolition of national borders and the simultaneous change in national legislation and regulations across several countries. Multinational players (e.g. buyers, suppliers, research and development bodies and competitors) become transnational in search of economies of scale and scope. Much focus is on building products that are 'global' while meeting 'local' needs (Bartlett and Ghoshal, 1987a). However, time and cultural differences, difficulties in communication, distance, a variation in technological standards and intense competitive rivalry create problems. These result in new challenges for organisations.

New dimensions also appear to gain momentum in the competitive game. Organisations seem to shift emphasis to time as a means to acquire and sustain competitive advantage. Indeed, time is coined as the current source of competitive advantage (Stalk and Hout, 1990). Stalk (1988) notes that, like competition itself, competitive advantage is a constantly moving target and that today, the way leading companies manage time, *in new product development and introduction*, represents one of the most powerful new sources of competitive advantage.

Stalk also notes that, while time is a basic business variable, management seldom monitored its consumption explicitly – almost never with the same precision it accorded to sales and costs. Yet, time is a more critical competitive yardstick than traditional financial measurements. It is already forty-five years since Jay W. Forrester (1958), the person who created the system dynamics approach, established a model of time's impact on an organisation's performance. He tracked the effects of time delays and decision rates within a simple business system consisting of a factory, a warehouse, a distributor and retailers, and showed the adverse effects of lengthy operations. The cycle period from the finished product to the retailer was sufficient as long as demand was stable and forecasts were accurate. When unexpected changes occurred, they resulted in lengthy delays that distorted the flow of production, procurement, sales and consequently finances. Distortions that reverberate throughout the system not only produce instability within the organisation, but can also undermine the organisation's position in the eyes of its customers. Stalk continues, saying that, to escape distortions, companies have to reduce the time delays in the flow of information and *product through the system*, and that the new approach to do so is to reduce time consumption.

Stalk explicitly recognises the need for a reduction in the time spent on new product development and product introduction to markets. This indicates that an organisation that can develop and roll out new products faster and on schedule enjoys an advantage over its competitors. It also means that product rollout patterns may have changed for good. More and more companies develop products and product innovations targeting markets in several countries, and they co-ordinate their launch on a global basis. Ford's new Escort is an example. This is the company's second global car after the Mondeo. Several companies opt for a simultaneous launch across markets world-wide, as in the case of Microsoft's new operating platform, 'Windows 95', launched on 24 August 1995. The same happened with Microsoft's subsequent product launches (e.g. Windows 98 and 2000). Fast and timely rollout becomes an integral part of organisational adaptation and alignment with these evolving environmental conditions, and is pivotal for organisational survival.

2.2.3 Timeliness in rolling out new products across international markets

The notion of timeliness of rollout across international markets may comprise decisions regarding the order of entry across country markets (which country first, which second?) and against competition (pioneer or follower?). Nonetheless, what underlines and cuts across both aspects is how long it will take to market the product across all target country markets.

First, this time period concerns a choice between simultaneous versus sequential new product rollout. Simultaneous means that the company makes the product available across all its target markets at the same time. Sequential means that the company makes its product available first in some markets and later in others. Secondly, this time period concerns the timeliness versus delay in such availability. Timely (on schedule) availability of the new product means that the company rolled out its new product as planned, calculated and expected. Delay in the schedule means that the company did not roll out its new product as planned, calculated and expected. It is likely that the longer the delay, the worse the outcome, because the new product will not be available for sale across several countries.

Such definition of timeliness is similar to that used by Cooper and Kleinschmidt (1994) in their study of timeliness in new product development. It is also similar to the one used by Olson *et al.* (1995) in their discussion of timeliness in new product commercialisation. Authors in both contributions perceive timeliness as the time required to complete the activity relative to its scheduled/anticipated time frame (see for instance, Olson *et al.*, 1995, p. 56). Timeliness of new product rollout across international markets therefore revolves around two factors:

- the company decision on the simultaneous versus sequential rollout of its new product across countries and the timing schedule; and
- delays in the rollout schedule.

The time schedules for new product rollouts across all company European target markets, and the causes of delays in the rollout schedule, are the focus of the present empirical study.

The emphasis on avoidance of delays in new product rollout across countries is crucial, yet it is often underestimated by many companies. It is easier for managers to obtain the crude measures of overall company performance than to isolate the softer, very complex and daunting effects of delays in rolling out new products across countries. However, the advantages associated with timely new product rollout across international markets are substantial. Among these advantages are the following:

- Enhancement of competitive advantage. A delayed introduction of technology (e.g. VCRs, compact discs) not previously available in the market increases the issues at stake. Increasing lead-time in individual country markets also helps a pioneer to establish a stronger brand name (Schmalensee, 1982) and to move customers' ideal points closer to the pioneer's mix of product attributes (Carpenter and Nakamoto, 1989). Research into consumer products suggests that consumer information processing is strongly influenced by what the consumer already knows about a product category. Consumers reduce the cognitive demands of processing new information by relying on previous learning (Fiske and Taylor, 1984). Thus, consumers use their knowledge of a pioneering brand as a measure against which to judge late brands in the category (Carpenter and Nakamoto, 1989, 1994), or may fail to integrate information about late brands into their existing knowledge structure at all (Kardes and Kalyanaram, 1992). Increasing lead-time in individual countries also helps the pioneer to further broaden its product line (Robinson and Fornell, 1985).

- Quick response to rapidly changing markets and technologies, and ever shortening product lifetimes. Increasing obsolescence and intensified competition mean shorter windows of opportunity if products are not rapidly available for sale. One report reveals that product lifetimes are becoming as short as two years in some industries (Patterson, 1990).
- Increase in profitability. There is evidence that it is better to develop a product on time but well over budget than to develop it on budget and late. A report suggested that, under a very specific set of circumstances, a six-month delay will reduce a high-tech product's profitability by one-third (Dumaine, 1989). Vessey (1991) adds that decreasing the development time by six months improves profits by 11.9 per cent (p. 14).
- Reduction in 'time to market'. In the case of products marketed to several countries, 'time to market' includes not only product development time, but also time to 'commercialise' the product (Olson *et al.*, 1995) across countries (Mascarenhas, 1992a,b). Consequently, rapid development is likely to be worth little, if the length of product introduction time across countries is longer than planned, calculated and expected.

Delays in rollout can also have a series of severe repercussions for the company. This happens because the expense of a newly developed product with no sales in its multiple international target markets goes beyond longer break-even times and reduction in product lifetime profits. No method of financial accounting or business monitoring can adequately report business costs. Some of them are:

- A burden on the company's resources, such as funds, facilities and management attention, that may be disproportionate to the product's future contribution to sales and profits. This may also happen at the expense of other products. Technical innovativeness cannot also be tested and psychological disappointment of personnel may reduce organisational effectiveness and efficiency in the short and long run.

- Non-revitalisation of the product portfolio across countries with new products. This is likely to result in decreased international sales, excess capacity and truncated company ability to sell. It is not only important to introduce new products across countries on time in order to compete head-on-head or to pre-empt competition in these countries, it is also important to keep to the schedule in doing so.
- Poor technological and social connotations for companies respected by marketing channels and the public across the world for innovativeness against competition and keeping pace with technology advances (Clark and Fujimoto, 1991). This can seriously affect corporate image.
- Early elimination of the new product. Technology has been the main agent in the birth, growth, decline and death of innumerable products in the past. The rapid diffusion of technology across countries, the abolition of trade barriers (e.g. European Union), the acculturation of executives with customer preferences across nations, advances in telecommunications and the multiplication of competitors rapidly render products outdated, outmoded and less efficient: in other words, obsolete. Products with delays in their availability across countries are quickly outlived and become prime candidates for elimination before the company recovers the costs of their development.

Rollout of new products across countries and identification of causes of delays therefore, seems to take a prominent position in managerial decision-making regarding the achievement of competitive advantage and organisational survival. Prompt rather than belated amendment can cut costs, free up resources, improve margins, and assist organisations in achieving and maintaining competitive advantage. Several insights from previous research can assist investigation of the issue. These are presented next.

2.3   Literature review

2.3.1   Introduction

This section reviews the literature concerning:

- the diffusion of innovations, a stream largely relevant to research in consumer behaviour;
- business strategy;

- product portfolio management, new product development and product elimination;
- international business; and
- research in international marketing.

2.3.2 Innovations and their diffusion across markets

The diffusion of an innovation is defined as the process by which that innovation 'is communicated through certain channels over time among the members of a social system' (Rogers, 1983). As such, the diffusion process consists of four key elements: innovation, communication channels, time and the social system (Mahajan *et al.*, 1990). Diffusion theory mainly focuses upon the communication channels – that is, media, verbal and non-verbal interpersonal communication – by which information about an innovation is transmitted to or within the social system. Modelling of diffusion is a relatively advanced area of research, with published work spanning several decades. Diffusion studies generally analyse the development of first purchases of a new product or service by a population over a period, the rate of diffusion, the cumulative number of adopters during that period, the total number of potential adopters in a population and the rate at which adoption occurs (see Mahajan *et al.*, 1990, 1993 for a literature review and directions for further research and Mahajan *et al.*, 1995, for a discussion of empirical generalisations and managerial uses of diffusion research). Various functional forms for the rate of adoption lead to models that imply different diffusion processes. Methodologies seem to follow a pre-specification of an analytical model and its fitting to data for a varying number of applications.

Researchers look at the diffusion of innovation from different perspectives. Several researchers have evaluated the applicability of the theory to consumer behaviour. A recent meta-analysis of 15 major articles on the subject (Sultan *et al.*, 1990) found that 213 sets of parameters were used in the estimations. Innovations examined included agricultural products, durable goods, industrial products, franchises in fast food restaurants and hotels, medical innovations and financial investments. Most diffusion applications were based on US and European data. The meta-analysis showed that diffusion of an innovation depends more upon such factors as word-of-mouth than upon the innate innovativeness of consumers. The estimated coefficients of innovation were fairly stable under a wide variety of conditions, although models fitted to data from European countries have higher coefficients than US models. The coefficient of innovation reflects the chance of adoption of an innovation by an individual. In contrast, the coefficient of imitation varied widely with (1) the type of innovation examined; (2) the estimation procedure employed, and (3) the use of other marketing-mix variables by the company.

Research in the area has largely developed by examining the major assumptions underlying the basic Bass (1969) model. Thus, research has examined what happens to the diffusion of an innovation under the following conditions:

- the market potential of the new product changes;
- the diffusion of an innovation depends upon other innovations;
- the nature of an innovation changes over time;
- the geographic boundaries of the social system change during the diffusion process;
- the diffusion process is not binary (potential adopters adopt or do not adopt);
- the diffusion of an innovation is influenced by marketing strategies;
- the product and market characteristics influence diffusion patterns;
- there are supply restrictions;
- there is more than one adoption by adoption unit.

Questions have been raised in recent years about the forecasting accuracy of diffusion models, asserting that the analytical elegance of most studies surpasses the empirical validation of their derived results (see Gatignon and Robertson, 1985; Robertson and Gatignon, 1986; and Mahajan *et al.*, 1990, 1993, 1995). Research on diffusion of innovations (henceforth DR) contributes relatively little to the present study. This is due to several issues:

- DR focuses mainly on domestic markets. Extension of the models in international markets is truly limited in number and scope. The few models applied to international markets take into account consumer-only variables like cosmopolitanism (Gatignon *et al.*, 1989) or consumer involvement, learning and culture (Wills *et al.*, 1991; Amine, 1993; Samli *et al.*, 1993). DR in effect understands that adoption of products across countries is fundamentally affected by communication between consumers. For instance, Mahajan *et al.* (1995) conclude that: 'an important concept of diffusion theory relevant to predicting the global diffusion is the nature of communication about the innovation between two countries. The ability of change agents or adopters of an innovation in one country, called the lead market, to communicate with the potential adopters in the second country, referred to as the foreign market,..., influences the rate of adoption among its potential adopters' (p. 381). Severe questions were raised about the applicability of the premises of the Bass model in international settings (Mahajan *et al.*, 1990, p. 21).

- DR does not consider all the firm-originated decisions and the time objectives regarding the geographic spread and time length of launch. DR also does not consider if the launch of an innovation is a (re)action to competition. Gatignon and Robertson clearly mention on these points that DR 'almost totally ignores firm intentions for marketing the innovation. Even the research on new product diffusion conducted by marketing and consumer behaviour researchers ignores the intentions of supplier firms' (Gatignon and Robertson, 1985; Robertson and Gatignon, 1986, p. 6). DR seems to assume in this respect that rollout is simultaneous across the world.
- DR does not consider any firm factors that facilitate or delay the launch of an innovation across borders (e.g. lack of resources, deficient communication with subsidiaries, few synergies with other products, inappropriate distribution, mistakes in the product development or product inferiority factors).
- Last, but not least, DR applies to first product sales. The same internal organisational circumstances and market dynamics may not apply to product replacements.

Despite the number of its limitations, however, research on the diffusion of innovations provides insights that are relevant to this study. These are:

- An increase in market potential in some markets (the first assumption in the Bass model) may trigger a shortage of available quantities of products and other resources. These may be due, for instance, to insufficiency of manufacturing capacity to satisfy the requirements of additional countries; or lack of resources, including marketing and technical staff time and funds, to serve these markets.
- The rollout of a product relates to other products (the second assumption in the Bass model). Synergies between this product and other existing products are likely to facilitate the timely rollout across countries. Lack of synergies on technological or marketing grounds (such as product concept, distribution channels, sales force education and maintenance requirements) are very likely to cause delays in rolling out a new product.

- Delays should happen if the nature of innovation changes over time (the third assumption in the Bass model). Product adaptations for individual markets require time and resources. The possession of the necessary resources will lead to enhanced technologies and marketing effort, which, in turn, will lead to more rapid diffusion because they will meet the customer needs sooner and better (Mansfield, 1982; Robertson and Gatignon, 1986, pp. 5–6). Insufficient quantity and inadequate quality resources (that is, the required resources exceed the current organisational capabilities), are likely to cause delays in rolling out the new product.

These are insights to be considered in the present investigation.

2.3.3   Organisational strategy

'Strategy' is defined in several distinct ways (see Kerin *et al.*, 1990 for a discussion). Perspectives range from idiosyncratic strategies that vary for every single business setting (Andrews, 1971) to contingent strategies (Chandler, 1962; Learned *et al.*, 1965; Mintzberg, 1978; Hambrick, 1980; Ginsberg, 1988) and generic strategies applicable to every business setting (Porter, 1980, 1985). These varying perspectives have a profound effect upon marketing and product portfolio strategy across borders. The deployment of a new product across multiple country markets reflects strategic decisions regarding product portfolios and constitutes the implementation of such decisions (Douglas and Craig, 1989). It therefore becomes important to look more closely at product portfolios, which we will consider next.

2.3.4   Product management

2.3.4.1   Management of product portfolios

During the twentieth century, firms generally developed from offering a single line to offering multiple lines and products. Organisations learned that they could not succeed without good management of their products. This 'involves an understanding of, and sensitivity to, consumer needs to identify good ideas for new products and services, knowledge about competitors, an appraisal of opportunities [and] a commitment to the process of developing new products' (Hisrich and Peters, 1991, p. v) and further is concerned with 'eliminating these products that do not serve the company goals any more' (Avlonitis, 1980; Hart, 1988).

Substantial literature on this subject has accumulated over the years (Cooper, 1979; Booz *et al.*, 1982; Johne, 1984; Johne and Snelson, 1989; Craig and Hart, 1992; Hart and Baker, 1994). Many researchers concentrated upon the composition of product portfolios (see Varadarajan,

1990; Mahajan and Wind, 1992; Wind and Lilien, 1993). Wind and Lilien (1993) classified product portfolio models on either a financial or business base. Thus, they grouped under the *business models* heading analytic models (e.g. Stratport), standardised and modified product business portfolios (e.g. BCG growth/share matrix; Shell International); and customised portfolio models (e.g. conjoint analysis based approaches, analytic hierarchy process based, etc.). Wind and Lilien (1993) grouped under the *financial-based models* heading basically risk-return and stochastic dominance models. They also identified hybrid approaches between business and financial-based models.

Other researchers concentrated on aspects such as the position of the product variable within the framework of the broader dynamics of competition (Gatignon *et al.*, 1989; Heil and Robertson, 1991; Bowman and Gatignon, 1995). Linking the above indicates the need to identify the position of a new product within the wider company product portfolio. The most important products for the company are likely to be the products that account for a substantial amount of company sales (Mahajan *et al.*, 1993). Because these products are important, they are more likely to reflect the main business focus of the company and the current strategic directions of a firm.

The rollout of these products is therefore more likely to attract managerial attention for accurate estimation of the anticipated rollout time, and should constitute a basis for the sampling rationale of the present project.

2.3.4.2 (Re)action against competition and the rollout of new products

Chen *et al.* (1992) and Heil and Walters (1993) argued that any company's incentive to act or react – probably through the launch of a new product – relates to at least four different elements:

- competitive impact and its pervasiveness;
- attack intensity (the extent to which the competitive action has affected the company's markets for the specific product);
- the type of action; and
- implementation requirements (the degree of effort that the initiating firm requires to execute an action).

These are explained in turn.

Competitive impact: It is likely that the greater the competitive impact suffered by a company under attack (the 'victim'), the greater the 'victim's' intention to (re)act. This is because the 'victim' company is more likely to become aware of, and motivated to respond to, an action that has great competitive impact upon its long-term survival. The pervasiveness of such competitive impact is also important. Competitors attempting to achieve their objectives in a manner that:

- is inconsistent with the rules of competitive conduct in an industry; or
- is overly self-serving; or
- threatens social and political norms; or
- benefits one party at the expense of another,

are sending signals of high hostility to other firms (Heil and Walters, 1993). These signals tend to stimulate the feeling of pervasiveness and trigger strong reactions (Kahneman *et al.*, 1986a,b; Scherer and Ross, 1990). Although competitors may initially be uncertain of the implications of such a move, its very pervasiveness will tend to impel the 'victims' to react (Chen *et al.*, 1992). This may create a snowball effect (Farrell and Saloner, 1985) which is likely to give a strong impetus to any company in the sector to (re)act, even unnecessarily (Chen *et al.*, 1992). By the same logic, a hostile competitive action with pervasive implications for the 'victim' company will tend to provoke speedy counteractions and a fast and timely rollout of new products. This is because a delay in the availability of the new product for sale may cancel out all potential benefits for the company from developing the product in the first instance. In contrast, when a competitor undertakes a market activity:

- in a conventional manner;
- that is not overly self-serving; or
- that is consistent with social and political norms; or
- that is unselfish

signals of low hostility are derived by the affected firms. Perception of the importance of competitive impact is weaker because the normal pattern of competitive behaviour is not disturbed (Nicholson, 1978; Kahneman *et al.*, 1986a,b). By the same logic, a less hostile competitive action with non-pervasive implications will tend not to create a speedy counteraction and a rapid timely rollout.

Intensity of the attack: Attack intensity reflects the degree to which the company under attack (the 'victim') perceives itself to be threatened by competitors' action across its markets (Chen *et al.*, 1992). This captures the direct threat of a competitive action to the company under attack. While competitive impact reflects the pervasiveness of the move, attack intensity focuses more on the depth and width of the effect upon the 'victim's' markets. A competitive move does not have the same overall impact on every market of the 'victims' it threatens. The degree of threat depends upon the number and the importance of the affected market(s) for the affected companies. The more the markets, the greater is the threat. This impact also depends upon the internationalisation of the attacking firms. The more international the attacking firm and the higher the intensity of the attack, the higher the overall force and the potential impact of that attack.

Type of action and implementation requirement: Nonetheless, firms are not always prepared to act or counteract. They need time not only to understand and analyse changes in competitive rivalry, but also to decide how to respond (Chen *et al.*, 1992). A company's response relates to the type of action concerned and the implementation requirements for that action. For instance, in some sectors, most new products introduced by competition are replacements of older ones. This influences the importance of technology changes incorporated in every new product generation, because the product life cycle is short and new products incorporate in most instances only few technological changes (Samiee and Roth, 1992). In other cases, the situation may be different and introducing a new product may demand the incorporation of important technological changes.

The rollout of such a new product may require major investment in assets (Galbraith and Kazanjian, 1986), major reorientation of the organisation (Thompson, 1967), major change in the definition of the business (Abell, 1980), reconfiguration of the organisational structure (Galbraith and Kazanjian, 1986) and radical changes in management practice (Dutton and Duncan, 1987). Such new products may be fewer, but their rollout is more likely to face obstacles in execution because of the difficulty in reorienting and structurally reforming the company (Chen *et al.*, 1992). Something similar was argued by Teece (1977) when he claimed that international transfer of technology may be deterred by substantial difficulties and costs.

Concluding, this research stream provides an important insight into the present investigation. This insight is that 'victim' companies will have different incentives to react and their response behaviour is shaped by the attack intensity and pervasiveness of competitive moves having an impact upon them. The degree of threat to the company's key markets across multiple countries is likely to be a key issue. Major implementation requirements due to substantial technological changes will delay the rollout of the new products.

2.3.4.3   Adding new products: new product development

Research in the area is diverse and large (this section has benefited from Brown and Eisenhardt, 1995). Even though new product development (NPD) is crucial to organisational survival and a major core competence, it is nevertheless challenging to group the various contributions into coherent research streams. Literature is fragmented and varied. Within a wider innovation literature, there are two broad areas of inquiry that complement one another (Adler, 1989).

The first area of inquiry is economics-oriented. It offers understanding of innovation across countries and industries, the evolution of technologies, and intrasector differences in the propensity of firms to innovate (e.g. Nelson and Winter, 1977; David, 1985; Dosi, 1988). Within this area, product development remains rather neglected. At best, this work describes the evolution of idiosyncratic innovation routines within organisations (Nelson and Winter, 1977).

The second area of inquiry is the NPD literature, explaining how firms develop new products. Research contributions in this second area have multiplied in parallel with the increasing importance of proficient NPD for organisations (Dumaine, 1991; *Business Week*, 1992; Schender, 1992). In the NPD literature, the primary focus has been to acquire a rich understanding of the actual process of developing new products and the reasons for 'success'. This research area indicates that organisational structures, managerial practices and product/project characteristics lead to an improved NPD process and greater new product success. Literature in the NPD area can be organised (Brown and Eisenhardt, 1995) into three major research streams, namely: (1) rational plan, (2) communication web; and (3) disciplined problem solving. These streams have followed diverse routes of development, but their findings are complementary. The three research streams are now presented.

NPD as rational plan

This rational plan perspective emphasises that successful NPD is the result of the combination of several elements. Put in simple terms, the basic rationale underlying this stream of research is that a product well-planned and implemented and appropriately supported will be a success (Brown and Eisenhardt, 1995). Typically, methodologies rely heavily on single informants quantifying subjective judgements surrounding long lists of success and failure factors. Researchers also use a variety of indicators to measure success (profits, sales, market share, etc.). There have been several attempts to integrate research in this area. A recent meta-analytical review (Montoya-Weiss and Calantone, 1994) examined 47 studies. They grouped the factors responsible for success in NPD into four sets: strategic, market environment, development process and organisational factors.

Strategic factors include product advantage, synergies in marketing and technology and company resources. Market environment factors include the competitive nature of the market and its potential. Development process factors reflect the proficiency of the company in the execution of the NPD process. Organisational factors complement the above by including strong internal and external relations and internal company co-ordination.

Studies in this stream remain largely exploratory. As Brown and Eisenhardt (1995) suggest, the exploratory state of current theory still causes several problems regarding the coherence of the developed theory. The basic finding, that a product that is well-planned and implemented and appropriately supported will be a success, does not seem to judiciously advance theory. The same is true of claims that products targeted at a large growing market are more successful. Such a finding could not be considered surprising (Brown and Eisenhardt, 1995).

Historically, the study by Myers and Marquis (1969) was among the earliest. They investigated the development of 567 successful products and processes in over 100 firms and 5 industries. Later studies added failures to the mix (e.g. Rothwell, 1972). The SAPPHO study (e.g. Rothwell, 1972; Rothwell *et al.*, 1974) looked at 43 success and failure pairs among chemical and instruments firms in the UK.

Similar studies in Finland (Kulvik, 1977), Hungary (Szakasits, 1974) and West Germany (Gerstenfeld, 1976) largely confirmed the findings of the previous studies. Later research sharpened the emergent emphasis on product advantages, market attractiveness and internal organisation. Particularly important were two studies by Cooper (1979, 1983a,b, 1984, 1985a,b, 1988, 1992); and Cooper and Kleinschmidt (1987, 1991). The first examined 102 successful and 93 failed products within 103 industrial firms in Canada (Cooper, 1979). The second study examined 203 products in 125 manufacturing firms, including 123 successes and 80 failures (Cooper and Kleinschmidt, 1987). More recently, the same authors conducted a third study of product development in the North American and European chemical industries. The authors replicated some of their earlier findings. They suggest that successful product development occurs when (see for instance, Cooper, 1994 and Cooper and Kleinschmidt, 1993a,b; 1995a,b):

- The product delivers unique benefits and superior value to the customer. It is developed by a cross-functional team, it is sharply defined early in its process and it receives time and resources.
- The process of product development is proficiently executed, multi-stage, strongly market oriented and focused upon the customer. This process also includes up-front preparation, namely screening, market studies and technical feasibility.

The findings of the Stanford Innovation Project in the electronics industry also emphasised product advantage, market attractiveness and internal organisation. A total of 70 product success/failure pairs were initially surveyed and, from these, 21 case studies were subsequently conducted (Maidique and Zirger, 1984, 1985). A third study expanded the first two by examining 86 success/failure product pairs (Zirger and Maidique, 1990). The authors' conclusions largely confirm Cooper's (1979) and Cooper and Kleinschmidt's (1987) studies. For example, the authors wrote: 'Products are more likely to be successful if they are planned and implemented well' (Zirger and Maidique, 1990, p. 879). More recently, other authors confirmed the importance of predevelopment planning (Dwyer and Mellor, 1991), the focus on marketing and R&D involvement (Hise *et al.*, 1990; Gupta *et al.*, 1986, 1991).

Of much interest to the present study is also a recent trend towards studying the acceleration of product development (e.g. Gupta and Wilemon, 1990; Cordero, 1991; Mabert *et al.*, 1992; Millson *et al.*, 1992), timeliness in NPD (Cooper and Kleinschmidt, 1994) or speedier overseas launches (Oackley, 1996). For example, Gupta and Wilemon (1990) polled the factors that accelerated the development processes. These factors included more resources, internal organisation, early cross-functional teamwork, customer and supplier involvement in the process and visible top management support.

Cooper and Kleinschmidt (1994) found that the top three time-savers during the NPD process are the organisation of the project, a solid up-front preparation and a strong market orientation of the NPD effort. Interestingly, these authors identified that timeliness in NPD shows only a small positive correlation with financial performance of a new product project; its impact is not nearly as strong as one might have expected. Timeliness in NPD emerged as an independent or stand-alone performance dimension in the factor analysis they conducted. More precisely, they identified a two-factor solution where factor 1 was a *financial performance factor* (comprising profitability, success/failure, market share, and impact on firm;

loadings > 0.65); whereas factor 2 was the *time-related factor* (p. 392). Further their correlation matrix revealed only a handful of significant correlations between the measures of time and the various financial performance measures and certainly 'far less than the direct or almost one-to-one links the "hype" seems to imply' (p. 393). They also noted that a correlation of 0.42 found between timeliness and profitability explained only 16 per cent of the variation in this possible causal relationship.

Oackley (1996) examined the association between commercial successes and international commercialisation of the new products. He found that there is a significant association between greater commercial successes and more ambitious and speedier overseas launches. He suggested that firms should commercialise their new products in foreign countries as boldly and as quickly as possible.

The distinction between 'new' products and product replacements is also important (Saunders and Jobber, 1988, 1994). These authors suggested that managers manage product replacements and 'new' products differently. The authors:

- identified that there are five different types of product replacement, namely inconspicuous or conspicuous substitution, tangible or intangible repositioning and a facelift;
- detected that the number and type of marketing and technological changes vary in accordance with the above types (a facelift replacement, for instance, has undergone only changes in its appearance and consumer promotion, whereas an intangible repositioning has undergone a change in price, target market and advertising);
- argued that launch-phase strategy is distinguished into a rapid or slow penetration and a rapid or low skim; and
- found that replacing the older products can be done on a national, segmental or regional basis.

NPD as a communication web

This second stream narrowly focuses only on communication. The underlying premise is that communication among project team members and with outsiders stimulates the performance of development teams (see Figure 2.1). Thus, the more the members connect to each other and with key outsiders, the greater the likelihood of successful development. Methodologically, studies have used multiple informants and sophisticated research designs. These methodologies yielded quality insights, an issue that is of interest to the present investigation too.

Two theoretical themes emerge in the literature. One, an information-processing view, emphasises that frequent and appropriately structured task communication (both external and internal) leads to more comprehensive and varied information flow to team members and, thus, to higher-performing development processes. The second, a resource dependence view, emphasises that increased resources (e.g. budget, personnel, equipment) available to the team lead to higher-performing development processes.

Some of the earliest empirical research along these lines focused on the flow of information in R&D groups (e.g. Allen, 1971, 1977; Katz and Tushman, 1981). The results of these early studies highlighted the importance of external communication, mainly between key product development individuals and people outside their specialities. This external communication brought information into the organisation that was then disseminated to fellow team members (Katz and Tushman, 1981).

The content of that external communication was examined by Ancona and Galdwell (1990, 1992a,b). They measured success by subjective team and management ratings of performance. The authors found that team members communicated more with outsiders who had similar functional backgrounds. They also found that, when the team comprised more functions, there was greater external communication by the team as a whole and greater performance (Ancona and Galdwell, 1992a). This external

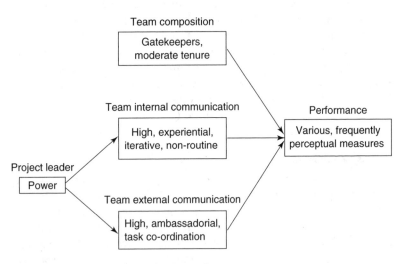

Figure 2.1   NPD as a communication web

Source: Brown and Eisenhardt (1995).

communication strategy was comprehensive. Teams combined 'ambassador' and 'task-co-ordination' activities that helped them to secure resources, gain information and so enhance success. 'Ambassador' (that is, political) activities involved lobbying for support and resources, buffering the team from outside pressure and engaging in impression management. 'Task co-ordination' involved the co-ordination of technical or design issues.

Finally, researchers focused on how communication affects the performance of teams over time. For example, Katz (1982) explored in a large US organisation the relationships among the degree of external communication, the mean tenure of a team and performance. He found that group performance increased with mean tenure of the group, but that this relationship reversed and performance dropped off after five years. The decline in performance was significantly correlated with a decline in external communication.

There also has been interest in the internal communication among team members. Keller (1986) found that internal group cohesion helped performance. Similarly, Ancona and Galdwell (1992a) found that teams with thorough internal communication had superior performance. They defined goals better, developed workable plans and prioritised work. Dougherty (1990) showed though, that the various functional departments were isolated in their own 'sphere' of knowledge and way of understanding. Not surprisingly, individuals from different departments interpreted the same information in different ways. What distinguished successful projects was not the absence or presence of these barriers, but rather how they were overcome. Failed products received sequential attention by functional groups, each function dominating a particular phase of the project. Successful products were developed by cross-functional personnel that convened in a highly interactive, iterative fashion. This increased information content (Dougherty, 1990) and participation (Dougherty, 1992b).

More recently, some researchers explored the link between the product development process and organisational structure. Olson *et al.* (1995) interviewed managers from different functions for 45 NPD projects. They found that the less experience cross-functional teams have with a new product, the greater:

• the amount of difficulty they encounter;
• the interdependency among the various functional areas;
• the flow of information and resources; and
• the reliance on less formal co-ordination structures.

In contrast, the more experience the functional participants have with a new product, the more mechanistic and formal the development process. Olson *et al.* (1995) also examined the time required for commercialisation. They found that projects with good 'fit' between newness and formality were likely to be completed within – or faster than – their anticipated time frame. 'Fit' was defined as the balance between the newness of the project and formality. The greater the extent of project newness, the lesser the need for formality to achieve successful NPD and timely product launch.

NPD as disciplined problem-solving

The disciplined problem-solving stream (Brown and Eisenhardt, 1995) evolved from case-based research (Imai *et al.*, 1985; Quinn, 1985; Takeutchi and Nonaka, 1986). Imai *et al.* (1985) studied seven successful product development projects, including Fuji-Xerox's FX-3500 copier, Honda's City box-car and Canon's Sure Shot camera. Methodologies are more complex and sophisticated than the single-informant ones that underlie much of the rational model research. The perspective extends the information-processing view of the communication web research by emphasising both information and problem-solving practices (see Figure 2.2). Successful product development results from balancing a relatively autonomous project team and a disciplined heavyweight leader, strong top management and overarching product visions (Brown and Eisenhardt, 1995). 'Heavyweight' team leaders co-ordinate the activities of a product development team and work with senior management to create an overarching product concept (part of the 'product integrity' concept – see below). Senior management can exercise subtle control through these 'heavyweight' team leaders, who manage their teams in the context of a product vision. The result is a fast and productive development process.

Later research concentrated upon two sectors with different speeds of technological change: automotives of medium and computers of rapid technology change. Clark *et al.* (1987), Hayes *et al.* (1988) and Clark and Fujimoto (1991) studied 29 cases of major car development projects across three American, eight Japanese and nine European companies. They reported that extensive supplier networks coupled with overlapping product development phases, communication, cross-functional groups, heavyweight team leaders and 'product integrity' improved performance. 'Product integrity' (Clark and Fujimoto, 1991) is a broad concept. It implies a clear vision of the product's intended image and performance, and its fit with corporate image, competences and customers. They

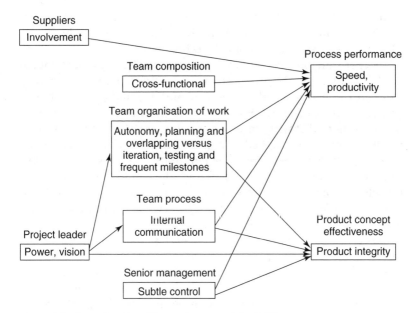

Figure 2.2 Disciplined problem-solving model of NPD

Source: Brown and Eisenhardt (1995).

measured three dimensions of product development process perform-ance: total product quality, lead time and productivity. Heavyweight team leaders are able to gain resources, command respect, break down traditional functional allegiances and build a strong product vision (Clark *et al.*, 1987; Hayes *et al.*, 1988; Clark and Fujimoto, 1991). Hayes *et al.* (1988) also emphasised predevelopment activities and described how resolving conflicts early is an important factor in speeding up the development process.

At the same time, Womack *et al.* (1990) examined lean versus mass production in the auto industry. Their conclusions replicate those of Clark *et al.* (1987), Hayes *et al.* (1988), Clark and Fujimoto (1991).

Two major studies were carried out in the electronics industry. Iansiti (1992, 1993) examined all the major products developed by the 12 chief competitors in the mainframe computer industry (from Japan, the USA and Europe) during the 1980s (27 in-depth studies). The author focused on the development of technologies associated with the packaging and interconnecting system of the mainframe processor. The primary result is that a high-system focus predicted both the lead-time and productiv-ity of product development teams. Similar to product integrity, system

focus implied concern for how technology choices for a given component fit with the product as a whole. System focus also involved early
planning for the integration of new technology.

Another study in the computer industry, by Eisenhardt and Tabrizi
(1995), considered 72 products in 36 Japanese, European and US
firms in the personal, workstation, mainframe and peripherals segments of the electronics industry. They contrasted a compression
model of fast NPD with an experiential approach. They found that
product teams who engaged in more experiential or improvisational
product design through frequent iterations, more testing, frequent
milestones, and powerful leadership developed products more
quickly. In contrast, attempts simply to compress the product development cycle by computer-aided design, rewards for schedule attainment, supplier involvement, overlapping development stages or
extensive planning not only did not accelerate pace but also in fact
often slowed it down.

In summary, the rational plan model offers a wide-ranging list of new
product success factors. The communication web stream seems to focus
on a single, yet fundamental dimension within the wider product development area. Although the findings do not form a fully coherent
picture, they substantiate the probable existence of highly influential
insights for the present research project. This is so despite their bias
towards product development for domestic markets. It is likely that
some of the new product success factors and communication issues
strongly affect the time to roll out a new product across international
markets. These studies suffer, though, from a major shortcoming: the
product rollout is seen as part of the product development process,
whereas in fact the purpose of each activity is different. The aim of the
NPD process seems to be the building of a new product. The aim of the
product launch seems to be its availability for sale across the company's
markets. Saunders and Jobber (1988, 1994) clearly demonstrate that
launch strategies are a different area from NPD.

It is likely that the development and rollout of products across international markets are also affected by other elements. These may include
market heterogeneity, sufficiency of company resources to adapt products, and co-ordination between the development team and overseas
subsidiaries/agents. These issues are not present in current NPD literature. Despite these deficiencies, however, the broader NPD literature
does offer insights of substantial importance to the present study.
It seems that factors affecting delays in product development may also
be responsible for delays in rollout. For instance, it is likely that a

product developed without customer opinion from several countries will not satisfy the needs of those countries. Sending the product back to the drawing board will automatically cause delays in rollout. In-depth case study methodologies may help to uncover some of the complexities of product rollout processes, and this is another element to take into account in the present investigation.

Furthermore, the disciplined problem-solving stream of research widens the focus of the 'communication web' on the amount and variety of information exchange, by adding a third dimension to the NPD literature: that is, on-time product development involves specific problem-solving practices. It is likely that there are different problem-solving models for sectors of medium (e.g. automotives) versus rapid (e.g. computers) technological change sectors. On the other hand, it is still too early to conclude that the problem-solving practices in NPD may be equally applicable to rollout. Problem-solving procedures are a refined conceptual area and need separate consideration in a later investigation. This is because we are not yet certain about the effects of delays in rollout of new products upon new product success. We also do not know the actual causes of such delays yet. Problem-solving procedures are therefore omitted from the present investigation.

2.3.4.4 Eliminating products from the product portfolio

The product elimination literature is in parts wide ranging and general, and in other instances narrowly focused and detailed (Avlonitis, 1980; Hart, 1988). Only a handful of empirical studies have been carried out. Cooper (1975), Avlonitis (1980) and Hart (1988, 1990) are among the most important ones. Table 2.1 presents the majority of studies on product elimination published so far. These studies suggest that elimination may occur both before and after the launch of the new product (Cooper, 1975; Avlonitis, 1980).

As candidates for elimination, products undergo a four-stage process. In the first stage, managers recognise the existence of such products using specific poor performance criteria (Rothe, 1970; Baccour, 1971; Avlonitis, 1980; Hise *et al.*, 1984). In the second stage, managers attempt to revitalise these products (Eckles, 1971; Hise and McGinnis, 1975; Avlonitis, 1980). In the third stage, managers evaluate the actual weakness of the products (Worthing 1971; Banville and Pletcher, 1974; Avlonitis, 1980). In the fourth stage, managers identify the phasing-out strategy (Rothe, 1970; Avlonitis, 1980; Salerno, 1983). The formality of the elimination process has also been examined (Avlonitis, 1985) alongside the influence of several contextual elements (Avlonitis, 1980;

Table 2.1 Empirical versus prescriptive and phase versus non-phase based studies

	Phase reported				Phase		
	1	2	3	4	approach	Sample	Sector
Empirical research							
Avlonitis (1980)	*	*	*	*	yes	20 + 94 firms	British engineering
Baccour (1971)	*	n.a.	*	*	yes	11 firms	n.a.
Banville and Pletcher (1974)	-	-	-	-	no	24 firms	small home appliances
Cooper (1975)	-	-	-	-	no	114 products	Canadian manufacturers
Eckles (1971)	*	*	*	*	yes	n.a.	veterinary, electrical
Evans (1977)	*	-	-	-	no	62 salesmen	one SME electronics
Gauthier (1985)	*	-	*	*	yes	17 interviews	French manufacturers
Hart (1988)	*	*	*	*	yes	33 + 166 firms	British manufacturers
Hise and McGinnis (1975)	*	*	-	-	yes	96 firms	sample of 500 largest US
Hise *et al.* (1984)	n.a.	n.a.	n.a.	n.a.	n.a.	299 firms	large US manufacturers
Kent (1984)	*	*	*	*	yes	12 interviews	Scottish food processing
Rothe (1970)	*	n.a.	*	*	yes		n.a.
Salerno (1983)	*	*	*	*	yes	64 firms	French manufacturing
Tavlaridis (1989)					yes	19 firms	Greek manufacturers
Worthing (1971)	-/*	-	-/*	-	no	1 firm	n.a.
Prescriptive studies							
Alexander (1964)	*	*	*	*	yes	n.a.	n.a.
Berenson (1963)	-	-	*	-	yes	n.a.	n.a.
Browne and Kemp (1976)	*	-	*	-	yes	n.a.	n.a.
Clayton (1966)	*	-	-	-	yes	n.a.	n.a.
Drucker (1963)	*	-	-	-/*	n.a.	n.a.	n.a.
Fluitman (1973)	*	-	-	-	n.a.	n.a.	n.a.
Hallaq (1976)	*	-	-	-	n.a.	n.a.	n.a.
Hamelman and Mazze (1972)	*	*	*	-	yes	n.a.	n.a.
Houfek (1952)	*	-	-	-	yes	n.a.	n.a.
Kotler (1965)	*	-	*	*	yes	n.a.	n.a.
Kotler (1974)	*	-	-	-	n.a.	n.a.	n.a.

Kratchman et al. (1975)	*	-	-	-	yes	n.a.	n.a.
McSureley and Wilemon (1973)	*	*	*	*	yes	n.a.	n.a.
Michael (1971)	-	-	-	*	n.a.	n.a.	n.a.
Sonnecken and Hurst (1960)	*	*	*	-	yes	n.a.	n.a.
Wind and Claycamp (1976)	*	-	-	-	n.a.	n.a.	n.a.
Winkler (1972)	-	-	-	*	yes	n.a.	n.a.

Note: Unit of analysis is the single research project and not the various publications derived from it.

Salerno, 1983; Kent, 1984; Hart, 1988, 1989). It is noticeable, however, that the elements transcending the extant literature on product elimination are:

- the descriptive versus prescriptive nature of studies;
- the phases versus non-phases based elimination decision-making; and
- the internal and external influences upon the elimination decision.

This has created some serious problems. Key ones are the following:

- The gap between prescriptive stances and empirical studies is sufficiently wide to impose problems of incomparability of findings and incomprehension of management practice.
- There is only anecdotal understanding of the relationship between product elimination and product replacement issues. There is also no empirical evidence on elimination decisions of products marketed in international markets.
- The examination of product elimination for new products targeting international countries is complementary, yet different from new product rollout. It is complementary because elimination may occur before or during the rollout of a new product across its international markets. It is also complementary because there may be a link between product cannibalisation or optimal timing of product replacement and rollout. Here, though, attention is focused on the time it takes to commercialise the new product across countries and the causes of delays in doing so. It is likely that a poor performer becomes a candidate for elimination, but current knowledge does not permit one to conclude that delay in rollout correlates with poor new product performance in the first instance.

2.3.5   International business literature

The literature on international business spans almost 200 years but specific research traditions are isolated and there is limited interaction between them. Older contributions relevant to this project go back to international trade theories. More recent contributions have their roots in theories of organisational structure in multinational enterprises and international marketing.

2.3.5.1   *International trade theories: the international product life cycle concept*

Several decades ago, Heckscher (1919) and Ohlin (1933) extended the Ricardian trade model (Ricardo, 1817) and suggested that nations' trade success comes from product-related cost advantages. Later, Linder (1961) found that trade commodities are similar between countries with similar income levels and demand patterns. The reciprocity of product demand and supply was also used by Alfred Marshal in his theory of foreign trade (1879). Buckley and Casson (1976) also assumed within the framework of internalisation theory that the cross-border elimination of external intermediaries includes international product management operations.

In the mean time, Vernon (1966) and Wells (1968, 1969) introduced the international product life cycle (IPLC) theory. They argued that US firms technologically innovate and sell their products first in the domestic US market. This is because early home demand for advanced goods helps US firms to pioneer new products. These firms would export during the early phases of industry development and then establish foreign production as foreign demand grew. This happens because firm-specific advantages constitute a comparative advantage that is fully realisable for the companies only by moving production from one country to another. Eventually, foreign firms would enter the industry as technology diffused, and both foreign firms and the foreign subsidiaries of US companies would export to the United States. The concept of the IPLC was highly influential. Lutz and Green (1983) and Onkvisit and Shaw (1983) empirically confirmed that the theory has some explanatory relevance for specific cases.

Other studies, however, questioned this relevance. Mullor-Sebastian (1983) found that industrial groups of products behave in a manner predicted by the IPLC theory on world markets, but not the individual products in these groups. It seems that the IPLC theory is rather limited in explaining the early post-war foreign manufacturing investment of US companies possessing specific functional utility (e.g. washers)

(Onkvisit and Shaw, 1983). The IPLC theory does, however, provide an important insight into the present project. This insight is that the rollout may take place in either simultaneous or sequential manner across countries. A simultaneous rollout is when the product is made available in all countries at the same time. A sequential rollout is when the product is made sequentially available in one country after another. This is an insight to consider in the present investigation.

2.3.5.2 Internationalisation strategies

The internationalisation of the firm has long been an important issue in international business research and has received regular press coverage, as a series of recent overviews suggest (Young, 1990; Buckley and Ghauri, 1993). Internationalisation strategies are a broad concept and can be defined as the part of a company's strategies that takes place across national boundaries. These were first associated with describing a company's outward action during the first phase of its internationalisation (Johanson and Wiederscheim-Paul, 1975). Even though such a crossing of national boundaries in the process of a firm's growth may be argued to be a meaningless threshold (Buckley, 1990), development through internationalisation still has significant differences and unique features as compared with development in usually narrower domestic environments (Buckley and Ghauri, 1993).

From a research point of view, there has been a substantial focus on the 'process' content of a firm's internationalisation. Within this stream, evolution in 'stages' has historically attracted substantial attention. The 'stages' theory argues that firms proceed in a sequential fashion along some organisation continuum in the development of their international activities (Johanson and Wiedersheim-Paul, 1975; Bilkey and Tesar, 1977; Johanson and Vahlne, 1977, 1990; Cavusgil, 1980; Reid, 1981; Wortzel and Wortzel, 1981; Moon and Lee, 1990). This has been historically associated with a change in the state of a company's involvement across national boundaries (Johanson and Wiedersheim-Paul, 1975; Johanson and Vahlne, 1977, 1990). The 'stages' theory has been challenged both theoretically (Reid, 1984) and empirically (Young and Hood, 1976; Buckley *et al.*, 1979; Turnbull and Valla, 1986; Turnbull, 1987). Among the criticisms was that determination of stages and operationalisation in multiproduct, multidivisional firms are difficult (Turnbull, 1987). An evaluation of the theory was recently made in an attempt to delineate its boundaries (Rao and Naidu, 1992; Andersen, 1993).

Nonetheless, this research stream confirms the interest of the present investigation in simultaneous versus sequential rollout. Furthermore, it introduces the notion of resource sufficiency into the discussion of simultaneous versus sequential rollout of new products across international markets. Firms may be more or less developed in their internationalisation. Greater company involvement in some country markets is likely to be associated with greater resources devoted by the company to these markets. Such resources are likely in turn to facilitate rapid and timely new product rollout in these countries. This is another insight for the present study.

2.3.5.3 International strategies

'Content' elements of international strategies have also been examined. The mode of entry into foreign markets has long attracted attention, and various paradigms have been proposed. Thus, according to Dunning's *eclectic* explanation (Dunning, 1980, 1988), mode of entry depends on ownership-, internalisation- and location-specific advantages. Moreover, the *transaction cost* explanation (Caves, 1982; Hennart, 1982; Anderson and Gatignon, 1986; Gatignon and Anderson, 1988) considers the choice of entry mode on a continuum as different alternatives of vertical integration.

At the corporate level, the fountainhead of most ideas is Perlmutter's notion of the geocentric firm (Perlmutter, 1969). More recently, Bartlett (1986) and Bartlett and Ghoshal (1986) outlined how the management of operations on a global basis is critical to exploiting the resources of national subsidiaries by the larger corporation. Prahalad (1975), Barlett and Ghoshal (1987a,b) also explained the multitude of potential strategies for doing so. These strategies range from global integration to national adaptation.

There are also several proposed strategies at the business level (see Sullivan and Bauerschmidt, 1991; Doz and Prahalad, 1991). These strategies vary and depend upon several criteria. Among them are:

- Mobility barriers (Hout *et al.*, 1982; Caves and Ghemawat, 1992; Karakaya, 1993). Yeoh (1994) clearly indicated approvals and patents to be a major barrier for launch of new chemical entities across countries.
- Market imperfections and economic disequilibria that permit multi-market sourcing and production shifting (Kogut, 1985a,b).
- The nature of sector, namely global versus multidomestic (Prescott, 1983; Cvar, 1984; Porter, 1986; Roth *et al.*, 1991). An important

criterion in the assigning of sectors into one group or another is the standardisation of technology across countries (Porter, 1986). Kobrin (1991) extended the above. He created a list of several sectors and showed their degree of internationalisation.

- The flexibility of the company and its ability to transfer its acquired capabilities across borders (Kogut, 1989). This includes how managers manage efficiency, effectiveness and learning in organisations (Sullivan and Bauerschmidt, 1991).
- The nature of investment, company integration and attention to local government requirements (Morrison and Roth, 1992, pp. 400–1).
- The industry globalisation drivers, organisation structure, management processes and nationality (Johansson and Yip, 1994).

Morrison and Roth (1992) eventually found that these business strategies form four clusters. The first cluster comprises firms pursuing domestic strategy; the second cluster comprises exporting firms; a third cluster consists of firms pursuing an international product innovation strategy; the fourth cluster comprises firms that pursue a quasi-global manufacturing and marketing strategy.

The above suggest three additional key elements for the sampling and the discussion of the present project:

- The first is the high internationalisation of some sectors. Time to roll out new products across multiple countries is likely to be very important in environments of intense internationalisation.
- The second is technological heterogeneity between sectors and activities. Gatignon and Robertson (1985) clearly support this point when they mention that the speed of diffusion can be enhanced by a reasonable standardisation of a technology or retarded if competing standards prevail and that this factor is particularly important for high technology products, especially those dependent on software and auxiliary components. Substantial product technological customisation is therefore a fundamental dimension for companies when they develop and roll out their new products.
- The third is the existence of approvals as a barrier to entry.

2.3.5.4 Elements of organisational structure in multinational enterprises

Several researchers have examined the nature of structure and co-ordination mechanisms within multinational enterprises (MNEs). Historically, researchers first focused their attention upon the more

evident elements of structure, namely departmentalisation in companies. Later on, researchers moved their focus towards describing
structure through 'softer' and less apparent elements, like the nature
of administrative mechanisms.

Early research by Stopford and Wells (1972) and Franko (1976) identified structure in terms of world-wide product divisions, world-wide
functional divisions, geographic area divisions, international division
and a matrix system. Egelhoff (1988) found that MNEs with world-
wide product division structures tend to have high levels of foreign
product diversity. MNEs with area division structures tend to have a
greater percentage of foreign sales. MNEs with matrix structures tend
to have relatively high levels of both foreign product diversity and
foreign sales. Porter (1986) classified activities of MNEs in terms of
'configuration/co-ordination', and Takeutchi and Porter (1986) applied
the concepts in the marketing area. 'Configuration' is distinguished
into activity performed in a single country and activity performed
in multiple countries (Porter, 1986). Roth (1992) extended the above
when he found that configuration practices by MNEs are grouped into
the following different clusters:

- concentrated hub (firms locate only their marketing and sales activities in many countries);
- local innovators (firms have their activities geographically dispersed);
- transnational innovators (firms co-ordinate their marketing and
  sales regionally and their R&D, manufacturing and finance
  globally);
- regional federation (a federation of regionally co-ordinated activities);
  and
- primary global (activities are either performed in a single location or
  dispersed and co-ordinated globally).

Each one of these clusters comprises companies that have configured
their activities in a different way.

On the other hand, 'co-ordination' refers to the myriad of options
regarding how management of operations takes place. This area has
attracted multiple contributions. Martinez and Jarillo (1989) reviewed
the literature in the area and grouped the administrative mechanisms
used by MNEs in co-ordinating their international operations into two
groups. The first group comprised the 'harder', more structural and
formal mechanisms, namely:

- the grouping of organisational units (departmentalisation);
- the centralisation or decentralisation of decision-making;
- the formalisation of procedures (written policies, job descriptions, etc.);
- the extent of planning (functional plans, scheduling, etc.); and
- the output and behaviour control (reports, direct supervision, etc.).

The second group comprised the 'softer', more informal and subtle mechanisms, namely:

- the lateral cross-departmental relations (temporary teams, task forces, committees, etc.);
- the informal communication (management trips, meetings, personal contacts between managers, etc.); and
- the socialisation between managers (a common organisational culture, shared vision, etc.).

Martinez and Jarillo (1989) also found a pattern of evolution: as time has passed, researchers have concentrated more on subtler and more informal mechanisms, abandoning their older unidimensional focus on 'harder' structural issues. Examples of this trend are Roth (1992) and Sullivan (1992).

Bartlett and Ghoshal (1987a,b, 1989), however, clarified that there are different distinguishable organisational models for different sectors and company types. They have constructed in this respect, a 'transnational organisation model' for transnational enterprises similar to that which Hedlund (1986) discussed. Ghoshal and Nohria (1993) complemented the above by introducing the notion of 'fit' between individual sector or country situations and the administrative mechanisms. Their findings imply that companies must identify the most appropriate organisational model and use administrative mechanisms that 'fit' their business environment and individual markets. They found that such a 'fit' results in high performance. In support of this, the same authors found that the greater the technological dynamism, competition and local subsidiary resources, the greater the formalisation and integration, and the less the centralisation of international company activities (Ghoshal and Nohria, 1989). This means that, in volatile competitive environments, firms should opt for greater integration and more formal mechanisms.

Other researchers have looked at the impact of the culture and origin of parent companies on the use of administrative mechanisms. Rosenzweig and Singh (1991) argued that formal mechanisms of control are employed when there is cultural distance between MNEs' HQ and their subsidiaries. Kriger and Solomon (1992) found that American MNEs grant less autonomy than Japanese-parented MNEs to their subsidiaries.

Relationships between HQ and subsidiaries are of substantial importance for the present study. Previous research indicates that management of product activities may be performed in one, more than one or all countries where the company is present (configuration issues). The co-ordination of these activities is through specific mechanisms. MNEs seem to use 'softer' administrative mechanisms nowadays. An important question is whether extensive use of these 'softer' co-ordination mechanisms is necessary for timely rollout across countries. Limited use of them may well lead to delays in rollout schedule and they should therefore be included in the discussion of the present project.

2.3.5.5   Order-of-entry

Numerous conceptual and empirical studies also advanced the notion that first movers achieve long-term competitive advantages. These studies purport to demonstrate the presence of a systematic direct relationship between order of entry for products (Spital, 1983; Lilien and Yoon, 1990), brands (Whitten, 1979; Urban *et al.*, 1986), businesses (Robinson and Fornell, 1985; Lambkin, 1988; Parry and Bass, 1990) and market share. Kerin *et al.* (1992) soon highlighted, however, the complexity of the phenomenon and suggested that there are other factors that moderate the order of entry-market share. Szymanski *et al.* (1995) extended the work of Kerin *et al.* (1992). They proposed that there are at least 11 market strategy and 5 marketplace factors that play this moderating role. Market strategy factors include customisation of the product; development time for the new product and synergies in facilities, customers and marketing activities. Marketplace factors include the speed of technological change and the consumer versus industrial nature of markets.

Such first-mover effects were also examined within the context of wider international markets. Mascarenhas (1992a,b) examined the intermarket and intramarket orders of entry and their performance consequences for an industrial product (the semi-submersible rig used in oil-drilling industry and launched in 73 markets). He found that almost a quarter of a century elapsed before this industrial product was introduced to two-thirds of candidate markets, even though it catered for similar needs internationally. He argued that simultaneous entry into multiple markets occurs in the mature stage of the product life cycle and the smaller markets are served later when the uncertainty regarding the product future is reduced. His findings can be summarised in the following statements:

- Market entry occurs sooner in large developed and highly centralised markets.
- First entrants are MNEs and later entrants are small local firms. Surviving first entrants maintain the highest long-term market share, followed by early followers and later entrants.

The study by Mascarenhas (1992a,b) is a remarkable effort to identify the market share implications of some aspects of new product rollout across international markets. In doing so, it is essentially the only study which comes close to the focus of the present investigation and confirms the importance of the investigated subject.

The study has a number of notable features. It explicitly mentions the notion of simultaneous versus sequential entry that implicitly appeared first in the IPLC theory. It also looks at the individual project level, concentrates on a single sector and examines the product launch in a multitude of company markets. Third, it implicitly introduces the concept of key and secondary markets. Secondary markets are the less important markets for the company. These are important insights for the sampling rationale of the present investigation.

Mascarenhas (1992a,b) focuses, however, on two different aspects of the rollout of a new product across international markets. He looks at the macro order of market entry, namely which country first and which second. He then looks at the micro order of market entry, namely pioneer or follower. The study also suffers in at least two areas:

- The first concerns the adoption of market share as the performance indicator. This is probably due to the conceptual roots of the study in the order-of-entry literature which extensively uses market share as the preferred indicator of performance. The appropriateness of market share has long been questioned as a performance indicator (Thomas and Gardner, 1985; Jacobson, 1988).
- The second concerns the narrow conceptual framework of the study. By having its conceptual roots in the order-of-entry literature, the study neglects substantial insights from other research streams. The explanatory power of the study suffers accordingly. It is notable that more recent discussions of the order-of-entry literature have identified a much wider range of factors affecting performance (Szymanski *et al.*, 1995).

Despite such shortcomings, Mascarenhas' work provides important elements to consider in the present investigation.

2.3.6   Research in international marketing

Contributions in international marketing are also relevant to our focus here. Initial focus was on the standardisation of advertising (Elinder, 1964). Later, the discussion broadened to include other elements of the international marketing programme (Buzzell, 1968; Keegan, 1969; Aylmer, 1970).

Recently, Douglas and Craig (1989) developed a model of international expansion. They conceived the international marketing strategy as an evolutionary process in which not only product policy but also all organisational and marketing strategy elements vary at each successive phase. There are four successive phases: *pre-international; initial entry; local market expansion;* and *global rationalisation*. Douglas and Craig argued that there are influencing elements that interact with each other. Triggers drive companies to consider further expansion into international markets. Levers for this increasing international expansion are skills, proprietary assets and synergies. These foster strategic thrust, which leads in turn to decisions of strategic importance. Such decisions are development and adaptation of products for international markets, improvement of efficiency in operations, and development of global product strategies. Success drives the companies to continue into the next expansion phase.

Early research attention also focused upon market elements, particularly market diversification. Ayal and Zif (1979) indicated 12 potential market diversification strategies and the factors affecting their selection. These factors (Ayal and Zif, 1979) were: sales-response function, growth rate, sales stability in each market, competitive lead-time, spill-over effects, product adaptation, communication adaptation, distribution scale economies, control requirements, and extent of constraints. Their findings imply that market diversification produces superior profitability and profit stability. However, this diversification needs to be extensive (Kim *et al.*, 1989; Olugosa, 1993).

Kim *et al.* (1989) introduced the notion of relatedness to market diversification. They found that diversification in related segments is generally associated with favourable profitability, but inconclusively associated with profit stability. Unrelated diversification will be positively correlated with profit performance when firms become well diversified internationally.

At the same time, Levitt (1983) argued the existence of segments with similar characteristics across countries. This is due to the reduction of old-established differences in national preferences by mass culture, economic and cultural interdependencies across countries and expansion of world-wide communications. These permit the applicability of a standardised action internationally. There has been a vigorous debate surrounding the validity of this argument. In fact, much discussion has taken place over the opportunities of, and barriers to, such standardisation. This discussion gives the impression that fragmentation rather than homogenisation may more appropriately describe international consumers (Kreutzer, 1988; Jain, 1989; Samiee and Roth, 1992) and international marketing strategies.

Later, attention focused upon product elements (see Table 2.2 for a list of these studies and other details). It seems that firms with more innovative products tend to be of Japanese rather than European origin and pursue a world-wide product standardisation strategy (Kotabe, 1990). Firms from newly industrialising countries have not reached high levels of innovativeness, but are rapidly improving upon this (Ting, 1982). Samiee and Roth (1992) and Szymanski *et al.* (1993) found that a broad product line, high-quality new products, quality service and competing in high-growth segments are elements associated with superior financial performance.

Davidson and Harrigan (1977) and Hill and Still (1984) suggested that firms initially introduce home-conceived products overseas. Hill and Upknown (1992) argued that these products usually undergo adaptation if they are consumer goods. There are indications, though, that MNE product adoption strategies are not consistent for all regions (Still and Hill, 1984). Fewer adaptations are required for products targeting the Americas, Africa and less-developed Asian countries. More adaptations are required for products targeting developed Asian countries (James and Hill, 1993). Product adaptation can then take place on either a 'modules' or a 'core product + attachments' base (Walters and Toyne, 1989).

When time passes and local subsidiaries increase in size, they alter the content of their product lines. Local subsidiaries replace the products developed for the HQ's home base with products conceived and developed locally (Hill and James, 1991). They may, however, adopt products from other subsidiaries. This happens when there is strong integration and dense intra- and inter-unit communication. Strong integration and communication facilitate creation, adoption as well as diffusion of innovations within the broader corporation (Ghoshal and Bartlett, 1988). This means that new products developed either in the HQ or in other subsidiaries can be rapidly adopted by third units if there

Table 2.2 Empirical research in international marketing: product aspects

	Davidson and Harrigan (1977)	Davidson and Haspeslagh (1982)	Douglas and Rhee (1989)	Hill and Still (1984)	Hill and James (1991)	Hill and Upkhown (1992)	Gatignon et al. (1989)	Ghoshal and Bartlett (1988)	James and Hill (1993)
Level of investigation	Product	New products	PIMS defined business	Product	Product lines	Product lines	Innovation	Innovation	Product lines
Sample	Large MNEs	Large MNEs	PIMS based	Directory of American companies operating abroad	Directory of American companies operating abroad	Directory of American companies operating abroad	Euromonitor data	Large MNEs	Directory of American companies operating abroad
Sample size and nationality	n.a. US	57 US	437 US and European	19 US and UK	15 US	28 US	6 Europe 14 countries	75 Us, Japan, Europe	15 US
Other sampling details			Two geographical subsamples (US vs Europe)			MNEs with 6+ foreign subsidiaries		Multiphase/ multi-methodology	MNEs with 7+ foreign subsidiaries
Method of investigation	Secondary data and interviews	n.a.	Secondary data	Mail questionnaire	Mail questionnaire	Mail questionnaire	Secondary data	Interviews and mail questionnaire	Mail questionnaire
Analysis	Frequencies	Qualitative and frequencies	Quantitative	Qualitative and frequencies	Frequencies	Quantitative	Quantitative	Qualitative and quantitative	Quantitative
Aspects	I	Z, I	A, B, C, D	M, N	K, L, O	O	S, W	V	P

	Kirpalani and Macintosh (1980)	Kotabe (1990)	Manu (1992)	Ronkainen (1983)	Samiee and Roth (1992)	Hill and Still (1984)	Szymanski et al. (1993)	Ting (1982)
Level of investigation	Business	Product	Innovation	Product	Products	Product	PIMS defined business	Product category
Sample	SMEs	International Directory of Corporate Affiliations	PIMS (SPI4) based	Mainly Fortune 500	America's Corp. Families and Dir of Corp. Affiliations	Directory of American Companies operating abroad	PIMS (SPI4) based	n.a.
Sample size and nationality	34 US, Canada	n.a. Japan, Europe	473 US, Europe	4 US	147 US	50 US	1556 US, Canada, UK, and Western Europe	
Other sampling details			Two subsamples		Firms in 'global' industries		Companies serving only one national country	n.a. Far East
Method of investigation	Interviews	Mail questionnaire	Secondary data	Interviews, document analysis, observation	Mail questionnaire	Survey	Secondary data	Secondary data and primary sources
Analysis Aspects	Quantitative D, E, F, G, H, J	Quantitative R, U	Quantitative T	Qualitative Y	Quantitative J	Frequencies P, J	Quantitative J	Qualitative R

Table 2.2 (Continued)

Guide to investigated issues and aspects

Product and line aspects		Product transfers		Creation and diffusion of innovations		N.p.d.		Launch	
Relative product quality	A	Subsidiary line origins	K	Degree of innovativeness	R	Process	Y	Order of market entry	Z
Relative amount of new products	B	Transfer initiation	L	Propensity to innovate	S			Speed of initial launch	Z
Product age	C	Obstacles	M	Innovation orientation	T				
Relative line breadth/width	D	Adaptations	N	Intra- and inter-company creation and diffusion	V				
Product line complementariness	E	Subsidiary mix and mix localisation	O	Effects of market growth, nationality, standardisation and trade across the Triad	U				
Sophistication	F	Geographic variations	P	Simultaneity of diffusion	W				
Value added of features	G	Production location patterns	Q						
Position on PLC	H								
Frequency of launching products abroad	I								
Standardised or tailor-made	J								

is strong interaction in the corporation. There is some evidence that product development by MNEs is subject to the same rules and premises presented earlier under the NPD literature (Ronkainen, 1983).

In summary, studies in international marketing are also of substantial value to the present project. A key element is the extent of changes in the technology and marketing mix. Another is the relatedness between segments and the uniformity of technology and marketing changes across countries. Critical in this respect may be not the actual extent of product and marketing changes *per se*, but whether the organisation has adequate and sufficient resources, skills and proficiency to carry out these changes. Major changes in technology, distribution channel or salespersons' education may be more difficult to accomplish than changes in advertising or promotion.

2.4   Conclusions: the emergent theoretical framework

The above review shows that there is an inadequate literature and an insufficient number of contributions on the subject under investigation. Despite these limitations, however, previous research provides some insights into both the issue of new product rollout across international markets and the potential causes of delays in its schedule. This happens for reasons of cross-fertilisation between fields. When such insights are seen holistically, they form a more coherent whole than the sum of the constituent parts. The constructs included in the emergent conceptual framework, the items relevant to each construct and their conceptual roots are summarised in Table 2.3. Their linkages are depicted in Figure 2.3.

2.4.1   External and internal environmental factors

It seems that both external and internal environmental factors will affect the company's product/market and rollout decisions. External environmental factors include the speed of technological obsolescence, the marketing and technological heterogeneity across countries and the pervasiveness and attacking intensity of competitive action.

Internal environmental factors include the way the company develops its new product, the configuration of its international operations and the intensity of co-ordination between the HQ and subsidiaries/agents across countries.

Some of these factors are rooted in the wider organisational and business management research and they are assumed to apply at the much narrower product commercialisation area. For instance, Stopford and

Table 2.3 Constructs included in the theoretical framework, items relevant to each construct and conceptual roots

Constructs and items tapping each construct	Conceptual roots
External environment	
Legal and regulatory environment and approvals: Extent of local government regulations; Problems in acquiring government/technical approvals.	Ghoshal and Nohria (1989, 1993), Samiee and Roth (1992), Yeoh (1994)
Technological heterogeneity: Standardised product technology and specifications.	Samiee and Roth (1992)
Complexity of customisation of product technology: Substantial complexity of hardware and software adaptation.	Samiee and Roth (1992)
Rate of technological obsolescence: Speed of technology change within the industry; Product and production technology obsolescence rate; Rate of product modification instigated by main competitors.	Samiee and Roth (1992)
Market homogeneity: Customer needs/preferences are standardised Europewide; Product awareness and information exists Europewide; Competitors market a standardised product Europewide; Standardised purchasing practices exist Europewide.	Kirpalani and Macintosh (1980), Levitt (1983), Kreutzer (1988), Gatignon *et al.* (1989), Jain (1989), Wills *et al.* (1991), Samiee and Roth (1992), James and Hill (1993), Yeoh (1994)
Pervasiveness and attack intensity of competitive action: Firm was threatened by competitive action; Competitive action was very hostile towards the company; This action was resulting in sales at firm's own expense; Firm was threatened in all its key European markets.	Chen *et al.* (1992), Heil and Walters (1993), Bowman and Gatignon (1995)
Internal environment	
Nature and intensity of co-ordination of company activities across markets: *Assessment of performance:* Cost and profit centres for performance assessment; Comprehensive management information systems; Quality control procedures; Standard cost procedures for performance assessment. *Formalisation:* Formal performance appraisals; A written marketing strategy; Written manuals of procedures and fixed rules; Master marketing plans and schedules.	Stopford and Wells (1972), Franko (1976), Bartlett (1986), Miller and Dröge (1986), Porter (1986), Takeutchi and Porter (1986), Bartlett and Ghoshal (1987a,b), Ghoshal (1987), Egelhoff (1988), Lemak and Bracker (1988), Ghoshal and Bartlett (1988), Martinez and Jarillo (1989, 1991), Jarillo and

Centralisation: Who decides (HQs or subsidiaries) regarding : technology/ specifications for new product; Time to launch in their markets; Product appearance/features; Segments to serve in each country; Promotion and advertising; Pricing. *Integration:* Direct contact; meetings and interaction between Head Office and subsidiaries/agents and between staff in different European subsidiaries/ agents; Transfers of managers between Head Office-subsidiaries/agents and between subsidiaries/agents; Interdepartmental permanent committees set up to allow Head Office and subsidiaries/agents' staff to engage in joint decision making; Interdepartmental temporary task forces set up to facilitate Head Office and subsidiaries/agents staff collaboration on specific issues; Liaison personnel; Project managers with responsibilities over total operations across Head Office and subsidiaries/agents; A matrix system where Head Office personnel within specialisations is fully integrated with personnel in subsidiaries/agents; A set of shared goals, values, and beliefs shaping behaviour of subsidiaries/agents' staff across European countries.	Martinez (1990), Rosenzweig and Singh (1991), Kriger and Solomon (1992), Roth (1992), Sullivan (1992), Ghoshal and Nohria (1993), Ghoshal *et al.* (1994)
New product development process: *Integration:* Integration between technical, marketing and manufacturing functions; Integration between these functions when located in different countries; Technical and marketing personnel contribution of accurate, on time and high quality input; Subsidiaries/agents provided continuous feedback; Final customers were strongly involved and provided feedback. *Proficiency of execution of the NPD process:* Predevelopment project planning; Tests of prototypes by customers/trial sales; Co-ordination of distribution channels and logistics; Co-ordination of advertising and promotion; Technical development and sorting out of unexpected 'bugs'; Technical testing of the product. *Protocol/early known targets:* The intended users; Target countries and their needs and preferences; The product concept and product positioning; The final product specifications and technical requirements; The product final features and characteristics.	Ancona and Galdwell (1992a,b), Calantone and Cooper (1979), Cooper (1979), Ronkainen (1983), Maidique and Zirger (1984, 1985), Clark *et al.* (1987), Cooper and Kleinschmidt (1987, 1993a,b), Hayes *et al.* (1988), Zirger and Maidique (1990), Clark and Fujimoto (1991), Iansiti (1992, 1993), Brown and Eisenhardt (1995), Eisenhardt and Tabrizi (1995)

50

Table 2.3 (Continued)

Constructs and items tapping each construct	Conceptual roots
Company (re)action and strategy	
Diversification of target segments:	Ayal and Zif (1978, 1979), Kim *et al.* (1989),
Number of *key* European markets for this type of product; In how many of these *key* markets the product was launched; The number of *secondary* European markets for this type of product; In how many of these *secondary* markets the product was launched; European countries which are *key* markets for the company.	Olugosa (1993)
Availability of resources for implementation of marketing and engineering decisions for the new product:	Johanson and Vahlne (1977, 1990), Jain (1989), Chen *et al.* (1992), Heil and Walters (1993), Cooper (1994)
Marketing resources: Marketing personnel/funds to adapt advertising/promotion; Personnel to train sales staff and technicians; After-sales service personnel and equipment; Distribution channels	
Engineering resources: R & D personnel/funds to adapt product; Hardware and software adapted for European country markets.	
Product/market characteristics and synergies	
Extent of marketing mix and technology changes and synergies with existing operations:	Davidson and Harrigan (1977), Ting (1982), Still and Hill (1985), Robertson and Gatignon (1986), Saunders and Jobber (1988, 1994), Ghoshal and Nohria (1989, 1993), Jain (1989), Walters and Toyne (1989), Kotabe (1990), Zirger and Maidique (1990), Hill and James (1991), Hill and
Hardware and software platform/architecture; Product appearance/features; Brand names; Product positioning; Distribution channels; Logistics and delivery systems; Advertising spending; Promotion to trade and final customers; Market research, advertising, promotion, production, sales force and service, hardware and software development technical capabilities and	

resources; Product handling/'feeling' has changed for customer; Change in the way user is informed about product functions; Change in the way user interacts with and controls operation of product.

Product superiority: Unique attributes and clearly visible benefits to the customer; Superior quality, performance, value for money; Attributes also perceived as useful by the customers; Intended image consistent with corporate image.

Timeliness of new product rollout
Scheduled/anticipated and actual time across European markets: Length of planned and actual time for rolling out this product across key and all European markets. Adherence of new product to rollout schedule.

Success of the new product rollout across multiple country markets
Achievement of targets: Sales (value); Customer acceptance; Return on investment; Product development budget costs; Technical performance of product; Development of the new product ; Product rollout across the key European markets; Product rollout across all (key + secondary) European markets.

Upknown (1992), Samiee and Roth (1992), Heil and Walters (1993), Szymanski et al. (1993), Cooper and Kleinschmidt (1993a,b), Olugosa (1993), Cavusgil and Zou (1994), Dhebar (1995), Ali et al. (1995)
Cooper (1979), Clark and Fujimoto (1991), Cooper (1994), Brown and Eisenhardt (1995), Montoya-Weiss and Calantone (1994)

Vernon (1966), Mascarenhas (1992a,b), Cooper and Kleinschmidt (1994), Olson et al., (1995)

Griffin and Page (1993), Montoya-Weiss and Calantone (1994)

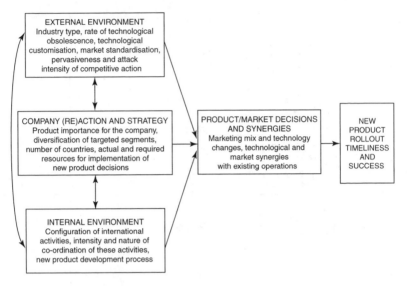

Figure 2.3   The emergent theoretical framework

Wells (1972), Franko (1976), Miller and Dröge (1986) and other researchers' findings on organisational structure and administrative mechanisms are also likely to be pertinent at the narrower areas of product/market, NPD process or product rollout decisions. Similarly, the pervasiveness and attacking intensity of competitive action factors rooted in Chen *et al.* (1992) and Heil and Walters' (1993) work are also expected to apply to product/market and rollout decisions.

Other factors such as the technological and market heterogeneity, rooted in the international marketing literature (i.e. Jain, 1989; Samiee and Roth, 1992; Wills *et al.*, 1991), have traditionally been close to the area under investigation and they are understood to have a major and direct influence upon product/market and rollout decisions.

2.4.2   Company (re)action and strategy factors

Factors such as target market segments, the desired technological and marketing customisation, the level of required investment and the company engineering and marketing resources available, which are rooted back to the research of Johanson and Vahlne (1977, 1990), Ayal and Zif (1978, 1979), Chen *et al.* (1992), Heil and Walters (1993), and Cooper (1994), are likely to be pertinent to the nature of marketing and technology incorporated in the new product as well as product rollout decisions.

2.4.3 Product/market decisions and synergies

These product/market decisions include the extent of technological and marketing changes for the new product as well as the synergies of the new product with existing operations (sales force, distribution channels, target markets). There is a multitude of research on these issues as it is indicatively reported in Davidson and Harrigan, (1977), Still and Hill (1985), Zirger and Maidique (1990), Samiee and Roth (1992), Cooper and Kleinschmidt (1993a,b), Cavusgil and Zou (1994), and Montoya-Weiss and Calantone (1994). These give an indication of the likely new product rollout strategies across countries and a potential linkage with the simultaneous versus sequential manner of rolling out new products and rollout timeliness. New product rollout will in turn affect the success of the new product.

Insights for the methodology and the sampling rationale include the following:

2.4.4 Rollout

This study should make a distinction between rolling out into 'key' versus secondary (in terms of importance of sales for the company) country markets (Mascarenhas, 1992a,b). It should examine the sequential versus simultaneous manner of new product rollout in many candidate markets (IPLC theory; Mascarenhas, 1992a,b).

2.4.5 Projects

Following traditional NPD literature and Mascarenhas (1992a,b) the study should concentrate on individual project level. It should also focus upon projects deemed important for the company in terms of sales (Mahajan *et al.*, 1993). It is likely that managers will pay substantial attention to scheduling and estimating accurately the anticipated rollout time for such projects.

2.4.6 Sophisticated research approach sample and research questions

The study should pursue a multiphase, in-depth case study approach. The study should also use samples in sectors with high internationalisation (Prescott, 1983; Cvar, 1984; Porter, 1986; Kobrin, 1991; Roth *et al.*, 1991) and different speeds of technology change (Porter, 1986; Ghoshal and Nohria, 1989, 1993; Samiee and Roth, 1992). It should consider customisation versus standardisation of product technology (Still and Hill, 1985; Porter, 1986; Ghoshal and Nohria, 1989, 1993; Samiee and Roth, 1992; James and Hill, 1993).

Insights for the research questions also include the following: (a) This study should investigate if timeliness of new product rollout is related to new product success; (b) It should examine if firms roll out their new products across international markets simultaneously or sequentially. It should also examine the link between the nature of product technology and sequential rollout and sequential rollout and delays; (c) It should explore the factors that lead to rollout delay; and (d) It should also look into the interaction between these factors and their direct and indirect effects upon rollout delay.

The methodology with more specific details of the research procedures used are presented next, in Chapter 3.

3
Methodology

3.1 Introduction

The importance of the timeliness of new product rollout, the insights supplied by previous literature on the subject and the emergent theoretical framework were explained in Chapter 2. This chapter describes in more detail the methodology of the present study. Discussion focuses, in particular on the nature of the dependent variable (section 3.2), the context of the study (section 3.3), the justification for selecting the case method (section 3.4), the research phases (section 3.5), sample selection (section 3.6), data collection, formulation of hypotheses and measurement issues (section 3.7), and the method of carrying out the cross-case analysis (section 3.8). The nature of the dependent variable is first explained.

3.2 The dependent variable

Delay (conversely, on-time), as a noun, is defined as 'the time during which something is delayed' (Oxford dictionary). There is in this definition an intrinsic comparative element of:

- a time difference between two periods used as yardsticks (i.e. reference); and
- initial expectations and final result.

Let us focus initially on the first issue (i.e. the reference periods). There are at least six different perspectives to use in comparing rollout time periods. The character of these perspectives is different. Some look internally into the company, others contrast what happens internally with what happens outside the company. Their aims are also different.

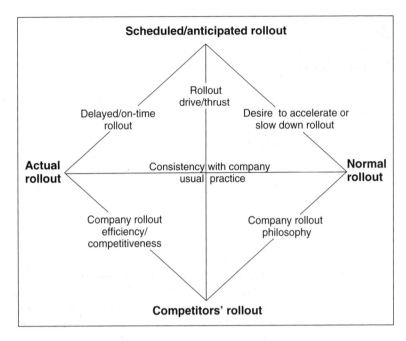

Figure 3.1   The rollout diamond

Some aim to judge timeliness, others to identify company efficiency, while others still may indicate company business philosophy.

Perspectives that look internally within the company involve comparisons between the usual time taken for the company to roll out its new products, the scheduled/anticipated time and the actual time taken to roll out a specific new product. Distinctly, the perspectives that contrast what happens internally with what happens outside the company involve, in turn, the same comparisons against competition. Figure 3.1 shows how these perspectives relate to each other.

At the four corners of the diamond are the company's *scheduled/ anticipated rollout* time period, the *actual rollout* time period (how long it actually took), the *normal rollout* time period (i.e. the usual company practice) and the *competitors' rollout* period (for similar products):

- Comparing the *scheduled/anticipated against the actual* rollout time shows whether managers achieved their initial expectations or plans regarding the necessary period to make the new product available for sale across its target markets.

- Comparing the *scheduled/anticipated against the normal* rollout time shows the desire of the company to accelerate or slow down the length of the rollout period for a specific new product against what is the usual company rollout period. A desire to diminish the scheduled time period may well depend upon the launch of products by rivals, the acceleration of technological change and rapid product obsolescence.
- Comparing the *actual against normal* rollout time shows whether the rollout period was eventually consistent with usual company practice despite managerial desire to accelerate the rollout.
- Comparing the *actual product rollout time against rivals'* rollout periods indicates if the company is efficient and competitive in terms of time.
- Comparing the *normal rollout time* (i.e. the usual company rollout periods) *against competition* also seems to be an indicator of the overall company philosophy towards the marketplace. It is possible that some firms will opt for longer or shorter rollout periods than their rivals.
- Comparing the *scheduled/anticipated against rivals'* rollout periods may well show differences in the ability of the company to innovate and renew its product lines. These differences may also show a variation of business philosophy in line with the arguments of Miles and Snow (1978).

Table 3.1 summarises the discussion on the aims of the six comparative perspectives. The dependent variable in this study is the *timeliness in new product rolling out across European markets*.

Table 3.1 Aims of comparative perspectives

dt in rollout periods	Aim
Scheduled/anticipated vs Actual rollout	Identifies rollout delay or timeliness
Scheduled/anticipated vs Normal rollout	Shows desire to accelerate or slow down rollout period
Actual vs Normal rollout	Shows if the actual rollout time was consistent with usual company practice
Actual vs Competitors' rollout	Indicates company efficiency and competitiveness
Normal vs Competitor's rollout	Describes company philosophy
Scheduled/anticipated vs Competitors' rollout	Indicates drive and thrust

Extending the definitions by Cooper and Kleinschmidt (1994) and Olson *et al.* (1995) regarding timeliness in NPD and launch, a rollout is timely when it is completed within – or faster than – its planned (scheduled/anticipated) time frame. A rollout delay occurs when the rollout is completed later than its planned time frame.

This time frame in new product rollout is dependent upon managers' perceptions regarding the period aimed at, or needed, to make the new product available for sale in target segments across the company's target country markets. Such managerial perceptions may well vary, with individuals overestimating or underestimating time periods systematically. Such perceptions may be influenced by personal attitudes, previous work experience, lack of experience in decision-making and planning, or simple misunderstanding of the actual strengths and weaknesses of the organisation. Despite potential variations in the causes and the cognitive processes by which individuals identify, plan the schedule of, and estimate the anticipated time to roll out products across country markets, it is reasonable to infer that the difference between the scheduled/anticipated time considered to be necessary to roll out during the planning stage and the time taken to roll out a new product during the implementation stage is due to elements that have not evolved in accordance with expectations at the initial identification stage. A delay shows serious managerial misjudgement and may have substantial implications for company activities. Such misjudgement is assumed of course not to be deliberate and intentional. Understanding the causes of delays is, therefore, of fundamental importance to managers.

It is important to reiterate at this point that the focus of the present study is on delays in the rollout phenomenon, not the reasons for late product development of a new product or the most appropriate timing of the order of such entry within or across country markets. Timeliness in international new product rollout is not the same as a timely order-of-entry into a domestic (Kerin *et al.*, 1992; Szymanski *et al.*, 1995) or a foreign (Mascarenhas, 1992a,b) market; a timely NPD process (Cooper and Kleinschmidt, 1994; Olson *et al.*, 1995) or a speedier new product crossing of the national borders (Oackley, 1996). The purpose of each activity is different:

- The aim of a timely NPD process seems to be the building of a new product within an anticipated time frame. It is assumed here that there is no time gap between the completion of the NPD process and the launch of the new product in the first country.

- The aim of the timely order-of-entry may be to pioneer product availability for sale within markets (micro order of market entry) or across countries (macro order of market entry).
- The aim of timeliness in new product's international rollout is the availability of the new product for sale across the company's country markets within the anticipated time frame, irrespective of which country the company enters first and whether the company is entering each country as a pioneer, early follower or late follower. It is assumed that the company has already decided to make its new product available internationally (Oackley, 1996). This is also independent of rollout strategies. Saunders and Jobber (1994) identified that there is a link between the launch and deletion strategies of older products. They found, for instance, that rapid rollout strategies are accompanied by rapid deletion of older products and low price launches are accompanied by lower priced deletions.

3.3 The context of this research

Unit of analysis: The individual project is the unit of analysis in this study. There are notable limitations associated with investigations of new product performance and rollout timeliness at higher levels (e.g. firm level). Considerable variations in the effect of individual factors upon timeliness and new product success often exist across various new product ventures and product groups of the same firm. It is unrealistic to expect that the same elements will be responsible for delays in all product cases. Consequently, investigation of the rollout timeliness at aggregate level (i.e. the level of the overall firm or a level higher than the individual project) will result in amalgamated findings and misleading interpretation. Therefore the position taken in this research is that the individual project must be selected as the unit of study, to obtain a more precise measurement of the factors affecting the timeliness relationship and potential effects upon new product success. This stance is in line with the majority of research in NPD (see Montoya-Weiss and Calantone, 1994) and Mascarenhas' (1992a,b) work.

Key and secondary markets: A distinction is made between *key* and *secondary* markets. A key market is a European country that is important for the company in terms of sales for the specific product. A secondary market is a European country that is less important for the company in terms of sales for the specific product. A company may not roll out a new product to less important target country markets (Mascarenhas,

1992a,b). Sales are also understood to take place in a regular and frequent manner. This study was restricted to a European context.

3.4   Case research

Case research methodology was followed. Bonoma (1985) has argued that there are identifiable sets of research situations where the qualitative, in-depth approaches are desirable, even if accompanied by some risks to data integrity. In particular, they are useful when a phenomenon is broad and complex, where the existing body of knowledge is insufficient to permit the posing of causal questions, and when a phenomenon cannot be studied outside the context in which it naturally occurs. The investigation of the rollout-across-multiple-countries is exactly such a phenomenon. Several problems are associated, however, with the use of case research methodology (Kerlinger, 1973). The goal here is to understand and generalise to theoretical propositions and not to theoretical universes. Also, we vigorously attempted to address problems of validity and reliability using psychometrics-based methodologies; establishing the domain for generalisation; and precisely identifying possible causal relationships. We also followed the structured approach proposed by Eisenhardt (1989) and Miles and Huberman (1984) on data analysis. This procedure comprised:

- accurate definition of the research question with some a priori constructs;
- specification of the population on theoretical grounds instead of randomly;
- use of multiple data collection methods combining both qualitative and quantitative measures;
- overlap of the data collection and analysis;
- a within-case and cross-case analysis using divergent techniques;
- use of iterative tabulation of evidence for each construct and search for 'why' behind relationships;
- application of the theoretical (cases that vary against key variables) and literal (cases with the same critical variables) replication logic for confirmation, extension and sharpening of theory based on cross-case analysis;
- comparison with previous literature whenever possible; and
- completion of the research process when data show that improvement is marginal.

Further, this research followed a multiple-phase development to enhance the robustness of the process. We also developed hypotheses to allow easier replication, extension, refinement and tentative confirmation of the earlier findings, purposeful for generation of propositions for future testing. (Worsley *et al.* (1970) have adopted an extreme stance on this matter. They argued on the representativeness of cases that 'it is of the same kind that enabled Sir Ronald Ross to announce the "cause" of malaria when he found the malaria parasite in the salivary gland of a single female Anopheles mosquito in 1897' (p. 112).)

3.5   Cases

This study is based on companies operating in high internationalisation sectors that are also subject to rapid technology change. A pilot study looked at six companies. The main study was implemented in two phases and included 30 more companies (see Figure 3.2).

Such a purposive sampling is appropriate when the goal is to obtain good insights and critical appraisals because of the special experience of the sample cases (Selltiz *et al.*, 1976). The use of judgement and a deliberate effort to obtain representative samples by including presumably typical cases is necessary (Kerlinger, 1973). Revealing of particularities are allowed and conditions for transferability of conclusions to other business settings are illustrated (e.g. Harrigan, 1983; McGee and Thomas, 1988).

3.5.1   Pilot study: 6 company cases

Six companies, belonging to specific sectors known for strong international activities (Prescott, 1983; Cvar, 1984; Porter, 1986; Roth *et al.*, 1991), were selected randomly from the Datamonitor directory. Table 3.2 shows the spread of firms in the UK and Europe in these sectors.

The marketing managers of the interviewed companies were contacted by telephone. The two key questions we posed to them concerned

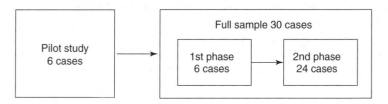

Figure 3.2   The pilot and the full sample study

Table 3.2 Sectors in the pilot study

Sector Dun & Bradstreet International (Europe) 1994 (SIC US 1987)	Firms in Europe	Firms in UK
Surgical and medical instruments, dental equipment and supplies, X-ray apparatus and cubes, electro-medical equipment	116	24
Mining machinery	43	19
Telephone/telegraph apparatus	127	69
Radio & TV communications equipment	121	24
Oil-field machinery	23	11
Construction machinery (inc. earth moving)	154	21

the major problems they faced in managing their product lines across international markets and the importance of timeliness in product launches.

One company (oil-field machinery and supplies) considered as a major problem the time to develop products. With development periods for 'new' products spanning over 30 years, the company introduces new product lines every 10 years on average. The UK HQ were facing substantial problems of co-operation with their US-based HQ for the international management of their product lines. Another company (construction equipment) mentioned that it experienced a serious new product failure. New product development takes 5–6 years. The company has also developed only two new products (line additions) in the last 20 years. The third company (a mining machinery firm) mentioned that geological characteristics are different for every mine and each country has different safety standards, thus requiring substantial product customisation. Delays in new product availability were common. The fourth company (a surgical equipment manufacturer) was in the process of concentrating on core products (through shrinkage of specialised lines). It was currently experiencing short product development phases of 1–2 years at maximum, yet competition managed to introduce new products quicker. The fifth company (a dental equipment firm), supplying both machinery and consumer goods, mentioned that it was diversifying its product lines and relaunching existing products. Sales of older products had collapsed and the company needed the rapid introduction of new products into its international markets and multiplication of the versions launched at each new round. New product types were launched every 8–9 months. The findings confirmed the managerial importance of the new product rollout timeliness issue, the appropriateness of insights from previous literature, and prompted us to:

- Concentrate upon highly international sectors of rapid technology change. In other highly international sectors of slower technology change (e.g. earth-moving equipment), NPD seemed infrequent and product lines narrow, resulting in limited occurrence of new product introductions to international markets.
- Select projects with both standardisable and customisable technology across countries; targeting both niche and mass/volume markets; of different novelty to the company ('truly' new products, product modifications, etc.).
- Carry out in-depth face-to-face interviews, given the apparent complexity of the investigated issues. The results of a postal survey was expected to undermine the robustness of the research design.
- Implement the sampling rationale for the full sample in two phases for reasons of a sequential step-by-step procedure, need to reinforce the emergent theoretical framework and qualitative methodology requirements.
- Select an equal number of timely versus delayed cases for greater comparability.

The method of selection of sectors and cases for the 30-strong sample is explained next. The implementation of the procedure follows.

3.5.2 Full sample: 30 cases

Sectors: An examination of Kobrin's (1991) list permitted the establishment of highly international sectors including telecommunications (Kobrin's international integration index of 0.404), electronics and computers (0.385), photographic equipment (0.324) and measuring instruments (0.286), where technological change is rapid and product launches are likely to be frequent. Eventually, 40 per cent of the investigated products had a product/production obsolescence period of 1–2.5 years, and an additional 40 per cent had an obsolescence period of 2.5–5 years. The Datamonitor directory was used to establish the number of companies active in each sub-sector in the UK. The Kompass directory was used for supplementary information. This was followed by:

- Identification of technology and likely product candidates through an in-depth investigation of multiple sources. The published issues of *BYTE* magazine were examined for the entire 1990–95 period. Information was further sought from other professional publications, and the F&S database of product announcements. Particular attention was given to technology and products that appeared in 1994 and 1995.

- Identification of companies that have launched products in the last three years in the technological areas of interest.
- Contact of these companies and mailing of the research project description alongside an invitation to participate in it.
- Pre-screen with the appropriate respondent over the telephone of the number and type of company product launches in Europe in the last three years in the product technology areas of interest and selection of a major product (in terms of sales). The product should have been launched in three or more European markets. An overall response rate of 50 per cent was achieved during these telephone calls. The rest mostly declined because marketing and sales to Europe were controlled from HQ located in other countries.

Table 3.3   First six cases: sectors and companies

	Product	Company	Delays in rollout	Origin	Customisation of product technology
Niche markets					
Telecommunication technologies	Private branch exchange	Nortel	no	North American	yes
Data/image acquisition technologies	Climatic data logger	Delta-T	yes	UK	no
	Dynamo-meter	Instron	yes	UK/USA	yes
Mass/volume markets					
Data/image acquisition technologies	Cameras	Halina	yes	Asian	no
	Cameras	Hanimex	no	North American	no
Image output technologies	TV sets	Panasonic	no	Asian	some

The two phases of data collection: The sampling rationale for the full sample was implemented in two phases. Six companies supplied information in the first phase: Nortel, Panasonic, Halina, Hanimex, Delta-T and Instron (see Table 3.3).

A total of 24 more companies provided input in the second and final data collection phase: Mitel, Toshiba, Hitachi, Motorola, Cray Computers, US Robotics, Taxan, OKI, Brother International, TEC, Citizen, LanArt, Allied Telesyn, Rhetorex, Orbitel, 3COM, Racal Datacom, Emulex, Hadland Photonics, Voltech, Amplicon Liveline, Laminex, Soundcraft and Sony.

Table 3.4 shows the list of focal cases and participating companies. The focal cases can be more precisely split into three areas: data and image acquisition technologies; data and image output technologies; and communication technologies.

Customisation of product technology and type of target markets: Cases belong to three groups (see Table 3.5). The first group includes products using similar technology that does not need customisation from country to country (i.e. the mobile GSM telephone, the Ethernet products, the sound mixing system, the hand stand still 35 mm cameras, the ISDN modem). The second group of products includes products requiring customisation (i.e. technology and specifications) from country to country, where such customisation is not difficult (i.e. the TV sets, the PC monitor, the laser and matrix printers). The third group includes products requiring extensive and complex customisation from country to country. Examples include a software-driven dynamometer (a vibration data acquisition and testing instrument) or some telecommunication products (analogue modems, PBXs) which also undergo laborious approvals from country to country. The 30 cases targeted 19 mass/volume markets (63 per cent of cases) and 11 niche segments (37 per cent of cases); 15 cases in the sample faced delays in rollout (50 per cent of the sample), while 15 cases were on time (50 per cent of the sample).

Project novelty and origin of parent companies: Almost half (47 per cent) of the cases concerned modifications of existing company products (type nos 6 and 7 in Table 3.6). The second place was shared between: products that are totally new to the world, for which there was an existing market (16.7 per cent); products that are new to the company, which offered new features versus competitive products (13.3 per cent); and product line extensions (13.3 per cent).

Table 3.4 Product technologies and selected companies

Area of technology		No. of cases	Nature of product technology	Product use	Software controlled	Company name(s)
Data/image acquisition technologies	Photographic equipment	1	High- and ultra-high-speed camera	Ballistic testing	yes	Hadland Photonics
		1	Medium-speed industrial camera	Control of production lines	no	Hitachi
		1	Medium-speed professional camera	Filming	no	Sony
		2	Hand stand still 35 mm cameras	General use	no	Hanimex, Halina
		1	Security identification and lamination system	Security control	yes	Laminex
	Measuring instruments	1	Climatic data recording instrument	Weather data acquisition	yes	Delta-T Instruments
		1	Dynamometer	Vibration data acquisition/testing	yes	Instron
		1	Electric data recording/ testing instrument	Component testing	no	Voltech

Category	Subcategory	Qty	Item	Use		Manufacturer
Data/image output technologies	Printing	2	Laser (B&W) medium/high-speed printers	Office printing	yes	OKI, Brother
		1	Solid ink colour printer	Portable colour printing	yes	Citizen
		1	Matrix (B&W) bar-code printer	Bar-code printing	yes	TEC
	Screen	2	TV sets	General use	no	Toshiba, Panasonic
		1	PC monitor	General/office use	yes	Taxan
	Audio	1	Sound mixing system	Theatre use	no	Soundcraft
Communication technologies	Local area networks (LAN)	2	Ethernet print servers	Computer networks	yes	Emulex, 3Com
		1	Ethernet 10/100 adapter card	Computer networks	yes	Allied Telesyn
		1	Ethernet port switch	Computer networks	yes	LanArt
		1	Ethernet multiplexer	Computer networks	yes	Cray Coms
		1	RS232 adapter (signal converter)	Computer networks	no	Amplicon Liveline
	Telephony	2	PBX systems	Switch telecommunication system	yes	Mitel, Nortel
		1	GSM mobile telephone	General use	no	Orbitel
	PC-telephony interface	1	Modem (ISDN)	Data/image transfer	yes	Racal Datacom
		2	Modems (analogue)	Data/image transfer	yes	US Robotics, Motorola
		1	PC-telephony integration platform	Data/voice routing	yes	Rhetorex
	Total	30				

Table 3.5   Sample cases: customisation of product technology and type of target markets

Type of target markets

Customisation of product technology	Mass/volume markets Total: 19	Niche segment/client-based sales Total: 11
Substantial (several standards) Total: 6	Analogue modems (2)	PBXs (2), dynamometer (1), PC-telephony integration platform (1)
Some Total: 7	TV sets (2), PC monitor (1), printers (2 B&W laser, 1 barcode printer, 1 colour solid ink)	
Limited Total: 17	Hand still 35 mm cameras (2), GSM mobile telephone (1), Ethernet LAN (5), RS232 adapter (1), ISDN modem (1)	Security identification and lamination system (1), high- and ultra-high-speed camera (1), medium-speed industrial and professional cameras (2), electric testing instrument (1), climatic data acquisition instrument (1), sound mixing system (1)

This shows a greater number of projects in 'existing' areas of product activity (60 per cent of cases; types 5, 6 and 7) than projects in 'novel' product activities for the company (40 per cent of cases; types 1–4). The existence of 'new' products of different novelty is important. It is necessary to have a spread of new product types as opposed to only one type. Internal company and external environment circumstances are likely to affect differently the novel product activities compared to the existing ones. Among the 30 cases, 11 companies are of North American origin, 9 are of UK origin while 10 are of Asian origin (see Table 3.7).

Multiple sources of data: Multiple methods of data collection were used. The first method consisted of a semi-structured, protocol-based interviewing with principal informants mainly in marketing. Table 3.8 shows some indicative titles of principal informants. Additional interviews were also carried out with engineering or manufacturing directors located in the UK. The interviews aimed to explore in depth the practice

Table 3.6* Sample cases: project novelty

Type of project	No. of cases	% of total cases	Cum. %
'Novel' areas of product activity			
1. Product totally new to the world, which created an entirely new market	1	3.3	3.3
2. Product totally new to the world, but for which there was an existing market	5	16.7	20.0
3. Product totally new to the company, which offered new features versus competitive products in an existing market	4	13.3	33.3
4. Product new to the company, which competed against fairly similar products on the market	2	6.7	40.0
'Existing' areas of product activity			
5. New item in an existing product line for the company, which was sold into an existing market	4	13.3	53.3
6. A significant modification of an existing company product	13	43.3	96.7
7. A fairly minor modification of an existing company product	1	3.3	100.0

Table 3.7 Sample cases: origin of parent companies

Origin	No. of cases	Total
North American		11
USA	8	
USA/Canada	2	
USA/Australia	1	
UK		9
UK	7	
UK/USA	2	
Asian		10
Asian (Japan)	9	
Asian (Hong Kong)	1	

Table 3.8   Indicative titles of principal informants

Company	Informant's title
Sony	Divisional Director
Nortel	European Marketing Manager
Emulex Europe	Director, European Sales Operations
Motorola, Info Systems Group	Marketing Director
Toshiba (UK) Limited	Group Product Manager
Brother International Europe	General Manager – European Development and Technical Services
Rhetorex Europe Limited	General Manager
Hanimex (Europe) Limited	Manager, European Operations

of international product rollout within the firms, verify the factors leading to timely/delays in rollout and expose their interactions.

The second method of data collection was through a questionnaire completed by all principal and additional interviewees. The questionnaire aimed to measure and test the relationships using psychometrics-based measurement methods. In doing so, completion of the questionnaire complemented the data from the interviews. Thirdly, information to confirm the findings was also sought from the web sites of participating companies and professional publications.

3.6   Influencing factors, propositions and measurement

The initial findings allowed the identification of a set of core and key antecedent factors seen as influencing timeliness of new product rollout. These are presented next. Research questions, propositions and measures employed follow.

3.6.1   Core and key antecedent factors

The core factors that influence timeliness of new product rollout relate to company sufficiency in marketing and technology for the specific new product, synergies in product handling and use, proficient execution of the NPD process and communication intensity between European HQ and European subsidiaries/agents. Their existence leads to timely rollout; lack of them results in delays in rollout schedule. These factors also influence each other (see Tables 3.9 and 3.10).

Antecedent factors influence the core set of factors in the following manner:

- The size of the firm, the extent of customisation of product technology, the extent of competitive threat and the strategic intention for the specific new product were seen to influence sufficiency in marketing and technology.
- The complexity of customisation of product technology, the difficulty of acquiring approvals and the speed of technology change were identified as influencing sufficiency in marketing, sufficiency in technology as well as synergies in product handling and use.
- The product European market share and the value of European product sales were seen to influence the intensity of internal communication between European HQ and its European subsidiaries/ agents.

The qualitative evidence does not provide clear indications regarding any additional influences from the antecedent upon the core factors.

Table 3.9 List of core factors that influence timeliness of new product rollout

---

Product specific factors
1. Sufficiency in marketing resources
2. Sufficiency in technological resources
3. Synergies in product handling by sales force and product use by customers
4. Superior product

NPD process factors
5. Quality integration during the NPD process: integration between functions and sites; input by subsidiaries/agents and customers
6. Proficiency of execution of the NPD process: technical and marketing activities
7. Known targets: knowledge by the firm of intended technical and marketing targets at the start of the NPD process; early product definition

Organisational factors
8. Internal communication between European HQ and European subsidiaries/ agents and between subsidiaries themselves: Direct informal contact between European HQ and subsidiaries/agents; formal contact through establishment of permanent committees and temporary task forces involving both HQ and subsidiaries/agents' staff; shared goals, values and beliefs in both HQ and subsidiaries/agents

---

Table 3.10   List of antecedent factors

| Antecedents | Direction of their effects | | | |
| | Sufficiency in | | Synergies in product handling and use | Internal communication |
	Marketing	Technology		
Firm size	yes	yes		
Extent of customisation of product technology	yes	yes		
Complexity of customisation of product technology/ approvals	yes	yes	yes	
Speed of technology change	yes	yes	yes	
Extent of competitive threat	yes	yes		
Strategic intention for the specific new product	yes	yes		
European market share and sales				yes

3.6.2   Propositions

A set of propositions was established and refined during the first phase of data collection for the full sample of the present study. They concern the core factors that influence timely new product rollout. They are expressed as hypotheses (see also Table 3.11):

Research question 1: Is rollout timeliness related to new product success?

Hypothesis H1a: New product success of timely and delayed rollout cases does differ.

Research question 2: Do firms rollout their new products across international markets simultaneously or sequentially?

This question looks at two different aspects:

(RQ2a):   Is there a link between the nature of product technology and sequential rollout?

(RQ2b):   Is there a link between sequential rollout and delays?

Hypothesis H2a: There is a relationship between the nature of product technology and sequential rollout.

Hypothesis H2b: There is a relationship between sequential rollout and delays.

Research question 3: What factors lead to rollout delay?

Hypothesis H3a: There is a relationship between sufficiency in marketing and timeliness in new product rollout.

Hypothesis H3b: There is a relationship between sufficiency in technology and timeliness in new product rollout.

Hypothesis H3c: There is a relationship between synergies in product handling by the sales force, use by the customers and timeliness in new product rollout.

Hypothesis H3d: There is a relationship between product superiority and timeliness in new product rollout.

Hypothesis H3e: There is a relationship between integration during the new product development process and timeliness in new product rollout.

Hypothesis H3f: There is a relationship between proficiency of the new product development process and timeliness in new product rollout.

Hypothesis H3g: There is a relationship between knowledge of intended targets at the start of the new product development process and timeliness in new product rollout.

Hypothesis H3h: There is a relationship between intensive internal communication between the European HQ and subsidiaries/agents, and between subsidiaries/agents themselves and timeliness in new product rollout.

The above factors were seen to interact with each other. The fourth research question concerns this interaction and the direct and indirect effects upon rollout delay.

Research question 4: What is the interaction between these factors and their direct and indirect effects upon rollout delay?

No specific hypotheses were established for this research question.

Table 3.11   Summary of hypotheses

Hypothesised effect – dependent variable

H1a: Timely rollout	yes	New product success
H2a: Nature of technology	yes	Sequential rollout
H2b: Sequential rollout	yes	Rollout timeliness
H3a: Sufficiency in marketing	yes	Rollout timeliness
H3b: Sufficiency in technology	yes	Rollout timeliness
H3c: Synergies in product handling and use	yes	Rollout timeliness
H3d: Superiority of product	yes	Rollout timeliness
H3e: Integration during the development process	yes	Rollout timeliness
H3f: Proficient development process	yes	Rollout timeliness
H3g: Early knowledge of intended targets	yes	Rollout timeliness
H3h: Intensive communication	yes	Rollout timeliness
H4a: Interaction between factors		Rollout timeliness

3.6.3   Measurement

Measurement of rollout timeliness: Mascarenhas (1992a,b) found that market entry occurs sooner in larger markets, the companies serving their smaller markets at a later date. In line with his findings and qualitative evidence, rollout timeliness was measured for both 'key' and 'all' (key + secondary) markets. New product rollout time was defined as starting 'when the product was launched in the first European country'. The end date was considered to be 'the date that launch was completed' (i.e. the product was available for sale) in the target (both 'key' and 'all' (key + secondary)) European country markets.

New product rollout timeliness was measured in two ways. One was a measure of time in months. Respondents were requested to indicate the planned (i.e. scheduled/anticipated) time period as well as the actual time the firm eventually spent on rollout of the investigated products across both *key* and all (key + secondary) European target markets. This first measure sought to identify:

- the approximate number of months companies aim to, and eventually, take to roll out their new products across multiple countries;
- the approximate number of months respondents consider to be a delay.

The time difference is then taken to give a relative measure, circumventing several potential problems of comparability of absolute time periods.

The second was a relative perceptual measure for rollout across 'key' and 'all' (key + secondary) markets. The two relevant questions considered whether the time spent on product rollout across (a) its *key* and (b) *all* (key + secondary) European target markets was slow or fast. The scale ranged from −5 for 'very slow to +5 for 'very fast'. This second measure aimed to identify the degree to which the project adhered to the 'time schedule' and it was 'time-efficient'. Evidence suggested that this measure was clearly understood by respondents and captured 'sticking to schedule', the importance of it and time efficiency. A low negative score (−5) indicates 'far behind schedule', 0 indicates 'stayed on schedule' and a high score (+5) indicates 'ahead of schedule'. The scheduled/anticipated time is seen as the yardstick against which to compare time importance and efficiency or inefficiency. A zero score was assigned by respondents for projects done in a time-efficient manner, (that is, 'as fast as it was expected to be done'), positive scores for projects done in a more time-efficient manner (that is, 'faster than it was expected to be done'), and negative scores for projects done in a time-inefficient manner (that is, 'slower than it was expected to be done').

Measurement of new product success: Griffin and Page (1993) report the findings of a multidisciplinary research project regarding the most commonly used measures for assessment of new product performance. The measures drawn from them to tap customer acceptance, financial, technical and speed-to-market product performance, included:

• customer acceptance: 'revenue (sales value) goals' and 'customer acceptance';
• financial performance: 'return on investment'; and
• product-level measures: 'technical performance of product' and 'speed-to-market'.

Scaling ranged from −5 for 'much below target' to +5 for 'much above target'. A negative value indicates that the new product has underperformed along the particular dimension. A zero value indicates that the new product has met the intended targets. A positive value indicates that the new product has exceeded its targets. A different approach was adopted regarding 'speed-to-market'. The NPD literature associates 'speed to market' with the timeliness of the NPD process (Cooper and Kleinschmidt, 1994). The same premise is adopted here. New product development time was defined as being from the managers' 'first meeting to consider the feasibility of developing the specific product to the date at which product stabilisation (i.e. no more changes are made to the product) is reached'. NPD timeliness was also measured in two ways. One was a measure of time in months. Respondents were requested to indicate the planned (i.e. scheduled/anticipated) and the actual time spent on NPD of the studied products in months. The time difference is then taken to give a relative measure, circumventing several potential problems of comparability of absolute time periods. The second was the relative perceptual measure. The relevant question considered whether the time spent on new product development was either very slow or very fast on an 11-point scale. The scale ranged from -5 for 'very slow to $+5$ for 'very fast'. The rationale for the above two measures is similar to that explained earlier in this section regarding timeliness of the new product rollout.

Sufficiency of resources: We first asked if the firm had sufficient availability of adequate quality (for the specific new product) of: (a) marketing personnel or funds to adapt product advertising and promotion for its European country markets; (b) personnel to train sales staff and technical personnel across its European country markets; (c) personnel and equipment for the after-sales service of this product in its European country markets; and (d) distribution channels in its European country markets. These questions indicate the sufficient availability of adequate marketing resources and were measured on a 1 (=not at all) to 5 (=very much so) scale.

We also asked if the firm had sufficient availability of adequate quality (for the specific new product) of: (a) technical personnel or R&D funds to develop product versions for particular European country markets; (b) hardware adapted for its European country markets; and (c) software adapted for its European country markets. These questions indicate the sufficient availability of adequate technological resources and actual product and were also measured on the same 1 to 5 scale.

The above correspond to what Montoya-Weiss and Calantone (1994) call 'strategic factors' (i.e. marketing, technology synergies and resources) and capture the number and quality of people assigned to the project (Gupta and Wilemon, 1990), the level of spending (Cooper, 1983a,b), and internal skills and capabilities (Johne and Snelson, 1989; Cooper and Kleinschmidt, 1993a,b). The absolute amount of people, funding, skills or capabilities, while reflecting company endowments, is not a satisfactory indicator on its own. There is a need to examine whether these resources were eventually put to use effectively and efficiently and whether other circumstances had adverse effects (Dougherty, 1992a,b; Parry and Song, 1993; Langley and Truax, 1994). What matters is the final result, namely if the company had sufficient availability of adequate quality elements (e.g. distribution channels).

Synergies in product handling and use: Two types of synergies were seen as of particular importance. The first type regards synergies in product handling by the sales force. We asked about the level of training the sales force needed to handle the new product compared to other new products. We measured this on a 1 (=much lower) to 5 (=much higher) scale. We also asked if this new product benefited from its closeness to the company's existing sales force and service capabilities and resources. We measured this on a 1 (=not at all) to 5 (=very much so) scale. These questions are rooted in Cooper (1983a,b), de Brentani (1991), Cooper and Kleinschmidt (1993a,b) and Cavusgil and Zou (1994).

Further, we asked three questions regarding product–user complementarity of the specific new product compared against previous or other products. Such complementarity is defined as no disruption in the way the user handles and interacts with a particular new product (Dhebar, 1995). We examined: (a) if the handling or 'feeling' has changed for the customer; (b) if the way in which the user is kept informed by the product and its function has changed; (c) if the way in which the user interacts with and controls the operation of the product has changed. These three questions were also measured on a 1 (=not at all) to 5 (=very much so) scale.

Superior product: We requested, also using a 1 (=not at all) to 5 (=very much so) scale, if the new product offered: (a) 'unique visible attributes' – uniqueness indicates that certain product characteristics are not available from competitive products, the visibility of the benefits indicates that these unique product characteristics are very obvious to the customer; (b) 'superior product quality, performance and value for money' – these terms indicate a positive impact for the customer, since the purchase and use of the product is understood to provide substantial benefits; (c) 'attributes perceived to be useful by the customers' – these examine if the importance of product characteristics and benefits is clearly communicated to the customer, product image is among the non-product advantages that strengthen the perceived superiority of a new product (Cooper, 1994); (d) 'consistency between product and corporate image' – discrepancy between the product and corporate image may not persuade the customer of the truthfulness of the product offering. These questions were drawn from Cooper (1994) and

Clark and Fujimoto (1991) and correspond precisely to what Montoya-Weiss and Calantone (1994) call 'the product advantage' factor.

Quality integration during the NPD process: We examined internal company integration and integration between the company and its markets during the development process of this specific new product. Thus, we asked: (a) if the integration between the technical, the marketing and the manufacturing functions was high; and (b) if the integration between these functions when located in different countries was also high. Thirdly, we asked the degree to which technical and marketing personnel contributed accurate, on-time and high-quality input to the NPD process. Fourthly, we explored the degree to which subsidiaries and/or agents provided continuous feedback. The reasons for including this question were:

- Respondents considered the integration between the senior marketing and engineering staff, which is usually dispersed across continents, to be a separate issue from the integration between European HQ and subsidiaries/agents for product and marketing decisions.
- In several cases, the European subsidiaries/agents had accounting, legal and operational independence from the European HQ. Subsidiaries/agents were also frequently the immediate buyers of the new products.

The fifth question concerned the strength of involvement of final customers and feedback in the NPD process. The above questions were drawn from Clark and Fujimoto (1991), Gupta and Wilemon (1991), Cooper (1994) and Brown and Eisenhardt (1995), and precisely correspond to what Montoya-Weiss and Calantone (1994) call 'internal/external relations' and 'organisational' factors. All questions were measured on a 1 (=not at all) to 5 (=very much so) scale.

Proficiency of execution of the NPD process: We further examined, using questions drawn from Cooper (1994), the proficiency of company actions during the new product development process for the specific new product. The first two questions tapped proficiency of: (a) predevelopment project planning Europewide; and (b) preliminary market assessment and market research Europewide. These aspects correspond precisely to what Montoya-Weiss and Calantone (1994) identify in their meta-analysis as 'proficiency in market pre-development activities'. We also checked the execution of pre-launch and customer testing activities asking specifically for the proficiency of (a) tests of prototypes by customers/trial market sales Europewide; (b) co-ordination of distribution channels and logistics Europewide; and (c) co-ordination of advertising and promotion Europewide. These correspond precisely to what Montoya-Weiss and Calantone (1994) identify in their meta-analysis as 'proficiency in market development activities'.

Last, but not least, we examined the company's preparation, actual technical development and testing of the new product. Thus, we asked the proficiency of: (a) preliminary technical assessment and setting of technical targets; (b) technical development and sorting out of unexpected 'bugs'; (c) technical testing of the product. These correspond precisely to what Montoya-Weiss and Calantone (1994) identify in their meta-analysis as 'proficiency in technology development activities'. All questions were measured on a 1 (=not at all) to 5 (=very much so) scale.

Targets known at the start of the NPD process: We also queried if the company knew its targets at the start of the NPD process and we used for this purpose Cooper's (1994) indicators. Thus, we asked if the company knew at the start of the NPD process: (a) the intended users, target countries and their needs/preferences; (b) the product concept and product positioning in the market; (c) the final product specifications and technical requirements; and (d) the product final features and characteristics. These are included in what Montoya-Weiss and Calantone (1994) call 'protocol during the NPD process' factor. All questions were measured on a 1 (=not at all) to 5 (=very much so) scale.

Intensity of co-ordination between European HQ and subsidiaries/ agents and between subsidiaries/agents themselves: This is a complex issue as there are many co-ordination mechanisms. Martinez and Jarillo (1989), in their review of research on co-ordination mechanisms in multinational corporations, classified these mechanisms into two groups. The first group consists of structural and formal mechanisms, including *formal structure, centralisation* and *formalisation* of decision-making, *planning* and *performance control*. The second group consists of more informal and subtle mechanisms including *lateral relations, informal communication* and *organisational culture*. As Martinez and Jarillo (1989) also argued, lateral relations cut across the formal structure and include direct contact among managers of different departments that share a problem, temporary or permanent task forces, teams, committees, integrating roles and integrative departments (Lawrence and Lorsch, 1967; Galbraith, 1973; Galbraith and Kazanjian, 1986). Internal communication supplements the formality of structures (Simon, 1976) by creating a network (Kotter, 1982) of informal and personal contacts among managers across different units of the company: corporate meetings and conferences, management trips, personal visits, transfers of managers, etc. The development of an organisational culture through this process of socialisation of individuals improves internal communication, the way of doing things, the decision-making style, and the objectives and values of the company (Pfeffer, 1982). Thus a veritable 'system of ideology' (Mintzberg, 1983) is 'internalised' (Simon, 1976) by executives throughout the organisation, something that generates identification and loyalty (Selznick, 1957). The questions we asked were adopted from Lawrence and Lorsch (1967), Galbraith (1973), Edström and Galbraith (1977), Miller and Dröge (1986), Martinez and Jarillo (1989, 1991), and Roth *et al.* (1991). Our aim was to capture the typical relationships between European Head Office and European subsidiaries/agents for marketing and product decisions in markets where the companies rolled out the new products. In doing so, first, we examined the extent of usage of the following co-ordination mechanisms:

- interdepartmental permanent committees set up to allow Head Office and subsidiaries/agents' staff to engage in joint decision-making;
- interdepartmental temporary task forces set up to facilitate collaboration between Head Office and subsidiaries/agents' staff on specific issues;
- liaison personnel;
- project managers with responsibilities over total operations across Head Office and subsidiaries/agents; and
- a matrix system where Head Office personnel within specialisations are fully integrated with personnel in subsidiaries/agents.

These questions indicate the extent of lateral or cross-departmental relations and cross-subsidiary/agent relations. Then, we asked the extent of employment of the following:

- direct contact, meetings and interaction between Head Office and subsidiaries/agents' staff on most decisions;
- direct contact, meetings and interaction between staff in different European subsidiaries/agents;
- transfers of managers between Head Office and subsidiaries/agents;
- transfers of managers between subsidiaries/agents.

These questions indicate the extent of informal communication and personal contact among managers in both the European HQ and European subsidiaries/agents. Lastly, we queried if shared goals, values and beliefs shaping behaviour of subsidiaries/agents' staff across European countries existed. This question captures the socialisation between managers and the establishment of a common organisational culture. All questions were measured on a 1 (=not at all) to 5 (=very much so) scale.

Firm size: We asked for details of the approximate number of full-time employees (across Europe) and the approximate European sales turnover of the business unit (average last 3 years).

Extent of customisation of product technology for the European market: 'Technology' was defined here as the set of those closely related technological advances and technical specifications that act as a coherent whole and give the product its main and distinctive character. These are, for example PAL/SECAM technology for TV sets, GSM technology for mobile telephones, ISDN or analogue signal transmission technology for modems, and so on. We asked if standardised product technology and specifications applied in Europe. We also asked if the extent of local government regulations in Europe is high. For instance, these regulations concerned government approvals and certifications for compliance to safety, electromagnetic interference, or radio interference. Both questions were measured on a 1 (=not at all) to 5 (=very much so) scale and were drawn from Samiee and Roth's (1992) market standardisation construct and Ghoshal and Nohria's (1989, 1993) discussion of the multinational and transnational environment.

Complexity of customisation of product technology/approvals: Using three separate questions, we examined if the company faced substantial problems in acquiring government or other technical approvals, and if complexity of adaptation of hardware and software specific for the new product to the requirements of different European country markets was substantial (the scale also ranged from 1 (=not at all) to 5 (=very much so)).

Speed of technology change: We sought information regarding the speed of technology change. In doing so, we employed three separate questions drawn from Samiee and Roth (1992). These questions and their measurement is presented in Table 3.12.

Table 3.12   Questions on speed of technology change

(a) Speed of technology change within the industry	no change well established	slow	mode-rate	rapid	very rapid and in major ways
(b) Product and production technology obsolescence rate	>10 yrs	5–10 yrs	2.5–5 yrs	1–2.5 yrs	<1 yr
(c) Rate of product modification instigated by main competitors	seasonally	periodically <1 yr interval	annually	periodically >1 yr interval	irregularly no pattern

The extent of competitive threat: We asked questions regarding the pervasiveness, depth and width of threat of competitive action for the company and how these related to the rollout of the specific new product. Competitive action has neither the same pervasiveness upon every competitor it threatens nor the same overall impact in all the markets. The degree of threat an action poses to a given company will depend, therefore, on both the importance to that company of the affected market(s) and the number of these markets. If this competitive action simultaneously threatens a company, is pervasive, and it is intense across the company's key European markets, the overall force of the competitive threat is raised for the company (see section 2.3.4.2). Our questions were drawn from Chen *et al.* (1992) and Heil and Walters (1993). We specifically asked if the following apply for the specific new product: (a) the company was threatened by competitive action; (b) this action was very hostile towards the company; (c) this action resulted in sales at the company's own expense; and (d) the company was threatened in all its key European markets. All questions were measured on a 1 (=not at all) to 5 (=very much so) scale.

The strategic intention for the specific new product: Nonetheless, important new products for the company are likely to have high sales potential, long-term prospects and long-lasting effects against competitors. We have drawn questions from Chen *et al.* (1992) and Heil and

Walters (1993) and asked: (a) if the new product had high potential to capture sales from competition; (b) if the new product was a short-term or interim move against competition; and (c) if the new product was targeted to have long-lasting strategic effects against competition. All questions were measured on a 1 (=not at all) to 5 (=very much so) scale.

European product market share and value of European product sales: We asked for details of the approximate yearly value of the European market for this product and the approximate yearly sales of this new product to European countries.

Definition of product 'newness': We defined product newness using a modified version of Booz *et al.*'s (1982) and Cooper and Kleinschmidt's (1993a,b) scheme. Seven categories of new product types exist in this scheme:

- a product that is totally new internationally, which creates an entirely new market (true innovations);
- a product that is totally new internationally, but for which there was an existing market;
- a product that is totally new to the company, but which offered new features versus competitive products in an existing market;
- a product line that is new to the company, but which competed against fairly similar products on the market;
- a new item in an existing product line for the company, which was sold into an existing market;
- a significant modification of an existing company product; and
- a fairly minor modification of an existing company product.

Number of target European markets for the new product and where the new product was rolled out: We asked for the number of company's target *key* and *secondary* European markets for this type of product, and in how many of these the company eventually launched the specific new product. The country names were also obtained.

3.7 Cross-case analysis

The data collection and individual case analysis had a certain degree of overlap in both the first and second phase of data collection in accordance with the premises for theory building and rigour in research (Miles and Huberman, 1984; Eisenhardt, 1989). The aim was to synthesise the knowledge gained up to each point, to integrate and refine conceptual linkages from the evidence. Analysis followed a systematic process in stages:

- Classification and structuring of information. The sequence was as follows: (a) compare the scheduled/anticipated time to roll out the new products; (b) compare the time it eventually took to roll out the new products across Europe and the causes of delays in each case; (c) establish a cross-case list of scheduled/anticipated versus actual rollout time and cross-tabulate causes of delays.
- Identification of interrelationships: (d) regroup the causes of delays into logical and coherent sets; (e) establish a cross-case list of relationships between the independent variables (i.e. the core and antecedent factors); (f) conceive the context of interrelationships and cross-tabulate the relationships between the independent and dependent variables.
- Contrast the interrelationships between settings (between companies in the same sector and between sectors).
- Conclusion at both individual and cross-case levels.
- Construction of a conceptual framework and contrasting the findings with extant literature.

Through a continuous process of induction and combination, the identification and categorisation of interrelationships became gradually apparent. Arguments were formed. A consistent and cohesive match between these arguments and qualitative evidence progressively emerged. These eventually formed a more comprehensive and detailed conceptual framework (Figure 3.3).

This figure shows the interrelationships between the core factors and the effects from the antecedent factors. The qualitative evidence does not provide clear indications for any other additional effects from the antecedent upon the core factors. Broadly speaking, heterogeneity and competitive difficulty of the external environment matters only if the company doesn't have sufficient quality and quality of marketing and technological resources at product level, as each product may largely be idiosyncratic. Nonetheless the bundle of resources will need an established and proficient new product development process, also supported by strong communication between HQ and subsidiaries to result in an efficient and effective rollout exercise. Each one of these 'agents' individually and together, reinforces, fosters and dictates the company's ability to serve its target segments across multiple countries. Company

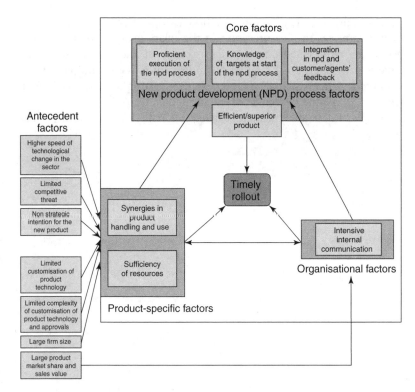

Figure 3.3 Timeliness in new product rollout: the interrelationships between the core factors and the direction of effects from the antecedent factors

failure in any one of these agents will cripple the firm's ability to roll out the specific new product on time.

3.8 Summary

A pilot study was carried out initially. This was followed by the identification of pertinent factors to the issues under investigation through six exploratory case studies. A cross-case analysis established coherent groups of core factors and key antecedents, which were largely confirmed later from data collected in 24 more companies. The initial conceptual framework was amended, and hypotheses were refined. Data collection took place with two complementary methods. The first method used a semi-structured case protocol that permitted the investigator to explore relevant issues in depth without abandoning a more rigorous research process. The second method used a detailed questionnaire whose aim was to measure and test the relationships. Additional data were also requested from secondary sources. Data were subsequently analysed through both qualitative and quantitative techniques. These allowed a richer explanation and permitted testing for internal consistency and explained variance of the individual factors.

Details of data analysis are discussed in Chapter 4.

4
Data Analysis

4.1 Introduction

In Chapter 3, the methodology of this study was presented. This chapter reports the cross-case analysis of the 30 investigated cases. Discussion commences with descriptive data regarding timely and delayed cases, including development and rollout periods, project novelty, number of European countries where the new products were rolled out, sales value and market shares, as well as the origin of parent companies. The frequency of causes of delays, grouped by importance, is shown followed by a summary of the qualitative findings. The quantitative analyses are presented next. The chapter concludes with the effects of the antecedent upon the core factors and a summary of key findings.

4.2 Timely versus delayed cases

4.2.1 Rollout periods

New product rollout time was defined as starting when the product was launched in the first European country. The end date was considered to be the date that launch was completed in the European target countries. The 30 sample companies *planned* to roll out the new products:

- across the *key* European target markets within 4.5 months on average;
- across *all* (key + secondary) their European target markets within 7.0 months on average.

The range of *planned* rollout periods is 1–34 months for the *key* and 1–45 months for *all* European target markets.

The *actual* time taken was:

* 6.8 months on average, for new product rollout across the *key* and
* 10.1 months across *all* European target markets.

Table 4.1 shows the *planned* and the *actual* rollout time for the sample cases. A *timely* rollout is defined in this study to occur when it is completed within – or faster than – its planned (scheduled/anticipated) time frame. A rollout delay occurs when the rollout is completed later than its planned time frame. Following the above definitions, the sample projects have been classified as either timely or delayed rollout cases. A total of 15 are labelled timely and 15 delayed rollout cases (see Table 4.1).

Table 4.1   New product rollout time (months)

Product	Rollout time				Rollout delay[†]	
	Key markets		All markets		Key months	All months
	Plan	Actual	Plan	Actual		
Timely rollout cases						
Laser (B&W) high-speed printer	2	same	2	same	0	0
Solid ink colour printer	4	same	4	same	0	0
Hand stand still 35 mm camera	1	same	1	same	0	0
Medium-speed industrial camera	2	same	2	same	0	0
Ethernet port switch	3	same	3	same	0	0
PBX	34	same	45	same	0	0
Laser (B&W) medium-speed printer	1	same	1	same	0	0
TV set	3	same	3	same	0	0
Medium-speed professional camera	12	same	12	same	0	0
Sound mixing system	1	same	1	same	0	0
PC monitor	3	same	6	same	0	0
Ethernet 10/100 adapter card	1	same	1	same	0	0
Matrix (B&W) bar-code printer	1	same	1	same	0	0
TV set	1	same	1	same	0	0
Analogue modem	3	same	3	same	0	0
Average	4.8	same	5.7	same	0	0

Delayed rollout cases

RS 232 adapter	3	12**	3	12**	9	9
Ethernet multiplexer	4	6**	12	14**	2	2
Climatic data recording instrument	3	4	6	9	1	3
Ethernet print server	1	2	3	4	1	1
High- and ultra-high speed camera	2	3	4	6	1	2
Hand stand still 35 mm camera	2	6	6	18	4	12
Dynamometer	3	9	3*	9*	6	6
Security identification and lamination system	18	36**	36	48**	18	12
PBX	3	8	6	12	5	6
Analogue modem	4	7	7	14	3	7
Mobile GSM telephone	1	5	3	7	4	4
ISDN modem	4	6	4	6	2	2
PC-telephony integration platform	6	14**	14	24**	8	10
Ethernet print server	3	9**	6	12**	6	6
Electric data recording/ testing instrument	6	6	12	24	0	12
Average	4.2	8.8	8.3	14.6	4.6	6.3
Average (timely + delayed rollout cases)	4.5	6.8	7.0	10.1	4.6	6.3

Notes: * The company does not have any secondary markets – score is assigned for comparative purposes.
** Rollout delays were still increasing in these four cases and rollout was indefinitely postponed in the fifth one (Security identification and lamination system). Scores are assigned for comparative purposes.
† Rollout delay in *key* markets and rollout delay in *all* (key + secondary) markets.

The rollout delays are calculated separately from delays that may have occurred during the development of the new product. More details regarding NPD delays are provided later (section 4.2.6).

Rollout time: timely versus delayed cases: The *planned* rollout period across *key* European target markets was almost the same for both timely and delayed cases (4.8 against 4.2 months on average). However, time periods were longer in delayed than in timely cases with respect to:

- the *planned* rollout period across *all* European target markets (8.3 against 5.7 months on average);
- the *actual* rollout period across *key* European target markets (8.8 against 4.8 months on average).

T-tests show that these differences are not statistically significant.

Table 4.2   Planned and actual rollout time: timely versus delayed cases (months)

Time	Timely cases		Delayed cases		Signif.
	Means	Std dev.	Means	Std dev.	
Planned, *key* markets	4.8	8.5	4.2	4.0	no
Actual, *key* markets	4.8	8.5	8.8	8.1	no
Rollout delay, *key* markets	0		4.6		
Planned, *all* markets	5.7	11.2	8.3	8.4	no
Actual, *all* markets	5.7	11.2	14.6	11.0	0.05
Rollout delay, *all* markets	0		6.3		

The *actual* rollout time across *all* European target markets was also longer in delayed than in timely cases (14.6 against 5.7 months on average). T-tests show that this difference is statistically significant ($p < 0.05$).

The rollout delay (*planned–actual* rollout time) is 4.6 months on average, for rollout across *key* target and 6.3 months on average, for rollout across *all* European target markets (Table 4.2). These correspond to 109 per cent (4.6/4.2) of planned rollout time across key markets and 75 per cent (6.3/8.3) of planned rollout time across all European target markets.

Eliminating the outliers: The above calculations are influenced though by the existence of one timely (Nortel) and one delayed case (Laminex) that act as statistical outliers. Each reported rollout period for these two

Table 4.3   Planned and actual rollout time: timely versus delayed cases when the two statistical outliers are eliminated from the calculations (months)

Time	Timely cases		Delayed cases		Signif.
	Means	Std dev.	Means	Std dev.	
Planned, *key* markets	2.7	2.8	3.2	1.5	no
Actual, *key* markets	2.7	2.8	6.9	3.2	0.001
Rollout delay, *key* markets	0		3.7		
Planned, *all* markets	2.9	2.9	6.3	3.7	0.01
Actual, *all* markets	2.9	2.9	12.2	6.2	0.000
Rollout delay, *all* markets	0		5.9		

cases is over 2 standard deviations distant from the respective averages of all other cases (*z-scores* range from 2.084 to 4.557). Table 4.3 shows the means and standard deviations for both timely and delayed cases when these two statistical outliers are eliminated.

The *planned* rollout period across *key* European target markets remained almost the same for both timely and delayed cases (2.7 against 3.2 months on average). T-tests show that this difference is still not statistically significant. Time periods were longer in delayed than in timely cases with respect to:

- the *planned* rollout period across *all* European target markets (6.3 against 2.9 months on average);
- the *actual* rollout period across *key* European target markets (6.9 months against 2.7 months on average); and
- the *actual* rollout period across *all* European target markets (12.2 months against 2.9 months on average).

T-tests show that these differences are statistically significant ($p < 0.01$). These figures indicate that managers in both timely and delayed rollout cases planned to make their new products available in their key European target markets at similar periods. However, managers in the delayed cases decided to postpone the rollout of their products to secondary markets until a later date. The delay in the rollout of the new product to its key target markets consequently impacts upon the actual time taken to roll out the new product to its secondary markets.

These actual delays were also reflected in the perceptual timeliness of the new product rollout measure (scale ranged from −5 for 'very slow' to +5 for 'very fast'). Correlations between the actual and perceptual rollout timeliness measures were also very strong (average 0.71, $p < 0.001$). The perceptual timeliness measure aimed to identify the degree to which the project adhered to the time schedule, where a low negative score (−5) indicates 'far behind schedule', 0 indicates 'stayed on schedule' and a high score (+5) indicates 'ahead of schedule'. Respondents indicated that they assigned a zero score for projects done in a time-efficient manner (that is, 'as fast as it was expected to be done'), positive scores for projects done in a more time-efficient manner (that is, 'faster than it was expected to be done'), and negative scores for projects done in a time-inefficient manner (that is, 'slower than it was expected to be done'). Table 4.4 shows the means and

Table 4.4   Perceptual timeliness measure: timely versus delayed cases (scale −5 to +5)

	Timely cases		Delayed cases		Signif.
	Means	Std dev.	Means	Std dev.	
Rollout time, key markets	1.1	2.2	−2.2	2.0	0.000
Rollout time, all markets	0.8	2.5	−2.9	1.8	0.000

standard deviations of the perceptual timeliness measure for both timely and delayed cases. Differences are strongly significant ($p < 0.000$). The assigned scores indicate that the timely cases were rolled out in a time-efficient manner (scores 1.1 and 0.8, on average) and that the delayed cases were rolled out in a time-inefficient manner (scores −2.2 and −2.9, on average). The difference in scores (scores 1.1 and 0.8 instead of the expected 0 score) for the timely cases may be attributed to cognitive biases of managers, in the sense that managers appear to inflate the timely rollout achievements in the perceptual measure.

4.2.2   Project novelty

The sample comprise 15 timely and 15 delayed rollout cases. The majority (80 per cent) of the 15 timely cases concern product line additions or modifications of existing products (product types 5, 6 and 7 in Table 4.5). In contrast, the majority (60 per cent) of the 15 delayed cases are 'new' products to the company or 'new' products to the world (product types 1, 2, 3 and 4 in Table 4.5).

A dummy variable was subsequently created. Each case belonging to the group of products in 'novel' product activities (product types 1, 2, 3 and 4) was assigned the value of 1. Each case belonging to the group of products in 'existing' product activities (product types 5, 6 and 7) was assigned the value of 2. T-tests show that the differences between timely and delayed cases regarding the product novelty are statistically significant ($p < 0.05$).

This shows that products which constitute 'novel' product activities for the company are more likely to face rollout delays than products in 'existing' product areas.

4.2.3   Number of European country markets

The timely rolled-out products have been made available for sale in all their European target country markets (4.93 key and 12.4 secondary

Table 4.5 Project novelty: timely versus delayed cases

Type of project	No. of timely cases	No. of delayed cases
'Novel' areas of product activity		
1. Product totally new to the world, which created an entirely new market	–	1
2. Product totally new to the world, but for which there was an existing market	2	3
3. Product totally new to the company, which offered new features versus competitive products in an existing market	1	3
4. Product new to the company, which competed against fairly similar products on the market	–	2
Sub-total	3 (20%)	9 (60%)
'Existing' areas of product activity		
5. New item in an existing product line for the company, which was sold into an existing market	3	1
6. A significant modification of an existing company product	8	5
7. A fairly minor modification of an existing company product	1	
Sub-total	12 (80%)	6 (40%)

countries) (see Table 4.6). The 15 delayed rolled-out products have been made available for sale in fewer than their target markets (3.66 out of 5.0 key and 4.4 out of 10.66 secondary countries). Key countries include in almost all cases the UK, Germany and France followed by Italy, Holland, Scandinavia and Spain.

Table 4.6 indicates that delayed products roll out to fewer target country markets than timely products. The delayed rolled-out products target both niche segments (7 out of the 15 delayed cases) and mass consumer/volume markets (8 out of the 15 delayed cases). The sample contains however, a lower proportion of products targeting niche segments (11 out of the 30 cases) than products targeting mass/volume markets (19 out of the 30 cases). This shows a greater propensity of products targeting niche segments to face delays in rollout.

Table 4.6 Intended and actual number of target key and secondary country markets: timely versus delayed rollout cases (average)

	Timely rollout cases		Delayed rollout cases	
	Intended no. of target countries	Actual no. of target countries	Intended no. of target countries	Actual no. of target countries
Key	4.93	4.93	5.00	3.66
Secondary	12.66	12.40	10.66	4.40

4.2.4   Product European market share and value of European product sales

A total of 55 per cent of the investigated cases ($n = 20$) concern products that occupied up to 10 per cent of the European market, 30 per cent between 30 and 49 per cent of the market, and 15 per cent over 50 per cent of the European market in value terms. T-tests show weak significant differences ($p \leq 0.10$) with respect to market share occupied by timely (average 30 per cent) versus delayed (average 12 per cent) cases. This may have happened for the following reasons:

- targeting, or the prospect of, a lower market share may not have put pressure on firms to achieve timely new product rollout; or
- the delay in the rollout of the new product results in a weaker market position and a smaller market share for the new product compared to timely rolled-out ones.

It is still possible however, that the timeliness of the new product rollout is independent of targeting, or the prospect of, a higher market share.

Value of sales varied from less than £300,000 (30 per cent of cases), to £500,000–2 million (30 per cent of cases) and over £8 million (40 per cent of cases) and the value of the European market for 35 per cent of the investigated cases was less than £8 million, for 30 per cent it was £10–200 million and for 35 per cent it was over £200 million. T-tests show no significant differences between timely and delayed cases with respect to either the actual product sales or the yearly value of the European market. The above indicate that rollout delays happen independently of the value of the new product sales or the value of the target market of the new product.

4.2.5 Origin of parent companies

There is a disproportionate representation of Japanese companies in 'timely' projects (see Table 4.7). All nine Japanese companies rolled out their products on time, in contrast with western (USA and UK) companies, whose majority (14 out of 19 cases) faced delays. The focus of this research was not to seek out a bias regarding rollout timeliness and firms' country-of-origin. Also, the sample size is too small to permit any generalisations about timeliness of multiple country rollouts and firms' country-of-origin, although future research might attempt to explore and confirm the existence of a nationality bias in the context of successful, timely international market rollout and the implications for international product management. The presence of Japanese companies in the timely rollout cases may also have happened for the following reasons:

- the area of product technology may have created certain demands and conditions where new product rollout timeliness was easier to achieve. For instance, almost all printer manufacturers rolled out on time. All printer manufacturers were of Japanese origin;
- firm- and point-in-time-specific circumstances; or
- the character of the necessary marketing action or the nature of competition may have placed different pressures on firms to achieve timely new product rollout.

Table 4.7 Origin of parent companies: timely versus delayed rollout cases

Origin	No. of timely cases	No. of delayed cases
North American		
USA	3	5
USA/Canada	1	1
USA/Australia	1	–
UK		
UK	–	7
UK/USA	1	1
Asian		
Asian (Japan)	9	–
Asian (Hong Kong)	–	1
Total	15	15

In the present study, the analysis concentrates on rollout timeliness irrespective of firms' country-of-origin. A striking feature is, however, that *all* seven British companies faced delays in rollout.

4.2.6   NPD time

NPD time was defined as being from the managers' first meeting to consider the feasibility of developing the specific product to the date at which product stabilisation (i.e. no more changes are made to the product) is reached. The average *planned* NPD time of the 30 sample cases was 14.4. months (the range is 3–36 months). The average *actual* NPD time was 21.2 months (the range is 4–60 months) (Table 4.8).

Table 4.8   NPD time, delays in NPD and rollout delays (months)

Product	Company name	Time		NPD delay	Case labelled	Rollout delay*
		Plan	Actual			
Laser (B&W) high-speed printer	Brother	18	16	−2	Timely	0
Solid ink colour printer	Citizen	24	24	0	Timely	0
Hand stand still 35 mm camera	Hanimex	12	12	0	Timely	0
Medium-speed industrial camera	Hitachi	12	18	6	Delayed	0
Ethernet port switch	LanArt	12	12	0	Timely	0
PBX	Nortel	36	60	24	Delayed	0
Laser (B&W) medium-speed printer	OKI	15	18	3	Delayed	0
TV set	Panasonic	12	12	0	Timely	0
Medium-speed professional camera	Sony	24	36	12	Delayed	0
Sound mixing system	Soundcraft	9	12	3	Delayed	0
PC monitor	Taxan	9	12	3	Delayed	0
Ethernet 10/100 adapter card	Telesyn	3	5	2	Delayed	0
Matrix (B&W) bar-code printer	TEC	18	24	6	Delayed	0
TV set	Toshiba	12	12.5	0.5	Delayed	0
Analogue modem	US Robotics	4	4	0	Timely	0

RS 232 adapter	Amplicon	4	5	1	Delayed	9
Ethernet multiplexer	Cray Comms	24	36	12	Delayed	2
Climatic data recording instrument	Delta-T	18	36	18	Delayed	3
Ethernet print server	Emulex	8	10	2	Delayed	1
High- and ultra-high speed camera	Hadland	9	15	6	Delayed	2
Hand stand still 35 mm camera	Halina	12	24	12	Delayed	12
Dynamometer	Instron	12	24	12	Delayed	6
Security identification and lamination system	Laminex	12	24	12	Delayed	12
PBX	Mitel	12	24	12	Delayed	6
Analogue modem	Motorola	4	4	0	Timely	7
Mobile GSM telephone	Orbitel	12	14	2	Delayed	4
ISDN Modem	Racal	18	20	2	Delayed	2
PC-telephony integration platform	Rhetorex	24	60	36	Delayed	10
Ethernet print server	3COM	18	28	10	Delayed	6
Electric data recording/ testing instrument	Voltech	24	36	12	Delayed	12
Average		14.4	21.2	6.8		

Note: * Figures correspond to rollout delays in *all* (key + secondary) target European countries.

A *timely* NPD is defined in this study to occur when it is completed within or faster than its planned (scheduled/anticipated) time frame. A delay in NPD occurs when the NPD is completed later than its planned time frame. Following the above definitions, 7 cases are labelled timely and 23 delayed NPD cases (see Table 4.8). The average delay in NPD is 6.8 months.

NPD time: timely versus delayed rollout cases: The *planned* NPD time is the same for both timely and delayed rollout cases (14.6 against

14.0 months on average). Both timely and delayed rolled-out cases faced delays during their NPD period (planned–actual NPD time), irrespective of the timeliness of their future rollout (Table 4.9).

The frequency of delays in NPD is higher, however, in delayed than in timely rollout cases. A total of 14 out of the 15 delayed rollout cases have faced delays in their development. In comparison, only 9 out of the 15 timely rollout cases faced delays in their development.

The *actual* NPD time is longer in delayed than in timely rollout cases (24.0 against 18.5 months on average) (Table 4.9). This results in a longer NPD delay in delayed (14.0–24.0 = 10.0 months) than in timely rollout cases (14.6–18.5 = 3.9 months) on average. T-tests show that this difference is statistically significant ($p < 0.05$). These NPD delays correspond to 26.7 (timely rollouts) against 71.4 per cent (delayed rollouts) of planned NPD time. This means that delayed rollout cases experienced almost three times as much overrun NPD time than timely rollout cases. The data from Tables 4.2 and 4.9 show that the 15 delayed rollout cases faced:

- an NPD delay of 6.1 months on average (3.9 – 10.0 = −6.1 months); and
- a rollout delay of 4.6 months, for rollout in *key* European target markets and 6.3 months on average, for rollout in *all* European target markets.

The 15 delayed rollout cases appear therefore, to be 10.7 months late (−6.1 + −4.6 = −10.7) in their *key*, and 12.4 months late (−6.1 + −6.3 = −12.4) in *all* their European target markets. For reasons that will be explored later, NPD delays also have serious repercussions on the completion of sequential international market launch.

The NPD delays were also reflected in the perceptual NPD timeliness measure (scale ranged from −5 for 'very slow' to +5 for 'very fast').

Table 4.9 Planned and actual NPD time: timely versus delayed rollout cases (months)

NPD time	Timely rollout cases		Delayed rollout cases		Signif.
	Means	Std dev.	Means	Std dev.	
Planned NPD time	14.6	8.4	14.0	6.7	no
Actual NPD time	18.5	13.9	24.0	14.3	no
Delays in NPD	3.9	6.5	10.0	9.0	0.05

Table 4.10 Perceptual NPD timeliness measure: timely versus delayed rollout cases (scale −5 to +5)

	Timely rollout cases		Delayed rollout cases		Signif.
	Means	Std dev.	Means	Std dev.	
Timeliness in NPD	−0.6	1.4	−2.0	1.69	0.05

Correlations between the actual and perceptual NPD timeliness measures were also very strong (0.60, $p < 0.001$). The perceptual NPD timeliness measure aimed to identify the degree to which the project adhered to the NPD time schedule, where a low negative score (−5) indicates 'far behind schedule', 0 indicates 'stayed on schedule' and a high score (+5) indicates 'ahead of schedule'. Table 4.10 shows the differences between timely and delayed rollout cases regarding the perceptual NPD timeliness measure. Differences are significant ($p < 0.05$). Section 4.2.7 gives more details on the causes of delays in new product rollout.

4.2.7 Causes of rollout delays and their frequency

Causes of delays in the cases that encountered rollout delay ($n = 15$) were grouped into several sets of closely related elements. Three different answers ('not a problem', 'minor' and 'MAJOR') have been assigned to each set of elements after careful consideration and cross-checking across cases and technologies:

- 'Not a problem' ('No') means that the firm did not face problems in the specific area under investigation or this is not applicable (i.e. no need to customise the product technologically to different country markets);
- 'minor' means that the problem existed, but it was not serious;
- 'MAJOR' means that the problem existed and was a major obstacle.

Table 4.11 shows the frequency of experienced problems of minor and MAJOR importance by type of cause. In 40 per cent of delayed cases, there were problems in 2–4 areas. In 40 per cent of the delayed cases, there were problems in 5–8 areas. In three cases, problems were experienced in 9 of the 13 areas.

Table 4.11 Delayed rollout cases: frequency of minor and MAJOR causes of rollout delays (*n* = 15)

Cause	Minor causes of rollout delays		MAJOR causes of rollout delays		Minor + MAJOR causes of rollout delays
	Occurrences in delayed rollout cases	Frequency (%)	Occurrences in delayed rollout cases	Frequency (%)	Cumulative frequency (%)
Insufficient availability of adequate quality of:					
(a) marketing/ customer support, personnel and related	0	0	11	74	74
(b) distribution channels	1	7	8	54	61
(c) engineers, technical resources, personnel and related	4	27	4	27	54
(d) hardware or software	2	14	7	47	61
Lack of synergies in product handling by:					
(a) sales force	1	7	6	40	47
(b) user unfamiliar	1	7	3	20	27

Problems during development of the new product:

(a) Non-proficient new product development process	1	7	6	40	47
(b) Internal communication between European HQs and new product development teams	1	7	3	20	27

Internal co-ordination and communication:

(a) Internal communication between European HQs and subsidiaries/agents and between subsidiaries/agents themselves	3	20	5	34	54

Other elements:

(a) Extensive customisation of product technology	3	20	1	7	27
(b) Complexity of customisation of product technology	1	7	2	14	21
(c) Approvals	1	7	2	14	21
(d) Low European product market share or value of European product sales	5	33	2	14	47

Frequency of minor and MAJOR causes together
Problems existed in the following areas.

In 74 per cent of delayed cases: inadequate marketing personnel and resources.

In 61 per cent of delayed cases: inadequate distribution channels; and inadequate hardware or software.

In 54 per cent of delayed cases: inadequate engineering and technical personnel and resources; and lack of internal communication between European HQ and agents/subsidiaries and between subsidiaries/agents themselves.

In 47 per cent of delayed cases: lack of synergies in product handling by the European subsidiaries/agents' sales staff; non-proficient NPD process; and low European product market share and value of European product sales.

In <47 per cent of delayed cases: lack of synergies in product handling by user (27 per cent); communication between European HQ and NPD teams (27 per cent); extensive customisation of product technology (27 per cent); complexity of customisation of product technology (21 per cent); and government or other approvals (21 per cent).

Frequency of MAJOR causes only
In terms of MAJOR causes, the picture is different. Marketing insufficiency (marketing incapabilities, insufficient expertise, personnel and resources) is the single most frequently experienced cause of delayed rollouts (74 per cent) followed far behind by other causes.

In 54 per cent of delayed cases: inadequate distribution channels.

In 47 per cent of delayed cases: inadequate hardware or software.

In <40 per cent of delayed cases: lack of synergies in product handling by the European subsidiaries/agents' sales staff (40 per cent); non-proficient NPD process (40 per cent); lack of internal company communication between European HQ and agents/subsidiaries and between subsidiaries themselves (34 per cent); inadequate engineering and technical personnel and resources (27 per cent); lack of communication between European HQ and NPD teams (20 per cent); and lack of synergies in product handling by user (20 per cent).

Almost none of the timely cases faced any problems in the above mentioned areas. Table 4.12 gives the details for each investigated case.

Table 4.12 Causes of rollout delays: problem areas

Company	Engineering/ technical personnel/ resources	Marketing personnel/ resources	Hardware/ software	Distribution channels	By sales force across Europe	By end user	Communication European HQs and npd teams	Proficient new product development	Eur. HQs and agents/ subsidiaries and between	Extent of	Complexity of	Complex or other problems	European market share or sales
Timely rollout cases													
Brother	no	no	no	no	no	no	no*	no	no	no	no	no	no
Citizen	no	no	no	no	no	no	no*	no	no	no	no	no	no
Hanimex	no	no	no	no	no	no	no*	no	no	no	no	no	no
Hitachi	no	no	no	no	no	no	no*	no	no	no	no	no	no
LanArt	no	no	no	no	no	no	no*	no	no	no	no	no	no
Nortel	no	no	no	no	no	no	no*	no	no	minor	no	no	no
OKI	no	no	no	no	no	no	no*	no	no	no	no	no	no
Panasonic	no	no	no	no	no	no	no*	no	no	minor	no	no	no
Sony	no	no	no	no	no	no	no*	no	no	no	no	no	no
Soundcraft	no	no	no	no	no	no	no	no	no	no	no	no	no
Taxan	no	no	no	no	no	no	no*	no	no	minor	no	no	no
Telesyn	no	no	no	no	no	no	no*	no	no	no	no	no	no
TEC	no	no	no	no	no	no	no*	no	no	no	no	no	no
Toshiba	no	no	no	no	no	no	no*	no	no	minor	no	no	no
US Robotics	no	no	no	no	no	no	no*	no	no	minor	no	no	no

Table 4.12 (Continued)

Company	Sufficient availability of adequate quality				Synergies in product handling		New product development		Internal communication	Customisation of product technology		Approval	Importance of product
	Engineering/ technical personnel/ resources	Marketing personnel/ resources	Hardware/ software	Distribution channels	By sales force across Europe	By end user	Communication European HQs and npd teams	Proficient new product development	Eur. HQs and agents/ subsidiaries and between	Extent of	Complexity of	Complex or other problems	European market share or sales
Delayed rollout cases													
Amplicon	no	MAJOR	no	MAJOR	no	no	no	no	MAJOR	no	no	no	MAJOR
Cray	MAJOR	no	MAJOR	no	no	no	no*	no	no	no	no	no	no
Delta-T	minor	MAJOR	no	no	no	no	no*	no	minor	no	no	no	no
Emulex	no	no	MAJOR	no	no	MAJOR	MAJOR*	MAJOR	no	no	no	no	minor
Hadland	minor	MAJOR	no	MAJOR	MAJOR	no	no	no	minor	no	no	no	no
Halina	minor	MAJOR	MAJOR	no	no	MAJOR	no*	no	MAJOR	no	no	no	no
Instron	MAJOR	no	minor	no	MAJOR	no	no*	MAJOR	no	no	no	no	no
Laminex	MAJOR	MAJOR	minor	MAJOR	MAJOR	no	MAJOR	MAJOR	MAJOR	MAJOR	MAJOR	no	MAJOR
Mitel	no	MAJOR	no	MAJOR	MAJOR	no	MAJOR*	minor	MAJOR	no	no	MAJOR	minor
Motorola	no	no	MAJOR	minor	no	no	no	no	no	minor	minor	minor	no
Orbitel	minor	MAJOR	MAJOR	MAJOR	no	no	no	no	no	no	no	no	minor
Racal	no	MAJOR	no	MAJOR	no	no	no	no	MAJOR	no	no	no	minor
Rhetorex	no	MAJOR	MAJOR	no	minor	minor	no*	MAJOR	no	minor	MAJOR	MAJOR	minor
3COM	MAJOR	MAJOR	MAJOR	MAJOR	MAJOR	MAJOR	no*	MAJOR	no	no	no	no	no
Voltech	no	MAJOR	no	MAJOR	MAJOR	no	minor	MAJOR	minor	no	no	no	no

Notes: *if new product development is located in another continent.

Detailed case descriptions for four timely and four delayed cases are also available in the appendix. The particular cases are either 'extreme' or 'typical' cases (Yin, 1984), and they intend to communicate a range of different circumstances to the reader. Circumstances of extreme hetero-geneity in technological standards across countries and high complexity of the approvals' procedures are shown for instance, in two cases (TMT Telecom Ltd and RXE Europe Ltd). (The names of the companies are dispuised here and in the appendix). BtH International Europe Ltd, OEL Europe Ltd and Alme Tel International Ltd are examples of intensive organisational communication. Moreover, the Tmt Telecom Ltd and LxL International serve as cases of the lack of synergies in product handling by the sales force.

4.3 Factor analyses

The quantitative analysis of the questionnaire items followed the premises of psychometric literature (Nunnally, 1978). After an initial data screening, exploratory factor analysis (EFA) was performed for the establishment of factors and construct identification. EFA is a set of multivariate statistical methods for describing the relationships among the item scores in a correlation matrix by assigning them to a few relatively independent but conceptually meaningful composite variables called factors (Yaremko *et al.*, 1982). The steps involved are (1) the preparation of the correlation matrix; (2) the extraction of initial factors; and sometimes (3) various rotation procedures aimed at obtaining the simplest interpretable factors. EFA is particularly useful for the situation where links between the observed and latent variables (a latent variable is a variable that represents an abstract theoretical construct) are uncertain. The analysis proceeds in an exploratory mode to establish if factors exist and that the items (i.e. observed variables) which tap these factors can be identified (Hair *et al.*, 1995, pp. 366–8). The EFAs carried out in this study are listed in Table 4.13.

The factor items were then subjected to reliability tests. 'Reliability' is defined as 'the degree to which measures are free from error and there-fore yield consistent results' (Peter, 1979, p. 6). These are important for the establishment of construct validity. There are several reliability coefficients (see Churchill and Peter, 1984), but Cronbach's coefficient alpha, which is a generalised measure of the internal consistency of a multi-item scale, is considered among the most robust and widely used

(Peterson, 1994). While a Cronbach's alpha score of ≤0.5 denotes acceptable, a score of >0.7 signifies good scale reliability (Nunnally, 1978). The individual EFAs and results from reliability analyses are presented in Tables 4.14–4.16.

Table 4.13 Table of EFAs in this study

Core factors	Antecedent factors
New product success	Firm size
Sufficiency in marketing	Extent of customisation of product
Sufficiency in technology	technology for the European market
Synergies in product	Complexity of customisation of product
handling and use	technology for the European
Superior product	market/approvals
Quality integration during	Extent of competitive threat
the NPD process	Strategic intention for the specific
Proficiency of execution	new product
of the NPD process	
Targets known at the start	
of the NPD process	
Internal communication	
between European HQ and	
subsidiaries/agents and	
between subsidiaries/agents	
themselves	

Table 4.14 Factor analysis: new product success

Items	Orthogonal factor solution: factor loadings	
	Factor 1 'Financial performance'	Factor 2 'Timely NPD'
Sales	0.92	0.08
Customer acceptance	0.70	−0.45
Return on investment	0.87	0.26
Technical performance of product	0.69	−0.47
NPD timeliness	–	0.78
Eigenvalue	2.79	1.13
Factor explained variance (%)	55.9	22.7
Total explained variance (%)	78.6	–
Cronbach's alpha score	0.83	–

Table 4.15 List of core factors (CF) and their items

Code	Factor name	Items (summary of question)		Factor loading	e^{**}	Variance	α^{***}
CF1	Sufficiency in marketing	*Sufficiency of adequate quality of:*					
		Marketing personnel/funds to adapt adv/promotion	A1	0.91	3.43	86.0	0.94
		Personnel to train sales staff and technicians	A2	0.94			
		After-sales service personnel and equipment	A3	0.92			
		Distribution channels	A4	0.92			
CF2	Sufficiency in technology	*Sufficiency of adequate quality of:*					
		R&D personnel/funds to adapt product	A5	0.89	2.60	86.7	0.92
		Hardware adapted for European country markets	A6	0.95			
		Software adapted for European country markets	A7	0.94			
CF3	Synergies in product handling and use	Sales force	A8	0.71	2.71	68.0	0.84
		Product handling/'feeling' has changed for customer	A10R*	0.89			
		Way user is informed about product functions has changed	A11R*	0.88			
		Way user interacts with and controls operation of product has changed	A12R*	0.77			

Table 4.15 (Continued)

Code	Factor name		Items (summary of question)	Factor loading	e^{**}	Variance	α^{***}
CF4	Superior product		*The new product offered:*		2.70	67.6	0.83
		A13	Unique attributes and clearly visible benefits to the customer	0.81			
		A14	Superior quality, performance, value for money	0.85			
		A15	Attributes also perceived as useful by the customers	0.91			
		A16	Intended image consistent with corporate image	0.68			
CF5	Quality integration during the new product development process	B1	Integration between technical, marketing and manufacturing functions was high	0.71	3.07	61.6	0.83
		B2	Integration between these functions when located in different countries was also high	0.80			
		B3	Technical and marketing personnel contributed accurate, on time and high quality input	0.79			
		B4	Subsidiaries/agents provided continuous feedback	0.90			
		B5	Final customers were strongly involved and provided feedback	0.68			

109

CF6	Proficiency of execution of the new product development process		*The following were proficiently executed:*		4.18	69.7	0.91
		B6	Predevelopment project planning	0.87			
		B8	Tests of prototypes by customers/trial sales	0.88			
		B9	Co-ordination of distribution channels and logistics	0.86			
		B10	Co-ordination of advertising and promotion	0.78			
		B12	Technical development and sorting out unexpected 'bugs'	0.73			
		B13	Technical testing of the product	0.85			
CF7	Targets known at the start of the new product development process		*The firm knew at the start:*		2.62	65.6	0.82
		B14	The intended users, target countries and their needs and preferences	0.80			
		B15	The product concept and product positioning	0.78			
		B16	The final product specifications and technical requirements	0.80			
		B17	The product final features and characteristics	0.84			

Table 4.15 (Continued)

Code	Factor name	Items (summary of question)		Factor loading	e**	Variance	α***
CF8	Internal communication between European HQ and subsidiaries/agents and between subsidiaries/agents themselves	C1	Direct contact, meetings and interaction between European HQ and subsidiaries/agents	0.78	3.86	64.4	0.88
		C2	Direct contact, meetings and interaction between European subsidiaries/agents	0.89			
		C3	Interdepartmental permanent committees between European HQ and subsidiaries/agents	0.83			
		C4	Interdepartmental temporary task forces between European HQ and subsidiaries/agents	0.85			
		C5	The use of a matrix system	0.64			
		C6	A set of shared goals, values and beliefs shaping behaviour	0.78			

Notes: * R = scoring was reversed; ** e = eigenvalue; *** α = Cronbach's α.

Table 4.16 List of antecedent factors (AF) and their items

Code	Factor name	Items (summary of question)	Factor loading	e^{**}	Variance	α^{***}
AF1	Firm size	Number of full-time employees in business unit (Europe) Log10	0.86	1.73	86.7	0.81
		Sales turnover in business unit (Europe, 3 years) Log10	0.86			
AF2	Extent of customisation of product technology for the European market	Standardised product technology/specifications X1	0.83	1.40	70.1	0.57
		Extent of local government regulations high X2R*	0.83			
AF3	Complexity of customisation of product technology for the European market/approvals	Problems in acquiring government/technical approvals X3 (APPR)	0.78	2.10	70.0	0.79
		Substantial complexity of hardware adaptation X4 (CMHW)	0.91			
		Substantial complexity of software adaptation X5 (CMSW)	0.81			

Table 4.16 (Continued)

Code	Factor name	Items (summary of question)	Factor loading	e^{**}	Variance	α^{***}
AF4	Extent of competitive threat	Firm was threatened by competitive action	0.97	3.58	89.7	0.96
		Competitive action was very hostile towards the company	0.95			
		This action was resulting in sales at firm's own expense	0.93			
		Firm was threatened in all its key European markets	0.91			
AF5	Strategic intention for the specific new product	Product had high potential to capture sales from competition	0.86	2.23	74.3	0.82
	X11R*	Product short-term/interim move against competition	0.77			
	X12	Product targeted to have long-lasting strategic effects	0.93			

Notes: * R = scoring was reversed; ** e = eigenvalue; *** α = Cronbach's α.

4.4 Effects of antecedent factors upon the core factors

4.4.1 Introduction

As mentioned in the theoretical framework (Chapter 3), some antecedent factors (AFs) were identified to influence the core factors (CFs) in the framework. Factor analysis on a series of items and reliability tests established a series of highly reliable and easily interpretable factors. The scores provided by the respondents on the items loading high on each AF were averaged to create scales specific to each factor. Hair *et al.* (1995) argue that when the average or summated scale is valid (that is, the items correctly define the factor) and reliable (i.e. the alpha coefficient is high), then this scale is the best alternative for representation of the factor (p. 9 and pp. 390–1). A short discussion of the effects of the AFs upon the CFs follows.

4.4.2 Firm size (AF1)

Figures show that there is a strong positive correlation (0.40, $p < 0.1$) between firm size and sufficiency in marketing (see Table 4.17). This means that bigger firms have an advantage. They are able to shift marketing resources, capabilities, skills and expertise) from one product to another. Recall that the factor CF1 (sufficiency in marketing) concerns sufficient availability of adequate quality of:

- marketing personnel and funds to adapt advertising and promotion;
- personnel to train sales staff and technicians;
- after-sales service personnel and equipment; and
- distribution channels.

So, bigger firms can more easily reach a critical mass. This results in a rapid sufficiency of adequate quality of marketing resources to support the rollout of a new product. In contrast, smaller companies are at a disadvantage. Lacking capabilities, skills, expertise and resources, these companies cannot easily support the rollout of their new products across international markets.

In contrast, firm size does not have a statistically significant effect upon sufficiency in technology. This means that sufficiency in technology resources, capabilities, skills and expertise depends upon things other than the actual size of the company. More likely, such sufficiency is project dependent. Recall that factor CF2 (sufficiency in technology) concerns sufficient availability of adequate quality of:

Table 4.17 Product-moment correlation coefficients between antecedent and core factors (identified relationships only)

	Factor code	CF1 Sufficiency in marketing	CF2 Sufficiency in technology	CF3 Synergies in product handling and use	CF8 Internal communication between European HQs and subsidiaries/agents and between subsidiaries/agents themselves
Firm size	AF1	0.40*	0.29†	–	–
Extent of customisation of product technology for the European market	AF2	n.s.	−0.44*	−0.39*	–
Complexity of customisation of product technology for the European market/approvals	AF3	n.s.	n.s.	−0.37*	–
Speed of technology change					
(a) Rate of product modification instigated by main competitors††		0.29*	n.s.	n.s.	–
(b) Speed of technology change††		n.s.	n.s.	n.s.	–
(c) Product and production obsolescence rate††		n.s.	n.s.	n.s.	–
Extent of competitive threat	AF4	n.s.	n.s.	–	–
Strategic intention for the specific new product	AF5	n.s.	n.s.	–	–
Product European market share		–	–	–	0.36†
Value of European product sales		–	–	–	n.s.

Notes: *$p < 0.10$, †$p < 0.15$, ††Kendall-Tau b correlation coefficients, − = relationship not identified.

- R&D personnel and funds to adapt product;
- hardware adapted for different European countries; and
- software adapted for different European countries.

However, the marginal statistical significance of the correlation (0.29; $p < 0.15$) shows a tendency of bigger firms to have some advantages in this area too.

4.4.3 Extent of customisation of product technology for the European market (AF2)

There is a strong negative correlation between the extent of customisation of product technology for the European market and both:

- sufficiency in technology (CF2); and
- synergies in product handling and use (CF3) (see Table 4.17).

The above shows that companies operating in areas where product technology is standardised are more able to achieve the required level of engineering resources, capabilities, skills and expertise. This standardisation further helps sales staff to familiarise themselves with the technology so that they can easily handle new products. Similar effects exist for the customer who is acquainted with the operation of similar products, the way they function and how to interact with them. This increases the product complementarity for the user.

There is no statistical significance in the correlation between the extent of customisation of product technology (AF2) and sufficiency in marketing (CF1). Support for a potential linkage could include the easier task of marketing a product with limited requirements because of its standardised technology. It seems that technological and market standardisation are two separate issues. New products are likely to need customisable marketing approaches in different country markets independently of the extent of customisation of their product technology.

4.4.4 Complexity of customisation of product technology for the European market/approvals (AF3)

There is no statistical significance in the correlation between the complexity of customisation of product technology for the European market/approvals (AF2) and sufficiency in technology (CF2) (see Table 4.17). Qualitative evidence showed that this link holds strong in a few cases, but it is infrequently an issue across the entire sample. This bears upon the statistical significance of the correlation coefficient.

Such complexity of customisation of product technology/approvals bears in contrast, strongly and negatively upon synergies (CF3). This indicates that the higher the complexity of the customisation of product technology/approvals, the more difficult it is for the sales force to handle the product and for the customer to use it.

4.4.5　The effects of speed of technology change

Three ordinal-scale items were used:

- 'rate of product modification instigated by main competitors';
- 'speed of technology change within the industry';
- 'product and production obsolescence rate'.

An EFA, which was carried out, yielded no meaningful factor. For this reason, all the above three items were retained independently and used separately in the analysis. The Kendal-Tau b non-parametric correlation test for ordinal variables was employed. Only one relationship was found to be statistically significant (see Table 4.17). There is a positive relationship between rate of product modification (5 = seasonal; 4 = periodically <1 year interval; 3 = annually; 2 = periodically >1 year interval; 1 = irregularly – no pattern) and sufficiency in marketing. The frequent product launches seem to increase the likely number of replacement product generations and the similarity of new products. These impact positively upon company sufficiency in marketing resources, capabilities, skills and expertise. There were no significant correlations between speed of technological change and:

- sufficiency in technology (CF2); and
- synergies in product handling and use (CF3).

This may be due to the fact that engineering capabilities in competing companies exist in both rapidly and less rapidly changing environments. Technological change may also not bear upon the interface between the user and the product. For instance, companies may keep the same product-user interface despite major changes in product technology.

4.4.6　The extent of competitive threat (AF4) and the strategic intention for the specific new product (AF5)

There is no statistically significant link (see Table 4.17) between AF4, AF5 and

- sufficiency in marketing (CF1); and
- sufficiency in technology (CF2).

The reasons for this picture have their roots in the complexity of wider competitive dynamics for each of the sampled cases which evolved over several generations of replacement or new products. It is therefore less easy to capture statistically how the competitive threat and the strategic intention for the specific new product affect sufficiency in marketing and technology. Current data do not permit the development of a full and accurate picture of these effects. Such a discussion would require a different set of data, and a longitudinal research project tracing the long-term evolution of competition and product portfolios.

4.4.7   Product's European market share and value of European product sales

The high product market share in Europe and the high value of product sales to the European market were identified to influence the internal communication between European HQ and subsidiaries/agents. The supposed link was that the higher the product market share or product sales to Europe, the higher the importance attributed by the corporation to the European market. This was seen to have a positive impact upon the communication effort to keep abreast with developments in the local European markets. Only the correlation between market share and intensity of communication (CF8) is marginally significant (0.36, $p < 0.15$) (Table 4.17).

4.5   Conclusion

This chapter reported the cross-case analysis of the investigated cases in the main study. Before proceeding further, it is necessary to mention that the potential elimination of the two statistical outliers would have only marginal importance; thus, the analysis incorporated all 30 cases, unless otherwise stated. Descriptive information with respect to timely and delayed cases was first provided. There are several differences between timely and delayed cases, as follows:

- *The project novelty for the company.* Delayed cases are in 'novel' product areas for the companies. Timely cases are in product areas where companies are already active. These are usually product line extensions or replacements of older products.

- *The number of target markets where the company rolls out the new product.* Delayed products are made available to only a few of their target country markets. Timely products are made available to almost all their target country markets.
- *Type of target markets.* Delayed cases target small niche segments. Timely cases target mass consumer/volume markets.
- *Market share.* Delayed products generally have lower market share. The actual yearly value of the European market for that product or value of product sales level do not seem to relate to rollout timeliness.
- *The origin of parent companies.* UK or North American companies may be more prone to delay in the rollout of their new products. Japanese companies may be more prone to timeliness in the rollout of their new products.
- *Delays in development occur in both timely and delayed rolled-out new products.* Nonetheless, timely rolled-out cases show a less frequent and shorter NPD delay than delayed rolled-out cases.

Discussion continued with the summarised presentation of qualitative information on the causes of delays for each case. The importance and frequency of delays across cases was also presented. There are several causes of delays. Insufficiency of adequate quality of marketing resources is both the most frequent and the most important cause. Insufficiency of adequate quality of engineering resources and technology and lack of internal communication come second. Problems in the NPD process follow closely. Problems in customisation of product technology/ approvals and lack of synergies in product handling and use supplement the above.

A series of factor analyses and reliability tests followed. Several items reflecting the above were subjected to EFA. High factor loadings, good to excellent reliabilities in all but one case, and easily interpretable factors have confirmed the appropriateness of items used in this study. Table 4.18 summarises the results of the EFAs and reliability tests.

Some antecedents were identified as influencing the factors that lead to rollout timeliness. Section 4.4 examined the statistical significance of the relationships. Table 4.19 shows whether the hypothesised effects where statistically confirmed.

It was found that bigger firms have an advantage in reaching a critical mass in marketing for the rollout of the new product. Larger companies are likely to be better equipped to orchestrate the gathering of the necessary skills, expertise, market connections, people and funds to support

Table 4.18 Summary of results from the EFAs and reliability tests

Factor name(s)	Explained variance (%)	Cronbach's α
New product success	78	
(a) Financial performance	55.9	0.83
(b) Timely NPD	22.7	n.a.
Core factors influencing rollout timeliness		
(a) Sufficiency in marketing	86	0.94
(b) Sufficiency in technology	86	0.92
(c) Synergies in product handling and use	68	0.84
(d) Superior product	67	0.83
(e) Quality integration during the NPD process	61	0.83
(f) Proficient execution of the NPD process	70	0.91
(g) Targets known at the start of the NPD process	65	0.82
(h) Internal communication between European HQ and subsidiaries/agents and between subsidiaries/agents themselves	64	0.88
Antecedent factors		
(a) Firm size	87	0.81
(b) Extent of customisation of product technology for the European market	70	0.57
(c) Complexity of customisation of product technology for the European market/approvals	70	0.79
(d) Extent of competitive threat	89	0.96
(e) Strategic intention for the specific new product	74	0.82

a new product. Smaller companies may be more likely to have greater difficulties in doing so. Their problems may even increase if companies target markets with a wide variation of requirements.

However, bigger firms do not always have an advantage in reaching a critical mass in technology for the new product. Such sufficiency is positively affected by the standardisation of product technology. Standardised product technology assists organisations to achieve more easily a critical mass in engineering resources, skills, capabilities and expertise for the new product. Customisation of product technology makes it more difficult for companies to achieve a critical mass in technology for the new product.

Table 4.19　List of antecedents and the statistical significance of their effects

Antecedents	Factor code	Direction of their effects			
		CF1	CF2	CF3	CF8
(a) Firm size	AF1	yes	marginal		
(b) Extent of customisation of product technology for the European market	AF2	n.s.	yes	yes	
(c) Complexity of customisation of product technology for the European market/approvals	AF3	n.s.	n.s.	yes	
(d) Speed of technology change		partial	n.s.	n.s.	
(e) Extent of competitive threat	AF4	inconclusive	inconclusive		
(f) Strategic intention for the specific new product	AF5	inconclusive	inconclusive		
(g) European market share					marginal
(h) European sales value					n.s.

Within this wider framework, complexity of technological customisation does not seem to have a statistically significant effect upon either marketing or technological sufficiency. This may be due to the small number of cases that experienced substantial complexity in customising their products. In contrast, such complexity bears strongly and negatively upon synergies in product handling by the sales force and product-user familiarity. It seems that it is difficult for sales staff to learn about:

• country-specific hardware and software; and
• complex government approval procedures. Such approvals usually require an in-depth knowledge of both technical and administrative matters.

These may be due to lack of expertise or lack of time. The sales force may dilute their efforts in selling a wide range of products, they may not wish to devote substantial time in learning the functioning of complex hardware and software, and they may not have the depth of knowledge required for supporting complex high technology products. Customers also experience difficulties in learning how to handle and interact with products that need complicated adaptation from country to country. Both customers and sales staff appear better able to handle and use uncomplicated, technologically non-customisable new products.

The speed of technology change is positively associated with company sufficiency in marketing. Companies in sectors of frequent product modifications create a marketing infrastructure that facilitates fast and timely rollout of younger generations of new products. Rapid change of technology does not, however, mean sufficiency in engineering resources is easier or more difficult to achieve. Such sufficiency seems to be project-specific.

The study did not find any statistically significant effects of competitive threat and the strategic intention for the new product upon sufficiency in marketing and technology. This is likely due to the difficulty of capturing the complexity of competitive dynamics when the research focus is on the single new product project.

This study also found that there is a statistically marginal, yet positive link between market share and internal communication between European HQ and European subsidiaries/agents. There is greater managerial attention upon products that account for high market share across Europe, which, in turn, promotes internal company communication.

Further analysis concentrates on the core factors (CF1,..., CF8) of the theoretical framework, rollout timeliness and the interactions between these core factors. Answers to the four research questions, alongside confirmation or rejection of the hypotheses of the present investigation, are presented in Chapter 5.

5
Findings and Discussion

5.1 Research question 1: is rollout timeliness related to new product success?

5.1.1 Introduction

Hypothesis 1 stated that:

New product success of timely and delayed rollout cases does differ.

The EFA regarding new product success (section 4.3.1) has revealed a two-factor solution. The first factor comprised sales, return on investment, customer acceptance and technical performance of product and was named *'financial performance'*. The second factor comprised NPD timeliness and was named *'timely NPD'*.

5.1.2 Rollout timeliness and new product success

For the first new product success factor (factor 1), the item values of the items loading high on the factor were averaged. Table 5.1 shows the difference in means and the standard deviations for the factors 1 and 2 between timely and delayed rolled-out cases. T-tests show these differences in means to be significant.

Table 5.1 indicates that timely rolled-out new products are far more successful than delayed rolled-out new products. A rapid and timely

Table 5.1 New product success factors 1 and 2: means and standard deviations for timely versus delayed rollout cases

Factor name	Timely cases		Delayed cases		T-tests signif.
	Mean	Std dev.	Mean	Std dev.	
Factor 1	1.95	1.67	−0.86	1.80	0.000
Factor 2	−3.83	6.58	−9.93	9.07	0.05

rollout becomes, therefore, a fundamental element for the overall successful NPD effort.

5.1.3   Relationships between rollout timeliness and success dimensions

The analysis proceeded with an examination of the individual relationships between rollout timeliness and the different success dimensions (sales, return on investment, technical performance, etc.). Table 5.2 shows the correlation coefficients between the various success dimensions and rollout timeliness.

These relationships are explained below:

- There is a strong and positive relationship between timely rollout and sales ($0.66, p < 0.001$) and between timely rollout and return on investment ($0.57, p < 0.001$). These indicate a crucial relationship between rapid and timely product availability and sales and return on investment. The considerably high correlations at a strong level of statistical significance show how destructive delays are in new product rollouts across international markets. Surprisingly, there is a small difference in correlations between timely rollout and sales, and rollout and return on investment. A greater difference might have been expected, suggesting a smaller effect upon profitability. Apparently, missed sales for products with rapid obsolescence and short product life cycles (and probable declining prices in the late stages of the products' life cycle) have a direct and immediate impact upon profitability. This is also captured from an extremely high ($0.85, p < 0.001$) correlation between sales for the investigated products and return on investment.
- The relationships between timely rollout and technical performance and customer acceptance are not statistically significant. These are

Table 5.2 Relationships between the new product success dimensions and rollout timeliness: correlation coefficients

Dimensions	Code	S1	S2	S3	S4	S5	S6
Sales	S1	1.00					
Customer acceptance	S2	0.50**	1.00				
Return on investment	S3	0.85***	0.46**	1.00			
Technical performance	S4	0.57***	0.53***	0.35*	1.00		
Timeliness in NPD	S5	0.36*	n.s.	0.44**	n.s.	1.00	
Timeliness in rollout (across *all* markets)	S6	0.66***	n.s.	0.57***	n.s.	0.45**	1.00

Notes: $*p < 0.05$, $** p < 0.01$, $*** p < 0.001$.

important issues. A remarkable technical product performance may not accelerate availability of the new product across countries. The same happens regarding customer acceptance. This indicates that organisational and other company or product related elements play a more fundamental role than technical performance and customer acceptance in timeliness of new product rollout.

- The relationship between timely NPD and technical performance is also not statistically significant. This replicates Cooper and Kleinschmidt (1994) who also found a non-significant relationship between NPD timeliness and the technical success rating. Cooper and Kleinschmidt (1994) argued that how the project was organised proved to be the strongest determinant of time efficiency and staying on schedule. At the same time, the relationship between timely NPD and customer acceptance is also not statistically significant. Potential customer acceptance may not help the NPD team to overcome a series of technical and organisational challenges that may bear upon the timely completion of the NPD process.
- The relationship between timeliness in NPD and rollout is positive and strong (0.45, $p < 0.01$).
- There is a stronger correlation at higher significance levels between timeliness of rollout and sales (i.e. 0.66, $p < 0.001$) and return on investment (0.57, $p < 0.001$) than timeliness in NPD and sales (0.36, $p < 0.05$) and return on investment (0.44, $p < 0.05$). This has been confirmed by multiple regression where sales or return on investment are regressed upon timeliness in rollout and timeliness in NPD (the two independent variables). Timeliness in rollout has scored higher standardised beta coefficients and statistical significance levels. This means that the impact of delays in rollout is likely to be greater than the impact of delays in NPD despite a strong and positive correlation between the two timeliness measures. These demonstrate that rapid rollout may probably overcome the negative impact of delays during the NPD phase.

5.1.4   Conclusion

Hypothesis 1 is accepted. This hides, however, certain interesting elements:

- Timeliness in new product rollout is strongly and positively correlated to both sales and return on investment. In fact, timely rollout has a stronger effect upon sales and return on investment than a timely developed new product. This means that the impact of delays in rollout is greater than the impact of delays in NPD despite a strong and positive correlation between them. The reader is reminded that sales are captured through a perceptual measure. The measure used does not differentiate between sales concluded prior to the actual product availability, sales at the time of product availability or sales at a later stage. Return on investment is also captured through a perceptual measure.

- The actual time it takes to make the new product available for sale across countries (in months) does not seem to be linked to a remarkable product technical performance or customer acceptance contrary to conventional managerial wisdom. A remarkable technical performance or higher customer acceptance come second to the actual product availability for sale and potential new product uniqueness among competing products.

5.2 Research question 2: do firms roll out their new products across international markets simultaneously or sequentially?

5.2.1 Introduction

This question looks at two different aspects:

- Is there a link between the nature of product technology and sequential rollout? (Research question 2a).
  Hypothesis 2a states that:

  There is a relationship between the nature of product technology and sequential rollout.

- Is there a link between sequential rollout and delays? (Research question 2b).
  Hypothesis 2b states that:

  There is a relationship between sequential rollout and delays.

Managers interviewed generally implied that simultaneous rollout meant a rollout that was completed within 1–2 months from the date of availability in the first European country. In accordance with this, the cases were assigned into two groups. The first group comprised 8 cases (27 per cent of the sample) of planned completion of the new product rollout in 1–2 months across all target markets. The cases in the first group were defined and labelled as 'simultaneous rollout'. The second group comprised 22 cases (73 per cent of the sample) of planned completion of the new product rollout in periods of over 2 months across all target markets. The cases in the second group were defined and labelled as 'sequential rollout' (see Table 5.3).

Table 5.3 New product rollout time (months) (simultaneous planned time = Sm; sequential planned time = Sq)

Product	Rollout time				Rollout Labelled		Rollout delay[+]	
	Key markets		All markets					
	Plan	Actual	Plan	Actual	Sm	Sq	Key months	All months
Timely rollout cases								
Laser (B&W) high-speed printer	2	same	2	same	Sm		0	0
Solid ink colour printer	4	same	4	same		Sq	0	0
Hand stand still 35 mm camera	1	same	1	same	Sm		0	0
Medium-speed industrial camera	2	same	2	same	Sm		0	0
Ethernet port switch	3	same	3	same		Sq	0	0
PBX	34	same	45	same		Sq	0	0
Laser (B&W) medium-speed printer	1	same	1	same	Sm		0	0
TV set	3	same	3	same		Sq	0	0
Medium-speed professional camera	12	same	12	same		Sq	0	0
Sound mixing system	1	same	1	same	Sm		0	0
PC monitor	3	same	6	same		Sq	0	0
Ethernet 10/100 adapter card	1	same	1	same	Sm		0	0
Matrix (B&W) bar-code printer	1	same	1	same	Sm		0	0
TV set	1	same	1	same	Sm		0	0
Analogue modem	3	same	3	same		Sq	0	0
Delayed rollout cases								
RS 232 adapter	3	12**	3	12**		Sq	9	9
Ethernet multiplexer	4	6**	12	14**		Sq	2	2
Climatic data recording instrument	3	4	6	9		Sq	1	3
Ethernet print server	1	2	3	4		Sq	1	1
High- and ultra-high speed camera	2	3	4	6		Sq	1	2
Hand stand still 35 mm camera	2	6	6	18		Sq	4	12
Dynamometer	3	9	3*	9***		Sq	6	6
Security identification and lamination system	18	36**	36	48**		Sq	18	12
PBX	3	8	6	12		Sq	5	6
Analogue modem	4	7	7	14		Sq	3	7
Mobile GSM telephone	1	5	3	7		Sq	4	4
ISDN modem	4	6	4	6		Sq	2	2

PC-telephony integration platform	6	14**	14	24**	Sq	8	10
Ethernet print server	3	9**	6	12**	Sq	6	6
Electric data recording/ testing instrument	6	6	12	24	Sq	0	12
Average	4.5	6.8	7.0	10.1		4.6	6.3

Notes: * Rollout delay in *key* markets and rollout delay in *all* (key + secondary) markets;
** Rollout delays were still increasing in these four cases and rollout was indefinitely postponed in the fifth one (Security identification and lamination system). Scores are assigned for comparative purposes;
*** The company does not have any secondary markets – score is assigned for comparative purposes.

5.2.2   The nature of product technology and sequential rollout

New products in some product technologies are more prone to sequential rollout. All three cases in measurement instruments and all seven cases in telecommunications were planned to roll out sequentially (Table 5.4). These also have a higher incidence of delays. Eight out of these ten cases eventually faced rollout delays.

This happens because the technological component becomes an additional problem area for the companies. Tables 5.5 and 5.6 show the problem areas for the cases of substantial versus limited customisation of product technology. It is noticeable that cases of:

- Substantial customisation of product technology face problems in both technology and non-technology areas.
- Limited product customisation (=standardised technology) mostly face problems in non-technology related areas.

The computer–telephone integration market is a case in point of substantial product technology customisation. This market, which is part of the wider telecommunications industry, was, until a few years ago, an

Table 5.4 Product technologies, sequential rollout and delays: number of cases

Area of technology	Total cases	Simultaneous rollout	Sequential rollout	Timely cases	Delayed cases
Photographic equipment	6	2	4	3	3
Measuring instruments	3	–	3	–	3
Telecommunications	7	–	7	2	5
Others	14	6	8	10	4
Total all cases	30	8	22	15	15

Table 5.5 Timely rollout cases: extent of customisation of product technology and problem areas

Company	Sufficient availability of adequate quality			Distribution channels	Synergies in product handling		Communication European HQs and n.p.d. teams	New development Proficient new product development	Internal communication Eur. HQs and agents/ subsidiaries and between	Customisation of product technology		Approval Complex or other problems	Importance of product European market share or sales
	Engineering/ technical personnel/ resources	Marketing personnel/ resources	Hardware/ software		By sales force across Europe	By end user				Extent of	Complex-ity of		
Cases of substantial customisation of product technology													
Nortel	no	no	no	no	no	no	no*	no	no	minor	no	no	no
US Robotics	no	no	no	no	no	no	no*	no	no	minor	no	no	no
Cases of some customisation of product technology													
Brother	no	no	no	no	no	no	no*	no	no	no	no	no	no
Citizen	no	no	no	no	no	no	no*	no	no	no	no	no	no
OKI	no	no	no	no	no	no	no*	no	no	no	no	no	no
Panasonic	no	no	no	no	no	no	no*	no	no	minor	no	no	no
Taxan	no	no	no	no	no	no	no*	no	no	minor	no	no	no
TEC	no	no	no	no	no	no	no*	no	no	no	no	no	no
Toshiba	no	no	no	no	no	no	no*	no	no	minor	no	no	no
Cases of limited customisation of product technology													
Hanimex	no	no	no	no	no	no	no*	no	no	no	no	no	no
Hitachi	no	no	no	no	no	no	no*	no	no	no	no	no	no
LanArt	no	no	no	no	no	no	no*	no	no	no	no	no	no
Sony	no	no	no	no	no	no	no*	no	no	no	no	no	no
Soundcraft	no	no	no	no	no	no	no*	no	no	no	no	no	no
Telesyn	no	no	no	no	no	no	no*	no	no	no	no	no	no

Note: * if new product development is located in another continent.

Table 5.6 Delayed rollout cases: extent of customisation of product technology and problem areas

Company	Sufficient availability of adequate quality				Synergies in product handling		New product development		Internal communication	Customisation of product technology		Approval	Importance of product
	Engineering/ technical personnel/ resources	Marketing personnel/ resources	Hardware/ software	distribution channels	By sales force across Europe	By end user	Communication European HQs and n.p.d. teams	Proficient new product development	Eur. HQs and agents/ subsidiaries and between	Extent of	Complexity of	Complex or other problems	European market share or sales
Cases of substantial customisation of product technology													
Instron	MAJOR	no	minor	no	MAJOR	MAJOR	no*	MAJOR	no	MAJOR	MAJOR	no	no
Mitel	no	MAJOR	minor	MAJOR	MAJOR	no	MAJOR*	minor	MAJOR	minor	minor	MAJOR	minor
Motorola	no	no	MAJOR	minor	no	no	no	no	no	minor	minor	minor	no
Rhetorex	no	MAJOR	MAJOR	no	minor	minor	no*	MAJOR	no	minor	MAJOR	MAJOR	minor
Cases of some customisation of product technology													
No case													
Cases of limited customisation of product technology													
Amplicon	no	MAJOR	no	MAJOR	no	no	no	no	MAJOR	no	no	no	MAJOR
Cray	MAJOR	no	MAJOR	no	no	no	no*	no	no	no	no	no	no
Delta-T	minor	MAJOR	no	no	no	no	no	no	minor	no	no	no	no
Emulex	no	no	MAJOR	no	MAJOR	MAJOR	MAJOR*	MAJOR	no	no	no	no	minor
Hadland	minor	MAJOR	no	MAJOR	no	no	no	no	minor	no	no	no	no
Halina	minor	MAJOR	MAJOR	no	no	no	no*	no	MAJOR	no	no	no	no
Laminex	MAJOR	MAJOR	minor	MAJOR	MAJOR	no	MAJOR	MAJOR	MAJOR	no	no	no	MAJOR
Orbitel	minor	MAJOR	MAJOR	MAJOR	no	no	no	no	no	no	no	no	minor
Racal	no	MAJOR	no	MAJOR	no	no	no	no	MAJOR	no	no	no	minor
3COM	MAJOR	MAJOR	MAJOR	MAJOR	MAJOR	MAJOR	no*	MAJOR	no	no	no	no	no
Voltech	no	MAJOR	no	MAJOR	MAJOR	no	minor	MAJOR	minor	no	no	no	no

Note: * if new product development is located in another continent.

underdeveloped industry. Currently, it experiences a phenomenal and explosive growth that is strongly linked to the emergence of powerful PC microprocessor and robust operating systems (i.e. OS/2, Windows NT). Its applications comprise voice messaging, inbound and outbound call processing, information services, and database access via telephone. Manufacturers need to customise the technology embodied in their products for individual countries due, mainly, to cross-country differences in telecommunication protocols. The US, European and other international digital networks are technically very different, with some countries supporting digital technology, while others employ 'hybrid' analogue–digital protocols or various analogue telecommunication protocols. Public and private investments made in telecommunication infrastructure are so varied that it is virtually impossible to standardise the telecommunication products across countries. The above become even more complex to achieve nowadays because of the new much stricter European Union requirements for electromagnetic interference. The case study of RxE Europe Ltd (see Appendix I) clearly shows the company's difficulties in both non-technology and technology areas and how these have resulted in a sequential planned rollout time.

5.2.3   Sequential rollout and delays

Delays were consistently featured in the cases of sequential new product rollout (15 out of the 22 cases). In marked contrast, all the simultaneously planned launches were timely. The observation of a high occurrence of delays in sequential as opposed to simultaneous country market launches is surprising. Bearing in mind that the researcher had requested the principal informant to select a recent rollout project, but had not specified the mode of rollout (sequential or simultaneous), the observed distribution of timely and delayed cases among the two modes of rollout is instructive. The result challenges conventional arguments for risk reduction in sequential launches (Mascarenhas, 1992a,b). Managers have tended to view simultaneous multi-country launches as a difficult and high risk strategy, and have traded off speedy market penetration for risk reduction by opting for a sequential rollout. This may have had an opposite result for sequential rollout cases in this study since it entails:

- a delay in the anticipated time frame for new product commercialisation across countries. Managers seem to have underestimated the difficulties and most of them did not eventually achieve their targets; and
- a substantial risk of new product failure. Such a failure contradicts the managerial target of reduction of risk.

5.2.4 Conclusion

Both hypotheses 2a and 2b are accepted. Specific product technologies are prone to sequential rollout and subsequent delays. This probably relates to the extent and complexity of customisation of product technology. All products planned to roll out sequentially have eventually faced delays.

5.3 Research question 3: what factors lead to rollout delay?

5.3.1 Introduction

The eight hypotheses related to this question state in summary that:

There is a relationship between

- *sufficiency in marketing (H_{3a});*
- *sufficiency in technology (H_{3b});*
- *synergies in product handling and use (H_{3c});*
- *product superiority (H_{3d});*
- *integration during the new product development process (H_{3e});*
- *proficiency of the new product development process (H_{3f});*
- *knowledge of intended targets at the start of the new product development process (H_{3g});*
- *intensive internal communication between the European HQ and subsidiaries/agents, and between subsidiaries/agents themselves (H_{3h})*

and timeliness in new product rollout.

5.3.2 Factors that lead to rollout delay

The framework of the present study comprised eight core factors that lead to rollout delays. Factor analysis on a series of indicators and reliability tests (section 4.3) established a series of highly reliable and easily interpretable factors. For each factor, item values were averaged. Table 5.7 shows the difference in factor means and standard deviations between timely and delayed cases.

The means show higher values for timely than delayed cases for all factors. This confirms their relationship with rollout timeliness. The strength of this relationship was subsequently tested through a series of product-moment correlations. Both measures of rollout timeliness were used (see Table 5.8). First, the relationship between these factors and the perceptual timeliness measure on a -5 to $+5$ scale is discussed. This measure aimed to identify the degree to which the project adhered to the time schedule,

Table 5.7   Means and standard deviations: timely versus delayed cases (scale 1–5)

Factor name	Code	Timely		Delayed	
		Mean	Std dev.	Mean	Std dev.
Suff. in marketing	CF1	3.4	1.2	2.0	0.8
Suff. in technology	CF2	3.8	1.1	2.4	1.2
Synergies	CF3	4.2	0.6	2.8	1.0
Prod. superior	CF4	4.3	0.6	3.5	0.7
Integration in NPD	CF5	3.7	0.9	2.3	0.5
Proficiency in NPD	CF6	3.6	1.1	2.2	0.6
Targets known early	CF7	4.2	0.7	3.2	0.9
Communication	CF8	3.5	1.0	1.8	0.5

where low negative scores (-5) indicate 'far behind schedule', (0) indicate 'stayed on schedule' and high scores ($+5$) indicate 'ahead of schedule'. Second, a discussion of the relationships between the 8 factors and the actual timeliness measure (calculated in months) is provided. The latter measure refers to the difference: *scheduled/anticipated – actual* rollout time in months (timeliness = $dt \geq 0$ months; delays = $dt < 0$ months).

Perceptual timeliness measure

Correlation coefficients are strong between all factors and the perceptual rollout timeliness measures [*key* markets (PT – key) and *all* markets (PT – all)]. Figures range from a low of 0.48 to a maximum of 0.79, at high levels of significance ($p < 0.01$ and beyond) (see Table 5.8).

Actual timeliness measure (calculated in months)

When the measure changes to actual delay in months (timeliness = $dt \geq 0$ months; delays = $dt < 0$ months), the results still remain stable for all factors, with strong, although decreased, correlation coefficients. The means of correlation coefficients decrease from 0.63 to 0.45 for *key* markets (AT – key) and 0.64 to 0.51 for *all* markets (AT – all) (see Table 5.8).

It is also useful to note the statistical significance of correlation coefficients. The average of statistical significance of correlations in Table 5.8 for the 'timeliness to *key* markets' measure decreases from $p = 0.001$ for the perceptual to $p = 0.01$ for the actual timeliness measure calculated in months (see Table 5.9). The average of statistical significance of correlation coefficients in Table 5.8 for the 'timeliness to *all* markets' measure decreases from $p = 0.0005$ for the perceptual to $p = 0.005$ for the actual timeliness measure calculated in months.

Table 5.8 Correlation coefficients between factors and rollout timeliness (*n* = 30, 2 tail significance)

Factor name	Code	PT-key	PT-all	AT-key	AT-all	CF1	CF2	CF3	CF4	CF5	CF6	CF7	CF8
Perceptual timeliness, key markets	PT-key	1.00											
Perceptual timeliness, all markets	PT-all	0.96***	1.00										
Actual timeliness, key markets	AT-key	0.64***	0.58***	1.00									
Actual timeliness, all markets	AT-all	0.65***	0.66***	0.74***	1.00								
Suff. in marketing	CF1	0.67***	0.71***	0.43**	0.47**	1.00							
Suff. in technology	CF2	0.61***	0.58***	0.50**	0.49**	0.58***	1.00						
Synergies	CF3	0.48*	0.53**	0.51**	0.49**	0.58***	0.55***	1.00					
Prod. superior	CF4	0.62***	0.59***	0.33*	0.46**	0.57***	0.57***	0.54***	1.00				
Integration in npd	CF5	0.66***	0.65***	0.43**	0.55***	0.78***	0.72***	0.57***	0.69***	1.00			
Proficiency in npd	CF6	0.66***	0.67***	0.36*	0.52***	0.82***	0.70***	0.54***	0.66***	0.88***	1.00		
Targets known early	CF7	0.57***	0.57***	0.45**	0.57***	0.70***	0.74***	0.61***	0.70***	0.75***	0.78***	1.00	
Communication	CF8	0.76***	0.79***	0.52***	0.62***	0.68***	0.57***	0.53***	0.48**	0.81***	0.77***	0.58***	1.00
Average		0.66	0.63	0.47	0.52	0.67	0.64	0.56	0.63	0.81	0.77	0.58	
Standard deviation		0.11	0.07	0.11	0.05	0.10	0.08	0.03	0.10	0.06	0.00		

Notes: * $p < 0.10$; ** $p < 0.01$; *** $p < 0.001$.

Table 5.9 Means of the statistical significance of correlation coefficients in Table 5.8

	Perceptual timeliness		Actual timeliness in months	
	Key markets	All markets	Key markets	All markets
Means	0.001	0.0005	0.01	0.005

The differences in correlation coefficients and statistical significance first indicate some cognitive biases of managers, in the sense that managers appear to inflate the success achievements of their new products in the perceptual measure. The use of two different timeliness measures, however, permits us to identify the scale of these differences. They are of the order of 0.17 for timeliness to *key* markets and 0.13 for timeliness to *all* markets (average of differences between correlation coefficients). It is interesting to note that the biggest reductions in the difference between correlation coefficients lie in specific areas (see Table 5.10). Decreases are of the order of 0.21–0.27 for product superiority (CF4), proficiency in the NPD process (CF6), intensity of internal communication (CF8), and sufficiency in marketing (CF1). The smaller decreases in strength of correlation coefficients are in synergies (CF3), sufficiency in technology (CF2) and targets known (CF7). These mean that the biggest cognitive biases concern the superiority of the company's products and softer organisational elements such as communication, marketing ability and internal co-ordination. In contrast, biases seem to be smaller for

Table 5.10 Differences between correlation coefficients in Table 5.8 for both measures of rollout timeliness

Factor name	Code	Timeliness in key markets			Timeliness in all markets		
		Perceptual measure	Actual timeliness in months	Difference	Perceptual measure	Actual timeliness in months	Difference
Suff. in marketing	CF1	0.6721	0.4448	0.2273	0.7132	0.4526	0.2606
Suff. in technology	CF2	0.6102	0.5106	0.0996	0.5835	0.4668	0.1167
Synergies	CF3	0.4835	0.5373	−0.0538	0.5322	0.4814	0.0508
Prod. superior	CF4	0.6270	0.3479	0.2791	0.5983	0.4577	0.1406
Integration in NPD	CF5	0.6685	0.4523	0.2162	0.6544	0.5397	0.1147
Proficiency in NPD	CF6	0.6621	0.3840	0.2781	0.6761	0.5159	0.1602
Targets known early	CF7	0.5798	0.4612	0.1186	0.5769	0.5531	0.0238
Communication	CF8	0.7689	0.5400	0.2289	0.7992	0.6201	0.1791
Average				0.1742			0.1308

more 'tangible' elements, including sufficiency in technology, actual synergies in product handling by the sales force and customer difficulty in operating the product.

It is important, however, that the strong correlation coefficients and the small standard deviations of these correlation coefficients (as shown in Table 5.8) have remained stable despite some inherent managerial biases. This shows that the CF1 to CF8 factors strongly relate to and lead to rollout timeliness. This happens independently of what measure of timeliness is used.

Following these findings, the next step is to examine the strength of differences between groups (i.e. timely and delayed cases). Cases were assigned to two groups (one comprising the timely and one comprising the delayed cases). A dummy variable was created and subsequently used as dependent. The value of 1 was given to all timely rollout cases and the value of 2 was given to all delayed rollout cases.

A series of Kruskal-Wallis 1-Way Anova between the individual factors (the average scale of all items loading on each factor) and the dependent dummy variable were carried out. Kruskal-Wallis is a robust non-parametric test of differences in location for two (or more) independent samples with a total of n observations, and it is particularly appropriate for the present analysis.

The question answered by the test is whether the differences among the samples signify genuine population differences with respect to the variable under study, or whether they represent merely the kind of variations that are to be expected among random samples from the same population. The Kruskal-Wallis 1-Way Anova is an alternative to a single-factor analysis of variance or a k-sample median test. For one sample, the median test is a binomial test with observations dichotomised as being above or below the hypothesised median. In Kruskal-Wallis 1-Way Anova, the scores in the combined samples are ranked, and the sum of the ranks, R_i, is found for each sample.

The test showed all differences in factor means between groups (i.e. timely and delayed cases) to be significant ($p < 0.005$) (see Table 5.11).

This indicates that all factors univariately relate and lead to rollout timeliness.

5.3.3 Conclusion

All eight hypotheses in this research question (RQ3) are accepted. There is a relationship between the above factors and timeliness in new product rollout. The interactions between the factors is discussed in more detail in research question 4.

Table 5.11 Kruskal-Wallis 1-Way Anova for individual factors between timely and delayed cases

Factor	Code	Mean rank timely	Mean rank delayed	χ^2	df	Signif.	Corrected for ties χ^2	df	Signif.
Suff. in marketing	CF1	20.10	10.90	8.19	1	0.0042	8.25	1	0.0041
Suff. in technology	CF2	20.03	10.97	7.95	1	0.0048	8.07	1	0.0045
Synergies	CF3	21.40	9.60	13.47	1	0.0002	13.63	1	0.0002
Prod. superior	CF4	20.23	10.77	8.67	1	0.0032	8.85	1	0.0029
Integration in NPD	CF5	21.13	9.87	12.28	1	0.0005	12.34	1	0.0004
Proficiency in NPD	CF6	20.50	10.50	9.67	1	0.0019	9.71	1	0.0018
Targets known early	CF7	20.17	10.83	8.43	1	0.0037	8.57	1	0.0034
Communication	CF8	22.30	8.70	17.89	1	0.0000	18.08	1	0.0000

5.4 Research question 4: what is the interaction between these factors and their direct and indirect effects upon rollout delay?

5.4.1 Introduction

Eight core factors were identified as relating to timeliness in new product rollout. This section focuses on the interaction between these core factors. A model is then presented. The total effect of each factor upon timeliness is subsequently ascertained through path analysis.

5.4.2 Modelling and the modelling process

Modelling was considered to be an adequate method to communicate the relationships. This is because a model is 'a simplified description of a system [system = a group of things working together as a whole] used in explanations, calculations etc.' (*Oxford Dictionary*). Such simplification is important, since it expresses the linkages between elements and clarifies their interaction, thus facilitating the generation of additional theoretical insights into the topic at hand. A theory is an abstract set of ideas that links together concepts, and a model is its formal representation in a way that approximates to reality (see Vázquez *et al.*, 1996 p. 79). Social modellers seem to assume in this respect that social action can be captured in a rational, logical scientific model which may be depicted in a causal diagrammatic manner (Meadows, 1980, p. 25). Due to the approximate nature of models and the impossibility of observing causality, however, all causal inferences must be regarded as tentative.

The modelling process followed in the ensuing analysis was adapted from Randers (1980). It is divided into four stages: *conceptualisation, formulation, validation* and *implementation*. This four-stage process is considered to be powerful and its value is established in complex system dynamics modelling problems (Legasto *et al.*, 1980).

Model conceptualisation and formulation: The conceptualisation stage establishes the focus of the model. The formulation stage casts the chosen perspective into a formal representation. The resulting model gives a precise, though not necessarily accurate, description of a slice of reality and is capable of generating images of alternative figures. During the formulation stage, one attempts to select a means of relating model behaviour to system properties. The trial and error process to be followed can reflect one of two attitudes: viewing the model as a 'black box' where parameters are systematically changed and behaviour is then simulated and observed; or utilising the system equations to guide parameter selection. The first attitude was followed. The use of case research methodology in this project had already provided an oral, descriptive and experiential database that was large, comprehensive and rich in depicting causal relations and dynamic behaviour. This helped conceptualisation and model formulation.

Model validation and representation: The validation stage subjects both model structure and behaviour to various tests intended to establish the quality of the model. The goal is to identify weak points for further improvement and to establish the extent of model utility. Finally the representation stage seeks to transfer study insights to those who might use them (Randers, 1980). Forrester and Senge (1980) contend that validity is determined by the confidence one has in the model; its assumptions, its plausible arguments, the consistency between model behaviour, dynamics and perceived important relationships. They argued on the matter:

> Validation is the process of establishing confidence in the soundness and usefulness of a model. Validation begins as the model builder accumulates confidence that a model behaves plausibly and generates problem symptoms or modes of behaviour seen in the real system. (p. 210)

Such system verification is completed through a series of model structure and behaviour tests as follows (see also Legasto *et al.*, 1980):

- *Tests of model structure.* Verifying structure means comparing the structure of the model directly with the structure of the real system that the model represents. To pass the structure verification test, the model structure must not contradict knowledge about the structure of the real system. Other possible tests include parameter verification, the extreme conditions test, the boundary adequacy structure test and the dimensional consistency test.
- *Tests of model behaviour.* Behaviour reproduction tests examine how well model-generated behaviour matches the observed behaviour of the real system. Behaviour reproduction tests include symptom generation, frequency generation, relative phasing, multiple mode and behaviour prediction. The symptom generation test examines whether or not a model recreates the symptoms of difficulty that motivated construction of the model (Forrester and Senge, 1980, p. 217). Presumably the model is made to show how a particular kind of undesirable situation arises, so it can be alleviated. Unless one can show how internal actions and structure cause the symptoms, one is in a poor position to alter those causes. The multiple mode tests consider whether or not a model is able to generate more than one mode of behaviour (i.e. in the present model timeliness versus new product rollout delay). Behaviour prediction tests are analogous to behaviour reproduction test and focus on future behaviour. Within this type, the pattern prediction test examines whether or not a model generates qualitatively correct patterns of future behaviour. The event prediction test focuses on a particular change in circumstances which is found likely on the basis of analysis of model behaviour. Other tests include the behaviour anomaly test, the family member test, the surprise behaviour test, the extreme policy test, the boundary adequacy test and the behaviour sensitivity test (Forrester and Senge, 1980).

At least three possible criteria can be used when implementing the tests:

- Does omission (inclusion) of the factor lead to a change in the predicted numerical value of the system?
- Does omission (inclusion) of the factor lead to a change in the behaviour of the system? For example, does it dampen or induce fluctuations in the system?

- Does omission (inclusion) of the factor lead to rejection of findings that were formerly found to have had a favourable/unfavourable impact, or to reordering of effects?

The modelling process premises were followed for the present endeavour. A continuous reiteration between model formulation, validation and representation eventually assisted in the establishment of a model for timeliness in new product rollout across international markets. This model is presented hereafter.

5.4.3 Model of timeliness of new product rollout across international markets

In section 5.3, eight core factors (CF1,...,CF8) were found to relate to timeliness in new product rollout. Each one of them leads to or detracts from the timely rollout of new products across international markets. The effect of one factor often depends, however, on the state of others. They constitute a complex dynamic system, through which many organisational characteristics influence timeliness. Yet, the system is an evolving one, in which one factor influences others. Rapid and timely rollout of a new product grows out of the self-reinforcing interplay of these factors, thus creating a situation in which it becomes likely or unlikely to achieve timely rollout across countries. The system is as important as the individual parts, or more so. The model has been initially explained in Chapter 3. Nonetheless, the implementation of the four stages of the modelling process (i.e. conceptualisation, formulation, validation and implementation) has permitted to refine both the sequence and position of each individual element in the model as well as the interaction between them. Figure 5.1 shows the representation of the refined model. Arrows suggest an interaction between two elements, the arrow head indicating the direction of effect.

Explanation of symbols is as follows:

CF1 = Sufficiency in marketing
CF2 = Sufficiency in technology
CF3 = Synergies in product handling and use
CF4 = Product superior
CF5 = Quality integration during the NPD process
CF6 = Proficiency of the execution of the NPD process
CF7 = Targets known at the start of the NPD process
CF8 = Internal communication between European HQ and subsidiaries/agents and between subsidiaries/agents themselves

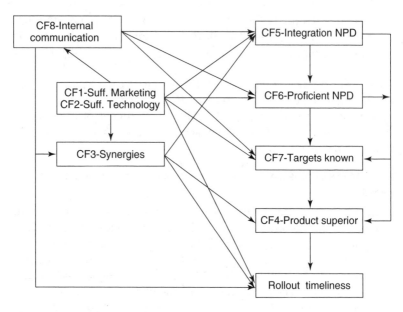

Figure 5.1   Model representation

The sequence of the model in its refined form is initiated with CF8 (communication) and CF1, CF2 (sufficiency in marketing and technology). CF3 (synergies), CF5 (integration in NPD), CF6 (proficient NPD) and CF7 (targets known) are intermediary elements that channel CF1, CF2 and CF8's effects upon CF4 (product superior) and rollout timeliness. These mean that new product rollout timeliness (conversely, delays) may be represented as a system of evolution where the first step of the evolutionary process regards resources (CF1, CF2) and communication (CF8) and the last regards rollout timeliness itself. There are two intermediary steps. The first intermediary step regards CF3 and the NPD related factors (CF5, CF6, CF7) while the second intermediary step regards product superiority (CF4). If a new product does not receive sufficient and adequate resources and there is weak organisational communication, the first to suffer will be synergies in product handling and use and the NPD process. Then, the products will be deficient, technically inappropriate, inferior to competition and unacceptable by customers, sales personnel and independent distributors. Furthermore, sales staff will not be familiar with the new products, product features and rollout dates, which will prevent them from informing and educating customers about the new arrivals. These create obstacles that oblige managers to lengthen the necessary periods to roll out the new products and run a higher risk of delays in the rollout schedules. New product projects will undergo this four-step system of evolution, though not necessarily one step at a time. Resources and communication exert their influence throughout the NPD. Similarly, a deficient NPD process, lack of synergies and a deficient product exert their influence throughout the new product rollout period. A positive standing of the new product project regarding all individual elements in each one of the above described four steps will result into new product rollout timeliness, a negative standing will result into delays in the new product rollout schedule. Having refined the sequence of the elements in the model and the interaction between them, the next step to investigate is the strength of the direct and indirect effects using path analysis. This is explained in turn.

5.4.4 Path analysis

5.4.4.1 Introduction

Path analysis is used to infer the existence of a causal relationship between the variables. It was first used by the geneticist Sewell Wright (1921) for untangling genetic and non-genetic influences. Path analysis employees a series of multiple regression analyses to describe the relationships among a set of variables that are logically ordered (Yaremko *et al.*, 1982). It is assumed that this reflects a causal order, so that each variable is determined by one or more of the variables that precede it, and in turn may determine variables that follow it. The model is shown in a path diagram, with arrows representing the direction of influence. Path analysis expresses the same relationships by a set of regression equations, with each variable expressed as a linear function of the preceding variables plus the error term. It is then concerned with estimating the magnitude of the linkages between variables and using these estimates to provide information about underlying causal processes (Asher, 1983). The simplest way to obtain the path coefficients is to regress each endogenous variable on those variables that directly impinge upon it, providing the regression assumptions are met, particularly the requirement that the residual variable in a structural equation be uncorrelated with the explanatory variables in that equation (Asher, 1983, p. 30).

One of the main advantages of path analysis is that it enables one to measure the direct and indirect effects of one variable on another. It must be recognised at the outset, however, that a causal model may never be established as proven by a given analysis; all that may be said is that the data are consistent with a given model or that they are not (Cohen and Cohen, 1983, p. 80). Furthermore, the conception of causality and the definition of cause have been the subject of intense discussion, a compelling resolution being available in Cook and Campbell (1979). For the purposes of the present study, the definition given by Cohen and Cohen (1983, p. 79) will be employed. They argued that causal analysis as a working method may require no more elaborate conception of causality than that of common usage, indicating that 'A' is a cause of 'B' when:

- 'A' precedes 'B' in time, although they may be measured at the same time.
- The mechanism whereby this causal effect operates can be posited.
- A change in the value of 'A' is accompanied by a change in the value of 'B'.

Ordinary least squares (OLS) regressions were used to identify the magnitude of effects in the model. Standardised path coefficients were used because of the difference in scaling between the dependent and independent variables. Measures used in the model are the factors established through factor analysis, tested for reliability and presented earlier in this document (CF1–CF8). Statistical assumptions regarding the use of regression were satisfied. T-tests were used to identify the statistical significance ($p < 0.05$) of each partial regression coefficient. Some of the linkages between variables were found to be statistically non-significant. For reasons of model purification, these linkages were eliminated from further consideration and a new series of OLS regressions were carried out. Figure 5.2 shows the paths that retained statistical significance and their standardised regression coefficients.

Eliminated linkages can be grouped into three sets:

- One set of eliminated linkages is from CF1 (sufficiency in marketing), CF2 (sufficiency in technology) and CF8 (internal communication) to the NPD process. CF1 does not directly influence early product and target market definition (CF7) in a statistically significant manner. CF2 does not influence directly in a statistically significant manner the proficiency of the NPD process (CF6). Furthermore, the linkages from CF1 and CF2 to rollout timeliness were also eliminated, although they were marginally significant. This indicates that marketing and engineering resources (CF1 and CF2) mostly channel their influence indirectly on rollout timeliness.

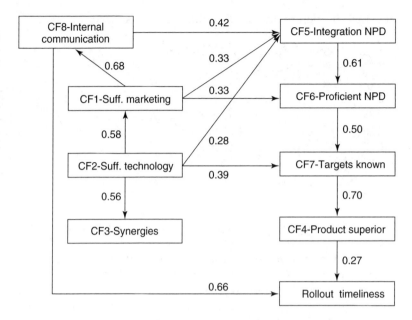

Figure 5.2 Model representation: statistically significant paths and standardised coefficients

Note: Adjusted R^2 values: Rollout timeliness = 0.67, CF1 = 0.31, CF3 = 0.29, CF4 = 0.47, CF5 = 0.79, CF6 = 0.80, CF7 = 0.66, CF8 = 0.44.

CF8 was also found to have a statistically significant influence only on the integration of the NPD process. CF8 affects neither the proficiency of execution of the NPD process nor early product and target market definition.

- A second set of eliminated linkages was between CF5 (integration during the NPD process), CF6 (proficiency during the process), CF7 (early product and target market definition) and CF4 (product superiority). Effects were found to be direct from CF5 to CF6, from CF6 to CF7 and from CF7 to CF4. These indicate that integration (CF5) leads to proficiency during the process (CF6), which leads in turn to early product and target market definition (CF7) and then to superiority of the product (CF4).
- The third set of eliminated linkages concerns CF3 (synergies in product handling by the sales force and in product use by the customers). CF3's effect upon rollout timeliness was marginal. The effect of CF1 (sufficiency in marketing) and CF8 (intensity of communication) upon CF3 were also eliminated, these also being marginal.

Model purification resulted in the following equations for the model:

TIMELINESS =		b_1 CF4 + b_2 CF8 + e
CF1	=	b_3 CF2 + e
CF3	=	b_4 CF2 + e
CF4	=	b_5 CF7 + e
CF5	=	b_6 CF1 + b_7 CF2 + b_8 CF8 + e
CF6	=	b_9 CF5 + e
CF7	=	b_{10} CF6 + e
CF8	=	b_{11} CF1 + e

where:

- b_n, $n = 1,\ldots,11$ are the standardised regression coefficients, e is the error term;
- **TIMELINESS = timeliness in new product rollout:** The perceptual timeliness to *all* markets measure was used to avoid skewness of the dependent variable in the regression equations. Recall the existence of two cases acting as statistical outliers (z-scores ranged from 2.084 to 4.557) (see also p. 106). At the same time, very strong correlations exist between the different rollout timeliness measures (average 0.71, $p < 0.001$).
- **CF1 = sufficiency in marketing** (distribution channels, marketing personnel and funds to adapt advertising/ promotion, personnel to train sales staff and technicians; after-sales service personnel and equipment);
- **CF2 = sufficiency in technology** (R&D personnel and funds to adapt product, hardware adapted for different European countries, software adapted for different European countries);
- **CF3 = synergies in product handling and use** (sales force, distribution channels, product handling/'feeling' remained same for the customer, way user is informed about product function remained same, way user interacts with and controls operation of product remained same);
- **CF4 = product superior** (unique attributes and clearly visible benefits to the customer, superior quality, performance, value for money, product intended image consistent with corporate image, attributes also perceived as useful by the customers);
- **CF5 = quality integration during the NPD process** (integration between technical, marketing and manufacturing high, integration between these functions when in different sites in different countries

high, final customers strongly involved and provided feedback, technical and marketing contributed accurate, on-time, high-quality input, subsidiaries/agents provided continuous feedback);

- CF6 = **proficiency of execution of the NPD process** (proficient execution of: tests of prototypes by customers/trial sales, co-ordination of distribution channels and logistics, co-ordination of advertising and promotion, predevelopment project planning, technical development and sorting out unexpected 'bugs', technical testing of the product);

- CF7 = **targets known at the start of the NPD process** (the firm knew at the start: the intended users, targeted countries and their needs and preferences, the product concept and product positioning, the final product specifications and technical requirements, the product final features and characteristics);

- CF8 = **internal communication between European HQ and European subsidiaries/agents and between subsidiaries/agents themselves** (extensive direct contact, meetings and interaction between HQ and subsidiaries/agents, direct contact, meetings and interaction between subsidiaries/agents, interdepartmental permanent committees between HQ and subsidiaries/agents, interdepartmental temporary forces between HQ and subsidiaries/agents, a matrix system between HQ and subsidiaries/agents, a set of shared goals, values and beliefs shaping behaviour).

The LMTEST (Byrne, 1994) was requested at this stage. The LMTEST provides Lagrange univariate and multivariate estimators regarding the direction of flows between the model factors. The LMTEST indicated that the direction of flows between the model factors was accurate.

5.4.4.2 Effect decomposition (standardised values)

Total and indirect effects are presented below:
Total effects upon:

Timeliness = + 0.518 CF1 + 0.390 CF2 + 0.274 CF4 + 0.058 CF5
          + 0.009 CF6 + 0.191 CF7 + 0.667 CF8
    CF1 = + 0.580 CF2
    CF3 = + 0.560 CF2
    CF4 = + 0.245 CF1 + 0.474 CF2 + 0.213 CF5 + 0.350 CF6
          + 0.700 CF7 + 0.089 CF8
    CF5 = + 0.610 CF1 + 0.636 CF2 + 0.420 CF8

$$CF6 = + 0.705 \ CF1 + 0.578 \ CF2 + 0.610 \ CF5 + 0.256 \ CF8$$
$$CF7 = + 0.352 \ CF1 + 0.653 \ CF2 + 0.305 \ CF5 + 0.50 \ CF6$$
$$+ 0.128 \ CF8$$
$$CF8 = + 0.680 \ CF1 + 0.394 \ CF2$$

Direct versus indirect effects upon:

Timeliness = Direct effect of CF8 = 0.665; indirect effect of CF8 = 0.002
   CF5 = Direct effect of CF1 = 0.33; indirect effect of CF1 = 0.28
          Direct effect of CF2 = 0.28; indirect effect of CF2 = 0.356
   CF6 = Direct effect of CF1 = 0.33; indirect effect of CF1 = 0.375
   CF7 = Direct effect of CF2 = 0.39; indirect effect of CF2 = 0.263

5.4.4.3 Discussion of effects: total effects

Upon timeliness = + 0.518 CF1 + 0.390 CF2 + 0.274 CF4
+ 0.058 CF5 + 0.009 CF6 + 0.191 CF7
+ 0.667 CF8

The decomposition of effects has noticeably shown that CF8 (internal communication between European HQ and European Subsidiaries/agents and between subsidiaries/agents themselves) and CF1 (sufficiency in marketing) have the strongest total effect (0.667 and 0.518 respectively) upon new product rollout timeliness.

This is followed by CF2 (0.390), which is sufficiency in technology and CF4 (0.274), which is superior product. CF3 was eliminated from the equation because its effect upon timeliness was marginally statistically significant.

Upon CF1 = +0.580 CF2; and upon CF3 = +0.560 CF2

CF2 has achieved a prominent position since it seems to influence all other variables in the model. This may be due, however, to the nature of sampled cases (in high-technology electronics) positing engineering resources at the very heart of rollout timeliness and sufficiency of marketing resources (effect upon CF1 = 0.580). CF3 (synergies in product handling and use) is particularly affected by CF2 (0.560). Marginally statistically significant effects of CF1 (sufficiency in marketing) and CF8 (internal communication) upon CF3 (synergies in product handling and use) were also witnessed. Yet, it is likely that abundant and high-quality technical inputs educate sales staff and customers rapidly, thus increasing their familiarity with the new product:

**Upon CF4 = + 0.245 CF1 + 0.474 CF2 + 0.213 CF5 + 0.350 CF6
+ 0.700 CF7 + 0.089 CF8**

CF4 (superiority of the new product) is excessively affected by CF7 (target known at the start of the NPD process), with a value of 0.700. It is also heavily influenced by both sufficiency in technology (CF2 = 0.474) and proficient execution of the NPD process (CF6 = 0.350).

The influence of internal communication (CF8) upon CF4 is small, however. This means that communication is only a means to achieve a superior product. Communication channels its influence upon CF4 only through the NPD process, an issue discussed next.

Upon CF5 = + 0.610 CF1 + 0.636 CF2 + 0.420 CF8
Upon CF6 = + 0.705 CF1 + 0.578 CF2 + 0.610 CF5 + 0.256 CF8
**Upon CF7 = + 0.352 CF1 + 0.653 CF2 + 0.305 CF5 + 0.50 CF6
+ 0.128 CF8**
Upon CF8 = + 0.680 CF1 + 0.394 CF2

CF5 (quality integration during the NPD process) is equally and strongly affected by sufficiency in marketing resources (CF1 = 0.610) and technology (CF2 = 0.636). CF8 follows closely behind (0.420). This indicates that quality integration leans upon adequate marketing and engineering resources, but communication backing is necessary. The importance of adequate quality marketing and engineering input is also apparent in the other equations, even though it is clear that a successful NPD process necessitates integration, proficient execution and early product and target market definition.

**Upon Timeliness = Direct effect of CF8 = 0.665; indirect effect of
CF8 = 0.002**

CF8 is affected by both CF1 and CF2 indicating that intra-organisational integration does not take place without appropriate quality marketing and technical resources. It also seems that subsidiaries and agents co-operate because the company has all the technology and products necessary to be competitive in the local European markets.

5.4.4.4 *Discussion of effects – indirect effects*

The most noticeable feature is the difference (+0.665 versus 0.002) between direct and indirect effects of CF8: that is, internal, HQ-subsidiaries and cross-subsidiaries' communication. This shows that almost the entire influence of CF8 upon timeliness is direct. It becomes clear, therefore, that without direct and strong integration between European HQ and subsidiaries/agents' operations, a new product will invariably experience delays in its international rollout:

Upon CF5 = Direct effect of CF1 = 0.33; indirect effect of CF1 = 0.28
Direct effect of CF2 = 0.28; indirect effect of CF2 = 0.35
Upon CF6 = Direct effect of CF1 = 0.33; indirect effect of CF1 = 0.37
Upon CF7 = Direct effect of CF2 = 0.39; indirect effect of CF2 = 0.26

CF1 influences both directly and indirectly most of the other elements in the model. Thus, it influences CF5 directly (0.33) and indirectly (0.28); and CF6 directly (0.33) and indirectly (0.37). The same happens for CF2 which also influences CF5 directly (0.28) and indirectly (0.35) and CF7 directly (0.33) and indirectly (0.26)

Both CF1 and CF2 (marketing and engineering resources) therefore become essential because they affect multiple aspects of the new product rollout. Their influence starts at the beginning of the NPD process through the necessary integration between functions, sites and people, leads directly and indirectly to a proficient NPD process (recall that indirect CF2 influence upon CF6 = 0.578), carries through an indirect influence upon the setting of targets, and remains strong through an indirect influence upon the superiority of the new product (recall effects upon CF4 = + 0.245 CF1 + 0.474 CF2). The role of the same elements (CF1 and CF2) persists through their influence upon the integration of operations between European HQ and European subsidiaries/agents.

Concluding, it seems that the three most important elements in the model are sufficiency in marketing (CF1), sufficiency in technology (CF2) and internal communication (CF8). More about the managerial implications of this finding follow in Chapter 6.

6
Conclusions and Implications

6.1 Overview

Rolling out new products across multiple country markets is important for the continued success of organisations. Although a small number of studies have begun to look at factors that are associated with timeliness in NPD and launch as well as the order-of-entry across international markets, none has attempted to investigate:

- whether timeliness in new product rollout across multiple country markets relates to new product success;
- whether companies do roll out new products across their international markets simultaneously or sequentially;
- the factors leading to rollout delay; and
- the interaction between these factors and their direct and indirect effects upon rollout delay.

Previous work on NPD and launch has shown that timeliness is an important issue; the current research extends these efforts to the timeliness of the international new product rollout. Nonetheless, it is important to remind the reader that rollout timeliness is a complex concept. The rollout diamond (see Figure 3.1) is useful in this respect. It provides a framework for the identification of at least six different comparative perspectives (see Table 3.1) in investigating the new product rollout phenomenon. This study has employed only one of the six possible comparative perspectives. Using multiple methods of data collection, this study reveals a number of important insights into the complex and risky decision of introducing new products across multiple country markets.

6.1.1   The relation between timeliness in rollout and new product success

Conclusion: Timeliness in new product rollout relates to new product success

The study found that a fast and timely rollout across multiple country markets strongly and positively correlates with higher sales and return on investment for the new product. This means that rollout speed and timeliness indeed play a fundamental role for a successful new product outcome. A wider number of countries is served in a relatively shorter time frame and the product's earlier availability results in higher sales and higher profits.

The product's earlier availability is clearly exhibited by the total period to develop and roll out the sample new high technology products. The completion of the 15 timely rolled-out projects was planned to last 20.3 months, on average (see Table 6.1). The completion of the 15 delayed rolled-out projects was planned to last 22.3 months, on average.

Eventually, the total time taken to develop and roll out the new products was 24.2 months for the timely rolled-out projects and 38.6 months for the delayed rolled-out projects, on average (see Table 6.1). The difference is 16.3 months (10.0 months delay in NPD and 6.3 months delay in rollout). This corresponds to a delay for the delayed rolled-out projects of 73 per cent of planned time for cross-country product availability (16.3/22.3 months). Of the total delay 40 per cent is caused by delays in new product rollout (6.3/16.3 months).

The new product rollout may be considered therefore, as a strong discriminator between failed and successful projects. This happens because project failures are available for sale more than a year ($3.9 - 16.3 = -12.4$ months) later than the successes. This period of 12.4 months is the time difference between timely and delayed rolled-out projects from first discussion of the new product idea to product availability in all European target country markets. This period of 12.4 months:

Table 6.1   Time from first meeting to consider the new product idea to product availability across country markets: timely versus delayed rollout cases (months)

	Timely cases (mean)			Delayed cases (mean)		
	Planned	Actual	Difference	Planned	Actual	Difference
NPD	14.6	18.5	3.9	14.0	24.0	10.0
Rollout	5.7	5.7	0	8.3	14.6	6.3
Total	20.3	24.2	3.9	22.3	38.6	16.3

- leaves a substantial amount of time for sales free of competition to successful projects. The market may thus become an oligopoly. Brand names will strengthen and customers will be compelled to buy the new product during this period, since there may not exist other substitute products available for purchase. Profitability will increase. The customers' ideal points will also move closer to the successful project's mix of product attributes; and
- is also a substantial proportion of the products' life cycle. Recall that 40 per cent of the investigated products had a product/production obsolescence period of 1–2.5 years and an additional 40 per cent had an obsolescence period of 2.5–5 years. The delayed rolled-out new projects are likely to appear in the market in the mature stage of their life cycle and they are closer to the end of their life cycle.

6.1.2 Simultaneous versus sequential new product rollout and the role played by the nature of product technology; the factors relating to delays in rollout schedule; the interaction between these factors.

1st conclusion: What matters is internal organisational elements including the existence of sufficient resources to support the new product rollout. External environment elements including the nature of technology have little direct effect upon the new product rollout and rollout delays.

The role of technology is not decisive regarding the simultaneous versus sequential new product rollout even though specific product technologies in the areas of telecommunications or measurement are more prone to sequential introduction of new products across countries and subsequent delays. Consider the following:

- Technological heterogeneity was anticipated to lead to rollout delays because of the need to adapt the new product to individual country requirements.
- Weak pervasiveness, weak attack intensity of competitive action and long technological obsolescence were anticipated to lead to long rollout periods and possible rollout delays because of no need for the firm to capture windows of opportunity, or to respond quickly to a competitor's new product.

The nature of product technology, the customisation of product technology across target country markets and the complexity of such customisation, like other external environment elements (i.e. heterogeneity of segments and the pervasiveness and attack intensity of competitive action), did not emerge as critical factors that impeded or slowed down the rollout of the sample new products. These broader external factors were only of secondary importance to rollout timeliness. Many of the principal causes of delays in international product rollout were associated with the firm's own internal environment, including failure in organisational communication and insufficient availability of adequate quality company resources for the development and rollout of the specific new product.

The broader external factors indirectly influence new product rollout in that they affect the accumulation of the necessary engineering and marketing resources allocated to the specific new product. It is more difficult to reach a sufficiency level of resources when the technological environment across countries is heterogeneous and where customisation of product technology is complex. Moreover, competitive pervasiveness and attack intensity may force the company to consider a rapid rollout, although without the resources to support such a rollout, the international launch will not succeed.

The capacity to 'leverage' resources is a strong indicator of the likelihood of successful fast and timely new product rollout across countries. Timeliness in rollout is constrained by, and dependent on, such 'leverage' of resources. Resources differentiate from a strategic point of view the chances a new product has for timely rollout. The underlying logic is that the current company products and activities constitute a unique bundle of tangible and intangible resources and capabilities, a notion similar to that argued by Penrose (1959) and Wernerfelt (1984) in the resource-based theory of the firm. This bundle of resources serves each individual new product differently and to a varying extent. As a new product targets specific segments and countries, it requires a unique bundle of tangible and intangible firm resources and capabilities. Each new product is idiosyncratic in this sense, since it necessitates a specific resource configuration, i.e. it asks for a portfolio of different organisational assets and organisational practices for both its development and rollout.

When there is 'leverage', a balance and compatibility exists between what is required for the development as well as the rollout of the specific new product (for example distribution channels or knowledge of the sales force) and what is already available in sufficient and adequate quality within the company.

The absence of the capacity to 'leverage' resources has a negative impact on the rapid completion of NPD and new product rollout, increasing the risk of product launch failure. The capacity to 'leverage' resources is thus, in aggregate, a fundamental determinant of the firm's 'positioning' and likelihood regarding:

- the launch of the new product across countries simultaneously rather than sequentially;
- shorter than longer rollout periods; and
- the timeliness rather than delay in new product rollout.

Recall that 73 per cent of the sample firms planned to roll out their new products in a sequential rather than simultaneous manner across countries. It is not surprising that all 15 delayed rollout cases were initially planned to roll out sequentially across countries. In contrast, all simultaneously planned launches were timely and they took place in a much shorter time frame. Firms with adequate resources can not only develop the new product sooner, but also roll it out rapidly and on schedule. Firms with inadequate resources will need more time to develop the new product, opt for a sequential rollout and tend to face delays. Constraints and resource needs are also higher for 'novel' product activities compared to product line additions or replacements of older products. A new project in 'novel' product areas is less likely to benefit from synergies in engineering and marketing resources. As a result:

- No project should be allowed to proceed to the development stage without considering the necessary resources to back up both its development and *rollout*. These include both engineering and marketing inputs.
- Companies should be extremely cautious when the new projects are in 'novel' product areas as these are more prone to problems that will lead to sequential rollout and rollout delays.

Specific product technologies (as in the measurement and telecommunications areas) also seem to negatively affect firm marketing and engineering resources. Product technologies in these areas are complex and seem to require a relatively higher level of organisational resources for a simultaneous, fast and timely new product rollout.

2nd conclusion: Internal communication elements between the subsidiaries/ agents in different countries, the NPD team and the HQ eliminate the obstacles to a rapid and timely new product rollout.

Internal communication between the subsidiaries/agents in different countries and the NPD team results in a more proficient NPD process.

Better integration ensures that there is early identification of the technical and market targets for the new product. The firm rapidly proceeds to the development of the new product guided by a concrete *protocol* and a '*sharp quality of feedback*'. Time and efforts are not wasted and resources are consciously 'leveraged' to achieve new product goals.

Internal communication between the subsidiaries/agents in different countries and the HQ *helps to set up an infrastructure* (sales force and intermediaries) *across countries* to service and support the new product. Extensive internal communications permit different country managers to:

- develop awareness of the new product, its embodied technology and target users;
- assimilate the new product technology and understand how to handle the sales of the new product; and
- complete all the necessary marketing actions for the product launch, ranging from the preparation of marketing channels to new product announcement.

These are explained in more detail here below.

Extensive internal communications are clearly important to assist the transfer of skills for new product commercialisation across countries. A simple transplantation of hardware/software (that is, 'ship the product, and let the subsidiaries/agents find out the rest') is likely to fail.

Communication differentiates from a strategic point of view the chances a new product has of timely rollout. The underlying logic is that different organisational procedures result in differences in the flow of knowledge, information, capabilities, skills and expertise between subsidiaries/agents, the European HQs and the NPD team. The more intensive the integration between them, the greater the information-processing capacity of the firm and the more effective the communication and co-ordination between units. Communication becomes, in this respect, another major determinant of an organisation's effectiveness in the speedier and timely rolling out of new products across multiple international markets.

Furthermore, intensive communication facilitates interaction between people, rapid transfer of knowledge, quicker resolution of conflicts and better understanding of customer requirements. It assists company adaptiveness to environmental uncertainty across countries; accelerates adoption of company innovations by subsidiaries/agents in various countries (see also Ghoshal and Bartlett, 1988); and strengthens the product's competitive advantage in the market place. Exchange of knowledge, expertise and other flows is engaged in two ways (see also Gupta and Govindarajan, 1991). One way is inflow from the (European) HQs to each individual subsidiary/agent, the other is outflow from every subsidiary/agent to the rest of the corporation. These result in the following:

- The amalgamation of country and organisational cultures quickly into a distinct sociocultural system with a set of shared beliefs and common goals for all managers and agents.
- The increase in interdependence between subsidiaries/agents, HQs and the NPD team in a conscious effort to benefit from comparative advantages available in different countries, units, and people.
- Sharing of marketing and technological resources. The most experienced and equipped subsidiaries/agents contribute more to the development, timely rollout and success of the company's new products.
- The rapid identification and provision of the resource bundle required by each new product.
- A more proficient NPD process which leads to higher product superiority. The integration between technical, marketing and manufacturing functions in different sites and in different countries is high, the views of final customers are rapidly transferred to the NPD team, and quality input is accurate and on time. This integration leads to proficient execution of tests of prototypes by customers/trial sales, technical development and sorting out unexpected 'bugs'. It also leads to technical testing of the product, co-ordination of distribution channels and logistics, co-ordination of advertising and promotion, predevelopment project planning and early product and target market definition.

When these occur, new products are more likely to offer unique attributes and clearly visible and useful benefits to the customer, superior quality, value for money and performance. This means that the new product is superior and likely to be successful. Distribution channels rapidly become familiar with the upcoming new products, and sales staff prepare the market and educate their customers. When the new product comes out, the scene is set for its reception.

6.1.3 Other important findings

The study also unveiled additional insights.

Timeliness in new product rollout facilitates customer acceptance: technical proficiency is of less relevance.

In terms of impact on new product performance, customer acceptance and technical performance are secondary to the actual product availability for sale. Rapid availability of the new product may force customer acceptance because of its uniqueness compared to competitive offerings. It even overshadows the importance of technical performance. A late arrival, although technically superior will achieve lower sales and profitability than a less technically outstanding product that is rolled out quickly and on time.

Many firms currently strive to produce new products that are technologically advanced. Innovativeness and pioneering technology may bring fame, but they will not necessarily yield higher product sales and profits. A technologically less advanced product that is rapidly and timely rolled out for sale across the world, will, in contrast, bring greater sales and profits. This happens for the following reasons:

- less time is spent on product development and education of the sales force;
- poorly educated customers failing to understand advanced product technology are not discouraged; and
- the company beats competition by capturing customers who can be satisfied by a product of less advanced technology.

Firms, therefore, must make a trade off. Not the 'better mousetrap' (i.e. technical performance), but the speed of product availability is the key to international new product success.

Timeliness in rollout is more important than timeliness in NPD for a successful new product.

Cooper and Kleinschmidt (1994) found a meagre positive link between timeliness in NPD and the financial performance of a new product project. These authors showed that this relationship is not nearly as strong as one might have expected and certainly 'far less than the direct or almost one-to-one links the "hype" seems to imply' (p. 393). This may be explained by the notion that a rapid timely rollout is more important than a timely NPD for both sales and return on investment for the new product.

This implies that high-tech firms wishing to maximise the potential of their new products should attempt to rapidly penetrate multiple country markets by quickly transferring their new products across the globe. It is the rapid rollout of the new product that makes the difference!

Timeliness in rollout relates to proficiency in NPD.

Executives should be careful. A timely new product rollout and a proficient NPD process go together. A non-proficient NPD process may imply that the company would face difficulties in achieving international new product rollout in a timely manner. A rapid and time efficient rollout is invariably accompanied, complemented and reinforced by a rapid and time efficient NPD process.

The potential effects of nationality bias

The focus of this research was not to seek out a bias regarding rollout timeliness and firms' country-of-origin. The observations did suggest, however, that the Japanese companies studied were more adept at achieving on-time rollout, compared to their western counterparts. Assuming that such nationality bias regarding speed and timeliness in new product rollout is confirmed by other studies, there are some longer-term effects at both sectoral and national level. These tentative effects are discussed here below in more depth:

Japanese companies in this study were strategically oriented towards specific product technology sectors (e.g. printers), where new products replaced older-generation products with minor technology and marketing changes, and where technology needed limited customisation across countries. As a result Japanese firms were easily able to deploy their resources and gain 'leverage'. Multiple timely new product rollouts and their positive effects upon sales and profitability may have been primary agents of growth for Japanese companies. These agents may have assisted the rapid accumulation of engineering resources, the building of a strong marketing base by Japanese companies over the years, and the entry and proliferation of new Japanese products in multiple markets. This, in turn, has assisted the rapid diffusion of Japanese technology in many high-technology sectors and further strengthened their marketing muscle. Organisational learning has increased, customer familiarity with the Japanese products has increased, resources have been better utilised, better resources have been acquired and complementary competencies have been achieved in many technological areas. Timely new product rollout may, in this respect, have sustained Japanese expansion across countries.

British and other western companies may, in contrast, have followed a different pattern. They may have remained in product technology sectors where timely rollout is difficult because of the nature of product technology. Multiple delayed new product rollouts by British and western companies may have:

- undermined the accumulation of engineering resources by British and western companies over the years;
- eroded their marketing muscle across many international markets;
- constrained their proliferation into new product areas and foreign markets;
- permitted the entry of companies from Japan or other nations into areas where western companies were once the major force.

Disassembling capability in this way may have weakened the ability of British and western companies to improve their market presence, sales and profitability. It may have affected their NPD process too. Organisational learning has not increased, customer learning of products has diminished, resources have not been better utilised, better resources have not been acquired and complementary competencies have not been achieved. The ultimate result is aptly described by Hart (1996) using the extreme case of the world shipbuilding industry. The British share of the market has declined from producing around 80 per cent in 1890 to less than 4 per cent in 1974, while by 1969 Japan's share had risen to 40 per cent (Ughanwa and Baker, 1989). Inferring further, it is likely that Japanese companies strategically enter technological areas which are complex and with no standards, as laser printer technology used to be. They remain in this area for a number of years, during which international technology standards appear, and then they fully exploit the potential. Keeping the complexity of their operations low, they can opt for a simultaneous rollout for their new products. This, combined with marketing competence and resources, leads to rapid and timely availability of their new products across countries, sales and profitability.

This research has helped shed some light on an issue which has been unexplored to date. Some of the drivers of a timely new product rollout, such as firm marketing resources across countries, were largely expected. The role of other drivers, such as the synergies in product use by the customer, was uncovered. Improvement upon the eight drivers identified by this research may help reduce time spent on new product rollout across countries. The link between timeliness in rollout and new product success also provides a warning to executives who may place a disproportionate emphasis on NPD at the expense of timely, rapid new product rollout.

The results of this study have several important theoretical and managerial implications, explained hereafter.

6.1.4 Theoretical implications

A number of theoretical implications emerged. These are:

- The likely existence of an evolutionary model of timeliness in new product rollout across international markets. The model which may consist of four layers is depicted in Figure 6.1 for illustrative purposes.

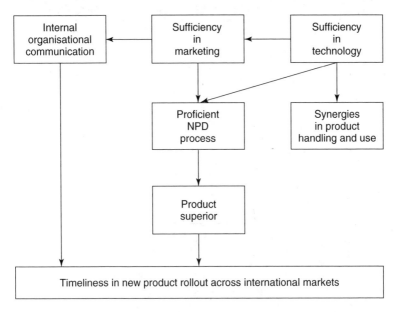

Figure 6.1 Conceptual evolutionary four-layer model of timeliness in new product rollout across international markets

Figure 6.1 constitutes a reshaping of Figure 5.2 in a more conventional manner for easier understanding. The marginal or additional potential effects are also included for the sake of completeness. Thus, the arrows suggest:

  – the probable causal loop between synergies in product handling and use and sufficiency in marketing and technology (see section 5.4.4.4);
  – the marginal effect of sufficiency in marketing and communication upon synergies in product handling and use (see section 5.4.4.1); and

– the marginal effect from synergies in product handling and use upon new product rollout timeliness (see section 5.4.4.1).

Elimination of the two intermediary layers can then result into a reduced two-layer model (Figure 6.2) where the most important factors for new product rollout timeliness are internal organisational communication and sufficiency in marketing and technology.

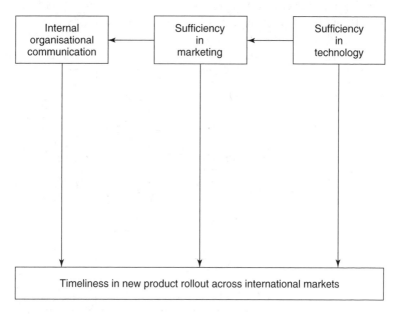

Figure 6.2 Conceptual evolutionary two-layer model of timeliness in new product rollout across international markets

- The position of the commercialisation stage in the NPD process. This study shows the need to rethink of the place of the launch step as among the last ones in the NPD process. It is necessary to take the rollout decisions far earlier in the NPD process and capitalise in the meantime for the co-ordination of the new product launch.
- Mascarenhas (1992a,b) examined the intermarket and intramarket order of entry and first-mover effects within the context of international markets. He argued that simultaneous entry into multiple markets occurs in the mature stage of the product life cycle and the smaller markets are served later when the uncertainty regarding the product future is reduced. This study shows that market entry does

not necessarily occur at the mature stage of the product life cycle as Mascarenhas (op. cit.) suggested. This may not be so. Despite catering for similar needs world-wide the 'quarter of the century elapsed' (see section 2.3.5.5) was probably due to product technology adaptation and lack of sufficiency in company marketing mix elements. Mascarenhas (op. cit.) also argued that market entry occurs in large developed and highly centralised markets. This study shows that this may happen because such countries may be the key target company markets. Moreover, simultaneous versus sequential launch may both happen, this depending upon the configuration of organisational marketing and technological elements for each individual product.

- Research in organisational structure in MNC has initially provided some insights about the importance of organisational elements in NPD and international new product launch. The findings of this research project and qualitative evidence from the case studies suggest that a hierarchical organisational model (Stopford and Wells, 1972; Franko, 1976) is likely to be inappropriate in today's environment. In contrast, it seems that a 'heterarchical' model (Hedlund, 1986) is more suitable. This happens because a 'heterarchical' model in developing and launching a new product increases the horizontal lateral decision making. This results in a better combination of activities and co-ordination of resources within the MNC boundaries and promotes innovation.

- Customisation versus standardisation debate. It is necessary to realise that some elements may become a 'bottleneck' in the companies' attempts to standardise marketing operations across countries. Customisation versus standardisation seems to take place at the individual product level. Thus, elements such as distribution channels, after-sales personnel, customer familiarity with each new product as well as the 'hidden' elements of product technology may become major obstacles in companies' attempts to standardise their operations across countries. The immediate result will be the sequential manner in launching the new product in international markets, while the ultimate result will be a likely delay in such rollout schedules.

- Globalisation strategy and diffusion research. This study suggests that the effect of likely external globalisation drivers (i.e. market factors, competitive factors, technology factors and environmental factors) is channelled through internal organisational and resource factors. This permits to argue that globalisation strategy is probably organisation-led and not consumer or market-driven. This affects in turn diffusion research in the sense that diffusion of company innovations is affected by internal organisational factors despite potential market demand due to rapid transcending of national boundaries of consumers' word-of-mouth. That is, international diffusion of new products is not consumer-pulled, but organisation-led.

- Douglas and Craig (1989) presented a model where the evolutionary process of international marketing strategy evolves through four phases: pre-international, initial entry, local market expansion and global rationalisation. Internal communication and resource elements may hinder on a product-by-product basis such evolution. Accumulation of multiple such obstacles may counter-affect and cancel any positive impact of favourable external triggers (i.e. market growth) or other positive internal triggers (i.e. management motivation), meaning that the company may not proceed further into its organisational evolution. On the other hand, rapid international new product rollout may exhibit the existence of facilitating agents for a quick company evolution through the same stages.

6.1.5   Managerial implications

A number of managerial implications also emerged. These are:

- New product rollout timeliness is fundamental for sales and profitability, and is an integral part of new product success. Managers have to monitor rollout time and accord to it the same precision they accord to sales and costs for the new product. Timeliness in rollout seems to be more important than timeliness in the NPD process in terms of new product success.
- Timely new product rollout across multiple countries occurs when the organisation has a clearly defined segment/technology focus and such focus is 'within the reach' of the organisation. This essentially means company involvement in specific product technology areas where there is compatibility between company resources and resource requirements for success. Incompatibility leads ultimately to confusion, disappointment, waste of time and resources and failure. Gaining competitive advantage through timely new product rollout across multiple countries may require for some organisations, therefore, new approaches to perceiving the market, whether this be segmenting, targeting or positioning; and new approaches to perceiving the way the technology can be applied. Identification of new segments

for existing technology may be preferable to delayed launch of new product innovations in current markets.

- Timely new product rollout across multiple countries is achieved when the organisation couples resources with communication. Their interaction creates the forces that shape the likelihood, direction and speed of NPD and rollout. These forces lead, in this respect, to simultaneous versus sequential and subsequently, timeliness versus delay in new product rollout. For a fast and timely rollout of new products, managers must create, redress or sustain the opportunity to 'leverage' engineering and marketing resources and manage communications between HQs and subsidiaries/agents. This requires thorough understanding of technical, marketing and organisational elements, and acute managerial judgement. Undiscerning, imperceptive or insensible judgement will result in either over or underestimation of the company's actual abilities, misinterpreted positioning and confusion. Gaining competitive advantage through fast and timely new product rollout across multiple countries may thus require a new approach to organising global and regional (i.e. European) procedures and activities. It requires procedures and mechanisms that help the organisation to screen and correctly capture the current internal resource and communication profile, and then redress or sustain it. Redressing and sustaining the profile needs continuous and subtle control over operations.

The availability and interpretation of information is central to all the above, first in the case of proper segment/technology focus, second in identifying the 'profile' regarding resources and communication. Timeliness occurs when managers realise the actual obstacles and perceive the areas for improvement. Inappropriate organisational functioning in the HQ, the NPD site or the various subsidiaries/agents may well stifle the development and rollout of new products. Organisational functions in this respect must be viewed as a system.

An analogy to human biology can be drawn. The human body needs to use a series of internal elements for its functions. Breathing, digesting and moving are such functions. The individual components/organs, work in harmony with each other. Breathing uses the heart, the lungs and the liver. Digesting uses the stomach, the pancreas, the kidneys and several other body organs. When one of these organs stops operating, execution of the function stops, other functions face difficulties and the entire body is driven into collapse.

6.2   Limitations and further research

This study is restricted to the UK and the views of personnel from the European HQs. A much larger study should investigate the views of subsidiaries/agents across Europe and the views of corporate HQs located elsewhere (e.g. the USA or Japan). The findings of this study are also based upon a limited number of cases. A larger study should expand on the number of investigated cases, the time spent in each company or the number of sites and countries where personnel are interviewed.

Attention should also be paid to the exploration of the nature of technology in each product. There is limited guidance in the extant literature concerning the way to define technology in a given product. Each new product contains multiple technologies from a number of different scientific disciplines and areas (e.g. technologies used in a laser printer are in the areas of plastics, toner, photocopying, metal, paper, microprocessing, data transfer, etc.). Unless there is a coherent framework for separating primary from secondary and major from minor technology, confusion arises. While there is substantive knowledge about the way to analyse marketing customisation to foreign markets (see Chapter 2), there is also limited guidance on how to measure technology customisation. The nature of technology and technological customisation were discussed in this thesis. However, the measures should be validated through a larger scale, empirical study.

An appropriate extension of this study would be to examine the simultaneous versus the sequential rollout pattern for larger populations of Japanese, UK, US and European companies.

Another extension of this study would be to examine new product rollout from an information-processing perspective (i.e. the nature of information and patterns of information flows). Also, what are the more effective and efficient methods of such communication (i.e. how meetings take place, where, who participates, how decisions are taken)? What are the more effective and efficient organisational structures to be used for rolling out new products across international markets? The 30 cases in the present study provide some preliminary evidence that would benefit from further and more detailed analysis. This evidence suggests that there may be specific methods, procedures and organisational structures that are particularly important in enabling the Japanese companies to be more effective and efficient than their western counterparts in occurring timely international new product rollout. It would be interesting to examine if similar or different methods, procedures and organisational structures have been adopted by western companies in their operations.

There is also much left to be done. It is important to recall that the data examined in the current study are cross-sectional and do not allow any strict causal inferences. Thus, the findings are tentative and would benefit from further confirmation by new studies. In this sample, technological resources were found not to influence directly proficiency of the NPD process in a statistically significant manner. This point needs further exploration. It would also be useful to investigate more precisely the financial and market performance implications of timeliness in rollout over several generations of new products. This would allow the role of rollout timeliness within the wider context of longer-term competitive dynamics. Finally, is rollout timeliness an issue for service organisations, and are the causes of delays the same? These questions all warrant further investigation.

7
Revisiting the Area

7.1 Introduction

The original research project commenced in 1993 and was completed in the mid to late 1990s. Nonetheless, time flies by. Both theory developed and empirical findings have been exposed to the world; I (with Veronica Wong) conducted additional analyses, thus refining our thinking on the subject; and comments and criticisms have been thankfully received. Interestingly, the business press continued to report problems of rollout delays – the Mercedes A class delayed rollout has been a prime example during this period (Wong, 2002). This is an indication that the topic is still important for businesses. I commerce revisiting the area with an overview of progress in the literature.

7.2 Review of the literature and progress in the area

The following contributions have been noted, but there is still an apparent need for further investigation of the subject.

7.2.1 A real-option approach to identify the financial and economic outcomes of a phased rollout across international markets

Pennings and Lint (2000) proposed a model to value a phased rollout, and to determine the optimal time of this rollout well as the optimal rollout area. Applying real option theory, the authors proposed that the economic value of a phased rollout strategy mainly depends on market and technology uncertainty and the expected net present value of the investment. They considered that uncertainty about future payoffs drives the rollout decision, and the higher the uncertainty, the larger the optimal rollout area and the longer the stage of phasing the rollout. They also considered as an important variable the cost of the investment. When the cost of the investment is small compared to the object's project value, the company will choose a global market introduction, and forgo the cost of a phased rollout. When the cost of investment is large compared to the project value, the company will abandon a global market introduction. A phased rollout appears to be optimal when the project value is close to the cost of investment. Other important parameters for the optimal rollout area and time include the abandonment costs and the risk free interest rate. The authors eventually illustrated their model on the rollout of Philips Electronics' CD-I product in the 1990s and they identified that the maximum value of phasing the rollout of CD-I was nearly 23 per cent of the investment cost, although they kept some of their assumptions, including uncertainty, constant and abandonment cost at zero levels.

Their contribution adds on the importance of the subject, and highlights the complexity of the financial and economic aspects of the international new product rollout decisions. Thus, it clearly shows that launching new products across international markets may require a multidisciplinary approach as financial, economic as well as strategic aspects, which haven't been looked at the present endeavour, are at work.

7.2.2 A game theory approach to sequential versus simultaneous rollout strategy

Kalish *et al.* (1995) used a game-theory based approach to explain simultaneous versus sequential rollout strategy choice. As also set out in the beginning of this book, at issue in the field of new product strategy is whether the country introductions should be sequential or simultaneous. The sequential one may be preferred, because of the lead effect – success in market one spreads the word or may facilitate entry into market two, so when the new item is marketed their results are superior. However, as in recent years competitors move in to new country markets fast, strategists have increasingly adopted a simultaneous entry into multiple country markets to establish positions. The authors investigated the argument: what strategy is best, and under what conditions? Some key considerations they considered included: (a) is there truly a lead effect, since sometimes there is more talk about a new item than other times?; (b) the status of market development may make a difference; sequential strategists typically move first into the most developed countries and then on down to the least developed countries; (c) there is competition – where does it exist, how aggressive will (can) it be? Can competitors erase the lead effect? The authors found that their game theory model does not select one over the other, overall. Neither simultaneous nor sequential is a preferred strategy. However, they attempted to examine if under a given set of conditions, one of the two may be clearly preferable. The conditions they considered relevant included:

- *The level of fixed costs.* If the fixed cost of a foreign market entry is high, sequential new product rollout is preferred; this way the firm has time to cover those costs and prepare for the next country market. But low fixed costs of market entry argue for doing it all at the same time.
- *Competition.* The more the competition, the shorter the market entry rollout time. The authors explained that this does not mean the more the 'competitors', because a competitor will not always launch an aggressive leap-frog entry programme. If competitors co-operate, sequential is still favoured. Monopoly is an extreme version of this; with no competition, sequential gives the most effect for the dollar.
- *Life cycle of the new product type.* The longer the life cycle, the greater the lead effect will be – the more time there is to gain communication into the non-entered markets.
- *Size of the particular foreign market.* This means that each market may be a separate decision, so the overall value of complete sequential or complete simultaneous is a composite of pluses and minuses. The larger the market, the less the lead effect, and thus the advantage of going all out. Given that larger markets will probably be entered first, there is a suggestion that a simultaneous into the first half of the markets might be followed by a sequential starting as the firm reaches into the smaller markets.
- *Foreign market growth rate.* Slow growth rate argues for sequential; the lead effect is greater than when the market is growing rapidly.
- *Degree of innovativeness in the new market.* The slower the people are to imitate, the more the value of advanced word from other counties (the lead effect), and thus the value of sequential.

Clearly, the larger number of conditions and how often these conditions change the more complex the situation analysis, and the more likely the rejection of an overall preference for either the sequential or the simultaneous new product rollout mode.

7.2.3   Launching product innovations in international markets

Golder (2000) collected insights from 64 senior executives, including many current and former CEOs and presidents of multinational companies regarding launching new product innovations in international markets. Interestingly, the views received related to several of the variables investigated in the present study. Among the issues that seem to govern successful rollout include: (a) the existence of superior products/product champions; (b) the collaboration between product development teams able to support the operating units that will introduce the new product; (c) strong local support, because it may determine where new products are introduced; and (d) informal processes, because they play a surprisingly important role in moving new products across countries.

Golder notes at the same time that a simultaneous rollout seems to be more likely in durables and high-tech sectors and in greater rather than less standardised markets. The author also notes that product pioneering in international markets may be weighted against associated costs and risks of this strategy and that there might be a national difference in preferences; US companies may be more likely to work towards big breakthroughs, i.e. products with limited technological synergies with past products, whereas Japanese companies may be more likely to rely on continuous incremental development.

Product standardisation is also preferred not because it is driven by the increasing similarity of customers: it is simply a better way to manage an international company (standardisation being easier, however, for image-based products). On the other hand, firms may not enter markets without a suitably differentiated product, meaning that some of the new product elements may remain similar, others may change from one country to another.

7.2.4 Launch of new products

The launch of new products has been a closely related area that has by far attracted the greatest attention. Several articles have recently appeared that examined various aspects of launch strategies (e.g. Hultink *et al.*, 1997; Thölke *et al.*, 2001; Debruyne *et al.*, 2002). Hultink and Robben (1999) also looked at the impact of launch strategy and market characteristics on new product performance and the stability of this impact across consumer and industrial products. They found that the impact of launch strategy was higher for market acceptance than for product performance. Overall, they found that market acceptance is influenced by the product's innovativeness, timing of market entry, breadth of assortment, branding, pricing, the objective of increasing market penetration, and competitor reactions. They also found that product performance is influenced by the product's innovativeness, breadth of assortment, and by the objective of using an existing market. Further-more, they identified that some launch decisions are more important in attaining new product success for consumer products than for industrial products, and vice versa. Thölke *et al.* (2001) sought to address what strategies are used by managers for launching new product features, how these strategies differ, what their opportunities and pitfalls are, and also they developed a typology of feature launch strategies.

The interplay between new product launch and minimisation of the likely competitive reaction has also been looked at. Hultink and Langerak (2002) developed a framework regarding incumbents' reaction to perceived market signals resulting from a new product's launch decisions as these may also depend upon industry characteristics (i.e. market growth) and entrant characteristic (i.e. aggressive reputation). Another study by Debruyne *et al.* (2002) that used a sample of 509 new industrial products launched in the US, the UK and the Netherlands also looked at similar issues. The authors found that the characteristics of the new product launch strategy had a significant impact on both the occurrence and nature of competitive reactions. Competitors failed to respond to radical innovations and to new products that employed a niche strategy. They reacted, however, to a new product that is assessed within an existing product category and thus represents an unambiguous attack. Both innovative and imitative new products meet reaction in this case. Their results also demonstrate that competitors are more inclined to react to the introduction of new products that are supported by exten-sive communication by the innovating firm. The likelihood of reaction is also higher in high growth markets than in low growth markets.

7.3　Own further refinement on the subject

In co-operation with Professor Veronica Wong, I continued to work on our data set and our work has lead us to refine our understanding on the following aspects:

- the link between timeliness in NPD and timeliness in rollout across international markets;
- the structure of the model that has been exposed in the previous chapters; and
- the likely applicability of the model in services.

Detailed thinking on these aspects has appeared in referred academic journal articles, and I will only attempt to summarise the findings here.

7.3.1 The link between timeliness in NPD and timeliness in rollout across international markets

The issue of market/product heterogeneity posed several unanswered questions, especially as far as the extent of product technology customisation was concerned. This happens because the offer of a standardised product for different country markets may enable companies to accomplish fast product development and multi-country rollout, while also enjoying substantial cost benefits. However, not all manufacturers serving multi-country markets can adopt a standardised product strategy. Where technological requirements, standards, and approval procedures vary substantially across countries, manufacturers invariably must adapt the product's technology to fit individual country requirements. Among the questions that required investigation was whether extensive customisation may lead to longer new product development and rollout times and may increase the likelihood of delays in the entire project, hence adversely affecting overall new product outcome. We examined the relationships between product technology customisation, the timeliness in completion of both the new product development effort and international market launches, and new product success. We found that timeliness in new product development and timeliness in rolling out the new product into different country markets mediate the link between product technology customisation and overall new product success. Customisation of product technology increases the likelihood of delays in the completion of new product development projects and multi-country rollout. This means that if the NPD project runs behind schedule, a fault-free multi-country rollout programme becomes increasingly unlikely, as problems encountered during product development spill-over into the rollout program. These points are further explicated in the next section (section 7.3.2) as they bear upon the structure of the theoretical model presented in the previous chapters of the present endeavour.

7.3.2 The structure of the model exposed in the previous chapters

Eight key causes of rollout delays including: insufficiency in marketing, insufficiency in technology, lack of synergies in product handling and use, a deficient product, lack of integration in NPD, lack of proficiency in NPD, targets not known early in the NPD process and poor internal communication between HQ and country markets were identified, and explained in earlier chapters, as causing delays. A model was formulated and explained in Chapters 5 and 6, which identified, for instance, that the NPD process does play an intermediate role in the relationship between organisational co-ordination, resources necessary for the new product project and the timely INPR outcome. Nonetheless further refinement was seen as necessary. An initial attempt was made in 1998 when we presented an evolution of the initial model at the PDMA Conference in Como, Italy (Chryssochoidis and Wong, 1998b). More recently, Wong (2002) proposed a further refined model, also reported here below (see Figure 7.1).

The differences between the original model presented in the earlier chapters of the present endeavour and the latter model presented by Wong (2002) include:

- a refinement regarding the impact of external environment antecedents;
- a simplification regarding NPD related operational efficiency, product superiority and firm resources factors; and
- the link between marketing and technology resources.

These are explicated in turn.

Impact of external environment antecedents. Evidence provided by other studies (for instance Cooper, 1979; Gatignon and Xuereb, 1997; Song and

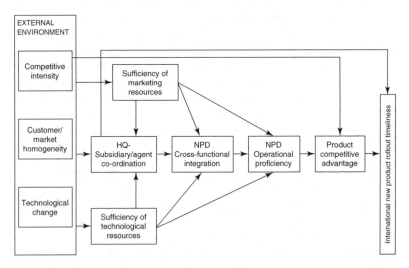

Figure 7.1 Conceptual model of antecedents of international new product rollout timeliness

Source: Wong (2002).

Parry, 1997) suggest a categorisation of external environment elements as follows: competitive intensity; customer/market homogeneity; and technological change. No evidence of direct impact upon the dependent variable (i.e. timeliness in international new product rollout) was identified in the present study. This means that the NPD and rollout process is somewhat insulated from the external environment. Nonetheless, it was identified that external environment variables may indeed play an antecedent/ancillary role in influencing timeliness and international new product success. This is a point of increasing importance. Although the external environment *per se* may not be a directly influencing factor upon international new product rollout timeliness, the firm's decisions and actions in response to external forces may indeed do so. The scenario where organisational setup and management action buffer the impact of external environment appears to increase in strength. In explaining this point, we will first turn to the examination of the nature of impact of technological market heterogeneity upon international new product rollout timeliness.

Mediating effects of NPD timeliness and rollout timeliness in the relationship: customisation of product technology (CPT) and international new product success. As it was originally shown (see also Table 4.17 and Table 4.19) in this book, product technology customisation impacts significantly and negatively upon sufficiency of technological resources but has no statistically significant association with sufficiency of marketing resources. Complexity of product customisation had also no statistically significant association with sufficiency of either marketing or technology resources. In further work Chryssochoidis and Wong (2000a):

- delved deeper into the precise nature of the customisation of product technology (CPT) construct (see Chryssochoidis and Wong, 2000a for a fuller explanation) and explicated that the extent of customisation of (factor code AF2 in Tables 4.18 and 4.19), as well as the complexity of (factor code AF3 in Tables 4.18 and 4.19), product technology are inseparable components of the same construct.
- identified mediating effects of *NPD timeliness* and *rollout timeliness* in the relationship: customisation of product technology (CPT) and international new product success. Mediation exists when the direct impact of one variable upon another, e.g.

   CPT → NPD timeliness;
   CPT → rollout timeliness;

CPT → product success;
NPD timeliness → rollout timeliness;
NPD timeliness → product success;
rollout timeliness → product success;

disappears in statistical significance in favour of an intermediating path solution which was eventually shown to take the following form:

CPT → NPD timeliness → rollout timeliness → international new product success.

A specific statistical and methodological procedure needs to be followed to test mediating effects (see Chryssochoidis and Wong, 2000a for details). The explanatory power of the mediating model was further enhanced when two control variables, namely: product newness and the number of target country markets were taken into account. A further explication for the presented path follows here below.

The overall effect of CPT upon new product success was initially shown to be moderate, explaining 16 per cent of the variance in new product outcome, suggesting that other unmeasured variables may provide additional explanation of variation in the new product performance dependent variable. Using the same data set as in this book, it was first shown that NPD timeliness was significantly associated with new product success ($\beta = 0.36$, $p < 0.05$). Significant relations were also found between INPR timeliness and new product performance ($\beta = 0.56$, $p < 0.001$). Nonetheless, the significance of the effect of CPT upon new product performance substantially declined (from $\beta = -0.49$, $p < 0.01$ to $\beta = -0.31$, $p < 0.10$) after controlling for NPD timeliness, while R^2 increased from 0.41, $p < 0.01$ to 0.49, $p < 0.01$. Similarly, when new product performance was regressed upon CPT and INPR timeliness, the negative impact of CPT on new product outcome was also reduced substantially (from $\beta = -0.49$, $p < 0.01$ to $\beta = -0.25$, $p < 0.10$), while R^2 increased from 0.41, $p < 0.01$ to 0.65, $p < 0.001$. These results show that both timeliness in new product development and timeliness in rolling out the new product into target country markets mediate the relationship between product technology customisation (CPT) and new product success. The greater the requirement for extensive technology customisation to meet different country needs, the more likely it is that firms face delays in completing both new product development and multi-country rollout, thus reducing the odds of new product success.

Additionally, the results showed that both NPD timeliness and INPR timeliness have enhanced the explanatory power of the mediational paths: the R^2 change with NPD timeliness mediating the CPT-performance relationship increased by 0.08, $p < 0.05$; the R^2 change with INPR timeliness mediating the CPT-performance relationship increased by 0.24, $p < 0.000$). Last, but not least, when the rollout timeliness became the dependent variable, NPD timeliness became a mediator variable. Evidence of mediation was shown by the reduction to non-significance in the effect of CPT on rollout timeliness when NPD timeliness was controlled for. The need for extensive adaptation of product technology to meet different country requirements reduces the firm's chances of completing new product development on time, subsequently reducing the likelihood of multi-country launches being accomplished within planned time durations.

These clarify the direction of refinement for the initially presented theoretical model, in that they clearly show that NPD activities and their timeliness play an intermediating role in the external environment (as it specifically regards market/technological heterogeneity) and *rollout timeliness* relationship. *Rollout timeliness* plays an intermediating role in the *NPD timeliness* → new product performance relationship too.

Another point here. It is likely that the greater the speed of technological change in international markets, the greater the pressures during customisation of product technology. This probably indicates that we need to ponder further regarding the exact position of technological speed as a variable in modelling. Is it possible that we have been erroneous so far, and speed of technology change may be a moderator variable in the market technological heterogeneity → timeliness relationship? So far, contributions (Chryssochoidis and Wong, 1998a; Wong, 2002) suggest that pace of technology change is an antecedent of the same level as market/technological heterogeneity.

It is also assumed here, that customisation of technical issues and product technology exhibits greater difficulty and requires a larger amount of organisational and other company resources compared to *marketing* related customisation elements (e.g. promotion). Let us reflect on Golder's (2000) findings based upon 64 interviews with senior executives. The author found that product standardisation is preferred not because it is driven by the increasing similarity of customers; it is simply a better way to manage an international company and that standardisation is easier for 'image'-based products (translated here as being easier to adapt marketing than technology elements). Increased market heterogeneity for marketing elements is expected to have a less pronounced effect upon timeliness and this impact is also buffered by the firm's capacity to allocate requisite resources, on the one hand, and the organisational arrangements that are subsequently enforced to deal with the pressures for structural integration and co-ordination, on the other (Porter, 1986; Ghoshal and Nohria, 1993).

The impact of competitive intensity is buffered by (a) organisational setup/ management action and (b) product superiority/ product's competitive advantage. As also noted earlier, it seems that the external environment *per se* may not be a directly influencing factor upon international new product rollout timeliness, but the firm's decisions and actions in response to external forces may indeed do so. In explaining this point, we first turned to the examination of the nature of impact of technological market heterogeneity upon international new product rollout timeliness, and it has been shown that the impact of CPT upon timeliness is mediated through company practice regarding NPD activities. Now we need to discuss the nature of impact of other external environment factors, namely the impact of competitive intensity. Extant literature seems to have clarified two points here:

First point: One of the paths, competitive intensity impacts upon rollout timeliness, is through organisational setup/management action.

As discussed in earlier chapters (see section 2.3.4.2) and further explicated by Wong (2002), firms may mobilise/adapt their resources in response to perceived or anticipated competitive threats (Chen *et al.*, 1992; Heil and Walters, 1993; Gatignon and Xuereb, 1997). The degree of threat is perceived to rise with the number of country markets in which the firm's sales and long-run performance are affected by competitive attack (Chen *et al.*, 1992; Heil and Walters, 1993). Proportionately with the intensity of competitive threat, the firm will commit a greater level of resources to the international NPD project and launch effort in order to ensure success (Wong, 2002). As shown by Song and Parry (1997), the level of competitive intensity significantly raises the firm's market and competitive intelligence, with greater expenditure of resources on information acquisition, which, in turn, affects new product outcome. By implication, competitive intensity may indirectly affect timeliness in new product rollout, through its direct effects on the firm's allocation of marketing and technical resources to the project (Wong, 2002).

Song and Parry (1997) tested the direct relationship between competitive intensity and cross-functional co-operation during NPD, but did not find a significant association between the two dimensions. They suggest that, at the operational, project level, the impact of external forces is buffered by the pervading organisational setup, such as top management commitment and support, and the use of integrative mechanisms and evaluation and reward procedures, yielding an internal culture of cross-functional co-operation (Song and Parry 1997, p. 45).

Wong (2002) argued that this applies to international new product launch and rollout too (p. 123). But there is a need for strong integration, not only at the operational, NPD project level, but also at the wider, cross-border level. It is insufficient merely to ensure co-operation and integration of activities of NPD team members and functional departments directly involved in the development process. There is a clear need for parallel alignment of goals and objectives in the new product process, resources and behaviour through the use of integrating mechanisms to generate a high level of co-ordination across headquarters, its subsidiaries and agents in different countries.

This has been explicated by Chryssochoidis and Theoharakis (in press) who found that attainment of competitive advantage across international markets requires both parts in an international exchange to bring complementary resources and that these resources need to be strategically aligned. Using an export/import setting, they explained that for an importer, it is necessary to obtain a superior offering (along several dimensions). This allows importers to operate in the market frontline knowing that they are not exposed. For the exporter, it is necessary to select a motivated importer whose strategic objectives are aligned with importing the particular product. This implies that the importer will allocate the necessary resources for attaining competitive advantage in the local market. Therefore, the dyad's attainment of competitive advantage depends both upon (a) the exporter to produce the right products and also to correctly support the products; and (b) the importer whose business strategy places substantial weight upon imports that serve as a vehicle for growth and efficiency gains. Therefore the resource profiles of the two partners that form the exporter-importer dyad have significant implications on the achievement of competitive advantage (Das and Teng, 2000) and require higher order strategic alignment.

Further, many individuals, ranging from country managers and local marketing, sales and channel members, may provide information to new product teams, without having direct involvement and influence in the development process (Wotruba and Rochford, 1995). Yet they rely on timely and quality feedback from new product teams to make adequate launch preparations (Wong, 2002). Cross-border, inter-departmental exchange and interaction create a greater sense of participation, shared understanding and commitment to new product outcomes (Erez *et al.*, 1985). Effective co-ordination, resulting in a high level of cross-border communication and integration, including a common vision, is also an important precursor for effective cross-functional project integration (Ghoshal and Bartlett, 1988; Roth *et al.*, 1991). Hultink and Atuahene-Gima (2000) add further in this respect, when they argue that adoption of the new product by the sales force is a precursor and major contributing factor to selling performance and new product success. Rackham (1998) also shows that feedback from the (international) sales force will highlight the true problems that new products may solve for the customer and not what management may consider to be the great new features ('bells and whistles') the new product offers. In a true customer-centred approach, the new product's features will be worthwhile only if they do meet customer needs; the sales force is at a prime position to be aware of this.

Concluding, internal organisational setups and management's response to the competitive threat, rather than competitive intensity *per se*, are seen to affect the firm's commitment of marketing and technological resources to the new product project, raising, in turn, organisational and management's emphasis on effective co-ordination of HQ-subsidiaries/agents' activities to achieve on-time new product launch across international country markets.

Second point: The second path, competitive intensity impacts upon roll-out timeliness, occurs through product superiority/product competitive advantage.

Song and Parry (1997) identified in their empirical research study that competitive intensity impacts not upon latter success-related dependent variables, but they impact upon *product competitive advantage* which in turn influences new product success, i.e. the path is:

increased (*decreased*) competitive intensity → *decreased* (*increased*) product superiority/competitive advantage → *decreased* (*increased*) product performance.

In intensely competitive markets, it is more difficult for companies to sustain a product or competitive advantage and for customers to perceive a new product's advantage relative to competitors' offerings

(Carpenter and Nakamoto, 1989; Song and Parry, 1997). As also explicated elsewhere (Chryssochoidis, 2000), late introduced differentiated products may be at a disadvantage compared to existing products in the marketplace as they suffer from consumer confusion regarding such differentiation, ultimately resulting in a slow diffusion and limited success of the late introduced differentiated products in the marketplace.

A simplification regarding NPD related operational efficiency, product superiority and firm resources factors. The variables taken into consideration in previous chapters of the present endeavour regarding NPD related operational efficiency and firm resources factors comprised: *sufficiency in marketing (CF1); sufficiency in technology (CF2); synergies in product handling and use (CF3); product superiority (CF4); integration during the new product development process (CF5); proficiency of the new product development process (CF6); knowledge of intended targets at the start of the new product development process (CF7).* Further work and empirical findings by other researchers implied the need for likely simplification of the picture through possible deletion or amalgamation of specific factors with the rest (this regards the CF3 and CF7 factors).

Synergies in product handling and use (CF3) may as a notion in fact be captured by the product superiority (CF4) factor and/or the sufficiency in marketing (i.e. marketing resources factor) (CF1). The CF3 factor was measured in the present endeavour as sales force, distribution channels, product handling/'feeling' remained same for the customer, way user is informed about product function remained same, way user interacts with and controls operation of product remained same. By pondering over the nature of the factor again, it looks like that these items may belong conceptually to either CF1 (i.e. sales force and distribution channels remained same) or CF4 (distribution channels and product handling/'feeling' remained same for the customer; way user is informed about product function remained same; way user interacts with and controls operation of product remained same).

Also, knowledge of intended targets at the start of the new product development process (CF7) is part of NPD operational efficiency and regards organisational professionalism applied during the NPD process. The reader is reminded here that the CF7 factor was measured in the present endeavour as: the firm knew at the start the intended users, targeted countries and their needs and preferences, the product concept and product positioning, the final product specifications and technical requirements, the product final features and characteristics. Knowledge of intended targets for the NPD effort is certainly inherently linked to proficiency of execution of the NPD process (CF6) which was measured in the present endeavour as: proficient execution of: tests of prototypes by customers/trial sales, co-ordination of distribution channels and logistics, co-ordination of advertising and promotion, predevelopment project planning, technical development and sorting out unexpected 'bugs', technical testing of the product. The lack of large sample in the present endeavour suggested the use of exploratory factor analysis on a factor-by-factor basis. This may have hidden the possible loading of both CF6 and CF7 items on the same factor during a larger sample-based analysis. Several other empirical research endeavours also consider these as part of the same concept umbrella, namely the one of proficiency of execution of operational NPD tasks and activities; or using alternative terminology: NPD operational efficiency (Song and Parry, 1996, 1997; Wong, 2002).

The link between technology and marketing resources. A path from technology resources upon marketing resources was also identified in the present endeavour (see section 6.1.3; Figure 6.1). This occurrence may relate however, to the nature of sample employed in the present endeavour that primarily consisted of firms in high-tech sectors. It is logical to consider that in technology driven sectors, sufficiency in technology resources may strengthen sufficiency and suitability of other company resources, including marketing. This is an issue that needs careful attention, however, as it may be still unclear whether there is a generalisable direct effect from technology resources upon marketing resources. Thus, it may be preferable to consider the effects of these two types of company resources upon the rest of investigated elements as distinct issues, until further analysis confirms/refutes and certainly clarifies the nature of their link in an NPD/rollout context.

7.3.3 Summarising the state-of-the-art regarding the topic under investigation

The empirical findings and contributions by other researchers as well as own further work, whose details have been explained above, suggest some alterations to the theoretical framework that was initially developed in this endeavour and presented in the earlier chapters. As explained at the beginning, this book has been based upon a PhD thesis whose findings have been later extended, expanded and refined by additional efforts and insights by other research works. We can conclude that the state-of-the-art regarding the topic under investigation is now characterised by the following:

(a) The topic of timeliness in international new product rollout is not an isolated subject. International new product rollout has major financial and economic implications (Pennings and Lint, 2000) that appear quite complex to study. This indicates that simplistic approaches may not be fruitful. Cost of investment compared to project value, degree of uncertainty about future payoffs and abandonment costs are some of the associated variables.

(b) International new product rollout, including the sequential or simultaneous rollout choice, needs to be looked at considering additional antecedent factors. Some of these have not been considered in the present endeavour, meaning that future research should take them into consideration. These include: the level of fixed cost (see also the points made in the previous paragraph); life cycle of the new product type (this is an issue that relates to speed of technology change); size of the particular market; foreign market growth rate; as well as degree of innovativeness across the foreign markets. Clearly, the larger number of factors and how often these factors change the more complex the situation analysis. Also, these factors may also impact upon organisational setups and management action/ allocation of company resources.

(c) There is an urgent need to consider the link between sequential/ simultaneous rollout strategy and pioneer-position-targeting strategy within markets (micro order of market entry) or across countries (macro order of market entry) (see also Mascarenhas, 1992a,b and section 3.2). The aim of timeliness in new product's international rollout is the availability of the new product for sale across the company's country markets within the anticipated time frame, irrespective of which country the company enters first and whether the company is entering each country as a pioneer, early follower or late follower. Nonetheless, the exact nature of the link is still unclear, it may make a severe impact upon the chosen rollout strategy, and may have an effect upon timeliness of the rollout effort.

(d) It is noted in the present endeavour (see sections 4.2.5 and 6.1.3), by Golder (2000) and by Wong (2002) that important differences may exist regarding the rollout strategies by companies of different country-of-origin. There is a need to observe for similarities (and differences) in the interrelationships and causal paths displayed by US, European and Far Eastern companies, rolling out new products into multiple countries in Europe, Asia or across the globe (Wong, 2002). Is there a consistency with the differences observed in NPD strategies, processes and practices of firms operating in different country environments (Hultink and Robben, 1999)? Launch strategies in domestic markets may also be strongly associated with rollout strategies across international ones.

(e) The scenario that external environment variables may indeed play an antecedent/ancillary role in influencing timeliness and international new product success seems strengthened. The external environment *per se* may not be a directly influencing factor upon international new product rollout timeliness, but the firm's decisions and actions in response to external forces may indeed do so. The point of importance of managerial choice regarding technological and marketing resources and their allocation along organisational setups seems to remain preponderant, as empirical findings and theoretical contributions that have appeared since the time the original work was conducted, suggest the same. Recall in this respect the mediating role of NPD timeliness and rollout timeliness in the relationship customisation of product technology (CPT) and international new product success; or the buffering role of organisational setup/management action and product superiority/product's competitive advantage with respect to the impact of competitive intensity.

(f) The need to simplify model structure, in parallel with the need to identify the precise nature of link between marketing and technology resources as such link may vary with context/type of industry.

7.3.4 The likely applicability of the theory in services

The initial project concentrated on manufacturing products in highly international and high-tech sectors. The rationale adopted at the time of design of the initial project was that sectors exhibiting rapid pace of technology change and stronger internationalisation were likely to require companies to develop and rollout new products more often than companies in sectors exhibiting slower pace of technology change and weaker internationalisation. Researching in the service sector was dropped then as an idea all together. Reasoning related to our belief that it would be wiser for the purposes of a PhD project to focus on manufacturing before preceding doing so in services. Also, we were not certain at the time (1993) that the phenomenon presented itself in the service sector.

Nonetheless, time and my position as lecturer at Cardiff University allowed to pilot test the theoretical framework in the service sector in the late 1990s through the research assistance of an MBA student. A pilot research project was undertaken using an exploratory case-based approach into service innovations launched by Cypriot financial institutions across three or more foreign country markets (see Chryssochoidis and Wong, 2000b). We did identify cases of delayed international new service rollouts. The analysis confirmed the overall appropriateness of the theoretical framework identified in manufacturing, showing that on-time introduction of service innovations rely heavily on: service innovation synergies with existing operations, sufficiency of marketing resources, extensive use of 'soft' integrating organisational mechanisms, and proficiency in the development process. Nonetheless, further empirical research is needed before generalising the findings, adaptation and further refinement of the theoretical framework may be required.

7.4   Some of the criticisms

Probably the most important criticism relates to the lack of deterministic manner by which someone can identify the initially planned period for rollout. In the earlier chapters, I basically reported that managers predetermine or do select a point in time by which the new product will have been developed and rolled out across international markets. The notion of an *initially planned* period has been one of the foundations upon which the present theory was based and lack of robustness of thinking on the matter may clearly diminish usefulness and applicability. One of the received comments regarded managers' ability to select the right length of rollout time. If managers initially form wrong impressions about the skills and abilities of their organisation, extension of synergies, or potential problems in the new product development process, things will go wrong, and delays will appear. All is a matter of managerial ability in selecting the length of period of time it will take for the project to be completed. Allocation of sufficient resources to ensure tasks that can be accomplished within planned time scales is also a highly relevant issue here. If the wrong length of rollout time is selected or resource planning is deficient, delays will occur. If the right length of time is selected and accurate resource planning is practiced, timeliness will occur. Where is theory behind that? Then, it is not important to develop theory on timeliness, but theory on managers selecting the right length of period of time in the first instance. The same applies for management accuracy during decision-making.

A lot of occurrences in managerial practice seem to do, however, with uncertainty, speed of change, nature of organisational life and managerial limitations. First, uncertainty may surround most of the variables identified as relevant to timeliness/delays in international new product rollout, meaning that managers may not always be decisively familiar regarding state of affairs for the variables relevant to the subject under investigation. Secondly, uncertainty may be introduced as some of the variables relevant to the subject under investigation can change during the course of development and rollout of a new product. Responsible experienced managers may also change during the course of development and rollout of a new project. Such managers may possibly be replaced by less experienced people who may also have limited knowledge of specific contexts. Thirdly, uncertainty may be introduced because managers may be under pressure and mistakes in judgement and management inaccuracies may occur. Fourthly, uncertainty may be initiated as management time is usually split among many activities. Managers may be responsible for, or involved with, a multitude of new product projects, meaning that some of these new product projects may not receive the needed attention, leaving room for wrong judgement and inaccuracies. The same may happen because of the likely, and in parallel, multiplicity of technologies developed by most companies in high-tech, high-internationalisation sectors year after year. As some of these technologies may be new, there might be insufficient managerial experience with the extent of actual synergies between products and the suitability of either organisational settings or marketing and technology resources. Last, but not least, uncertainty may be introduced as even strategies and the planning of actions are subject to continuous change. The volatile international and stock exchange environment we have witnessed in 2001 and 2002 clearly shows that even big corporations – especially in high-tech sectors – are subject to severe pressures and the most radical changes; unimaginable not long ago. A plan of actions regarding a single new product project that is well orchestrated at one point in time may become scattered because of alteration of corporate strategy, ownership changes or adjustment of organisational setup and resources. These may mean that managerial ability in selecting the length of period of time it will take for the project to be completed and management planning accuracy, may be undermined and hindered by the dynamics of managerial and organisational life. It is needless to say, that the greater the stability of the organisational environment, and the greater the managers' knowledge regarding the state of affairs for the different variables relevant to the subject under investigation, the more likely it is that these managers will select the right length of development and rollout time and the more likely it is that timeliness in new product rollout will be witnessed.

The above do not contradict the comment that it may be important to develop theory to assist managers selecting the right length of period of time. Such theory is needed but it is on a different subject and likely to have extensive roots in managerial and cognitive psychology. As also noted in Chapter 3, individuals may overestimate or underestimate time periods either systematically or unsystematically. Such perceptions may be influenced by personal attitudes, previous work experience, lack of experience in decision making and planning, or simple misunderstanding of the actual strengths and weaknesses of the organisation.

What I believe I do here is to present a view of the factors that facilitate timeliness, or conversely are the causes of delays from the initially planned period of rollout time. Despite potential variations in the causes and the cognitive processes by which individuals identify, plan the schedule of, and estimate the anticipated time to roll out products across country markets, it is reasonable to infer that the difference between the scheduled/anticipated time considered to be necessary to roll out during the planning stage and the time taken to roll out a new product during the implementation stage is due to elements which have not evolved in accordance with expectations at the initial identification stage. A delay shows managerial misjudgement, although it is assumed of course not to be deliberate and intentional.

7.5 Conclusion

Additional data is required to test the propositions that were initially established through this PhD-based work and refined aftermath, and to test the exact interactions between the constructs that appear to be relevant to the subject under investigation. This is important as the sample employed in the initial research has been small, posing potential problems of statistical analysis and generalisability. Future research will find however a fertile ground because of the additional contributions made by several works in the wider NPD literature and explained earlier, upon which it is possible to base an expanded and further refined theoretical framework. It is also important to recognise the impact of contributions rooted in diverging disciplines like real option theory and game theory that examined the same subject (Kalish *et al.*, 1995; Pennings and Lint, 2000). As proven by these contributions, international new product rollout is a highly complex yet highly exciting subject for further scientific exploration.

Appendix I: Delayed Cases

TMT Telecom Ltd

TMT Telecom Ltd (TMT) is the European HQ of the US$500 million TMT Corporation, one of the major world operators in telecommunication. Its competitors include AT&T, Nortel and Siemens. The US accounts for 52 per cent of TMT's corporate turnover. UK and Europe account for 26 per cent of TMT's corporate turnover (15 per cent of which derives from product sales and the rest from services). The focus in the present is upon TMT's main product, TMT2000 LT.

The product

The TMT2000 LT replaced three older products: the TMT2000SG developed in 1985 (800–3500 phone lines), the TMT2000S developed in 1988 (300–800 phone lines) and the TMT2000VS developed in 1990 (100–240 phone lines). The TMT2000 LT consists of modules serving needs of different sizes (100–3000 lines).

TMT also markets the TMT50 (from 4 lines and 8 extensions up to 32 exchange lines and 160 extensions). However, the TMT2000 LT is by far more important than the TMT50 for TMT's operations. The TMT2000 LT accounts for 95 per cent of TMT's product sales.

A private branch exchange broadly consists of the telephone network gateway, the central processing unit (CPU), the internal network interface and a variety of peripherals. The product discussed here consists of the network gateway, the CPU and the internal network interface seen in the figure below as 'network'.

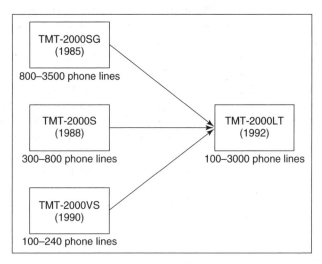

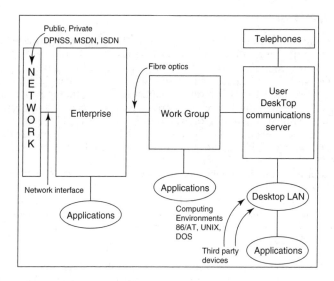

The product is designed around a central processing tower (18 inch tall) with individual modules interconnected by high-bandwidth fibre. Using fibre-optic connections and digital technology, the tower unit has an integral peripheral capability to support up to 128 universal devices, expandable through the addition of peripheral nodes to 768 ports (seen as 'applications' in the figure above). 'Applications' can be standard plain old telephones, modern voice routing platforms, networked computers or independent computer servers. Each 'application' can be customised with its own selection of software and peripheral support, enabling separate work groups to have the communications system that best meets their function. A system can be located in one site or at different sites through a public or a dedicated switched network.

Standardisation of the European market

Technological customisation of markets, complexity of such customisation and approvals

Some components of the product remain the same, others change:

- The main hardware components remain the same and they do not need customisation across countries. Machine software, and the set of modules to choose from, are standardised from country to country.
- The public switched telephone networks vary from country to country with a substantial, and several times incompatible, variety of analogue and digital standards.
- There is a substantial variety of peripherals. Applications (like voice mail or data-base information gateways) use many different technologies. These are client-specific and require extensive configuration to co-operate with the system.

Approvals' complexity

Local country approval is necessary for the TMT2000 LT. This has acted as an inhibitor to the launch of the new product because it is difficult to satisfy every country's own requirements. Countries like Holland have the shortest and France have the longest list of requirements, despite the European Community's attempts to harmonise the telecommunication standards. Safety, transmission, ringing tones, delays in ringing before connection, etc. vary. France and Spain also apply non tariff barriers during the approval procedures in an attempt to assist their local telephone operators (Alcatel and Telefonica). The company did not experience problems with approvals in the UK for the following reasons:

- Its own personnel has established strong connections with top executives in the UK approval mechanism.
- The company has permission to have an in-house Certified Testing Laboratory. This means that TMT's products have priority, they are free for sale when certified by TMT's own personnel and technical details are not disseminated to outside bodies.

TMT did not encounter problems with approvals in Germany either. The company hired a local engineer/approvals expert who completed the procedure on time. TMT faced, however, substantial problems in other European countries. The company explicitly avoided getting approval in France at that time, because the French PTT's nationalistic attitude would not let TMT's products be easily approved. Major obstacles were also faced at the same time in Italy for reasons which will be explained later.

Market

Purchasers of the TMT2000 product split into multinationals which purchase centrally and require the same telecommunication equipment throughout the world (some 15 per cent of total number of target clients) and independent purchasers. An estimated 80 per cent of buyers in Europe cluster in the services sector. Buyers are in the utility, financial and insurance services in the UK; media, IT and hotels in Europe. Applications and product requirements are sector-specific.

A short history of the company, the place of the TMT2000 for the sale of the company and the product failure in the German and Italian markets

By 1990, TMT was owned by a major European multinational. The major European multinational acquired TMT in its mid-80's diversification strategy. Increasing losses and a plunge in share prices forced the major European multinational's management to initiate a retraction strategy. Almost two years passed before a venture capitalist group bought TMT's shares in June 1992.

These two years were a period of high uncertainty for TMT. Investors had no interest in purchasing TMT shares and it had huge losses for a number of consecutive quarters. TMT's management decided to initiate an innovative new product programme that would improve the company's image. The new product development was initiated in 1991. Since the US market accounts for over half the total company sales, little consideration was given to the requirements of the European markets.

Eventually, the first internal announcement for the new product was made in 1992, by which time the company had changed ownership. Rollout across Europe was planned to start with an initial launch of the new product in the UK in September 1992, to be followed by Germany (December 1992), Italy and Ireland.

Inadequate communication between the TMT and European subsidiaries first resulted in a late initiation of the approval procedures. The product was unveiled in Germany the same month as in the UK (March 1993). It was not until the end of 1993 that the company installed two single systems in Germany on a trial basis. Turnover of TMT's German and Italian subsidiaries reached only 45 and 30 per cent of total company expenses in these countries in 1992–93. These losses mounted up to an estimated 20 per cent of total company turnover during the same period.

Table 1 TMT's revenues and expenses in the German and Italian markets in 1992–93

Country	Revenues Scale = 100	Expenses
Germany	100	222
Italy	100	361

These adverse developments are also apparent in the evolution of total company sales during the 1992–95 period.

Table 2 TMT's sales (1992–95)

Country	1992 (%)	1995 (%)
UK	78	82
Germany	6	2*
Italy	6	2*
Hong Kong	6	12
M. East – Africa	6	4**
Increase in sales (1995/1992)		+31

Notes: * = half the 1992 sales; ** = equal amount of sales.

Among the 30 people employed in the German subsidiary, 1 was responsible for approvals, 2 for marketing, 7 were the sales force and 7–10 were technical personnel. The structure was similar in Italy. In an attempt to break away from the deadlock (no sales in Germany and no sales or approvals in Italy), TMT transferred two Directors. One split his working time in the UK and Italy

(2 weeks in the UK and 2 weeks in Italy) and another one moved to Germany for 6–7 months. Unfortunately this decision was taken too late. Both offices closed soon afterwards. More details regarding the causes of failure follow.

Availability of adequate quality engineering and marketing resources – synergies in product handling by the sales force and in use by customers

Germany

- Deficiency in sales force and distribution. The previous TMT operations in Germany were strongly concentrated on sales of the TMT50 product (80 per cent of total company turnover in Germany). This product was targeting the segment of 30–100 lines, mainly consisting of small hotels. The sales force could not handle the TMT2000 LT because it is more complex than the TMT50. TMT also considers that recruitment of the sales force in the German market has not attracted talented and knowledgeable people.
- No distinctive advantage against other competing products and weak corporate and brand image in the German market:
  - Competitors capitalised on German nationalism suggesting to corporate clients that TMT is an 'outsider', a 'foreigner'. They were an 'English–Canadian' company that did not have anything to do with Germany. At the same time, Germany is the domestic market of Siemens and a manufacturing base for Alcatel.
  - Little consultation took place between TMT US and the local European Offices when the brand name TMT2000 LT was chosen in the US. The sound of the product name in the German language conjures up 'weak beer' and inferiority.
- Deficiency in engineering and marketing support and resources. A local third party company, which was used for technical support, did not have sufficient knowledge of TMT's products. TMT's own technical personnel had to fly out to Germany for training sessions, but this was not effective because of language barriers. Technical documents were also not translated into German.
- TMT did not attract any major and reputable initial buyers (show cases). This is very important since buyer decision is heavily influenced by existing installations at reputable sites. Two of its existing clients decided to test the product after an entire six months no-sale-period from actual product availability in Germany.

The German subsidiary closed in July 1995 with 30 redundancies.

Italy

- The Italian subsidiary failed to have the TMT2000 LT approved on time in Italy despite an earlier approval for the older generation products. Reasons relate to bureaucracy of the Italian State. It was characteristically mentioned in the interviews that the Italian Ministry of Communications has 72 departments in a 15 storey building. It was also reported that the financial failure of the company in Italy was also due to increased financial payments to the Italian Mafia in order to 'push' the approval procedure of the TMT2000 LT through the Italian Ministries. TMT expected the approval procedure to last 1 month. It eventually took $6^1/_2$ months.

- Inappropriate new project management in TMT. The initiation of approval procedures should have started much earlier.
- Deficiency of the sales force. The Italian sales force failed to expand into new sectors and acquire new clients. They also kept their sales concentrated in a narrow geographic area, did not segment its market and did not sell to big hotels where TMT has the biggest competitive advantages for the TMT2000 LT. TMT also considers that recruitment of salesmen in Italy, like in Germany, has not attracted talented and knowledgeable people.

The Italian subsidiary closed in March 1994 (just one year after the planned launch date in February/March 1993) with 40 redundancies amid financial losses, a series of law suits and court settlements.

The success – Middle East and Africa.

TMT decided that the Middle East and Africa would be the last markets to roll out the new product. Despite no remote training packages and the need to fly out for the training sessions, the product was rolled out on time and succeeded. Organisations in several African countries (Egypt, Bahrain, Kuwait, S. Arabia, Botswana, Tanzania) purchased the TMT2000 LT. Reasons include:

- The Middle East and Africa are served by a small number of TMT's expert personnel in an organisationally self-contained unit. They have substantial marketing and technical experience in these countries and a substantial number of links and acquaintances.
- The main PTT operators act as agents of TMT in these countries. There are no rigid telecommunication standards, so the time consuming approval procedures are avoided. Purchases are channelled through the main PTT operators. A within-24-hours quotation service provides rapid response to customer questions.
- The number of requests is small (a few hundred quotations per year). This permits central handling of TMT sales to these regions.

Co-ordination of relationships with subsidiaries/agents

The decision making and flow of information between TMT and European subsidiaries at the time of the launch of the TMT2000 LT were hierarchical. There was little direct contact between the subordinates at lower levels of the organisational structure. The German and Italian operations were reporting to their heads who, in turn, were reporting to the European UK-based VP for Sales. He would transmit information to the heads of the other company functions within TMT who would then pass the information to their own personnel. This has proved to be inadequate. Information was filtered and distorted. Deadlines were continuously postponed. The company has radically altered its internal structure and the structure of its channel relationships after the failed rollout of the TMT2000 LT. Changes include:

- Closing of all direct TMT operations in European countries. The TMT does not have its own marketing personnel in any of its target European markets.
- TMT agreed a pan-European distributorship with a pan-European consortium and separate agentships in the European countries. It is independent VARs and SIs that have undertaken the responsibility to market TMT's products.

TMT has since rolled out the TMT2000 LT into Italy, Germany, Jersey, Ireland, France, Holland, and Spain. For 'mature' agent relationships (like in Jersey), TMT conducts regular training sessions of several days, particularly at periods preceding local trade shows. For less 'mature' relationships (as in Holland) an account manager, a system architect and a system engineer regularly fly out at the time of the sale meetings to assist the local agent.

New product development process

The product development was initiated in the US in 1991 but faced delays. The product was initially developed for the US market by a US–Canadian team and it was inadequate for the European market. Limited communication took place between the US and TMT's European subsidiaries. The one-way communication flow from US to UK consisted of simple announcements regarding the evolution of the TMT2000 LT project. TMT was then passing the information to Germany and Italy. When the product was eventually announced, TMT were left with the task to adapt it for the UK and Europe. TMT decided to adapt the product initially for the UK and subsequently for the German and Italian markets.

TMT followed a 'list' approach, where the actions were summarised on a document, and personnel (in both the UK-located HQ and the European subsidiaries) were assigned specific tasks and deadlines for execution. Little communication with the local German and Italian subsidiaries took place. This communication was also difficult and hierarchical as explained earlier. The above were not effective or efficient and they resulted into continuous postponement of new product availability and rollout.

It is notable that in contrast to the problems faced during the development and customisation of the TMT2000 LT project, TMT has not faced any delays in the development and rollout of the TMT50 product. Even though information is dating, there was a strong agreement that the product was developed and rolled out on time. The TMT50 was launched in 1986 in the UK and shortly afterwards across other European countries. It was developed in the UK only, without the intermediation of the US or Canadian new product development teams. Variants for most European countries were also performed in the UK. Sales of the product, albeit not phenomenal, were satisfactory.

Following the failure of the European rollout, TMT drastically altered its internal organisational structure including the process of new product customisation. Due to these changes some 70 per cent of the people, who were employed at the time of the TMT2000 LT rollout, have left. The company's structure in February 1996 is depicted in the figure below. The existing structure is opposite to the structure the company used three years earlier:

- The top authority remains with a handful of personnel who meet every Friday and decide collectively, even though the Managing Director has the casting

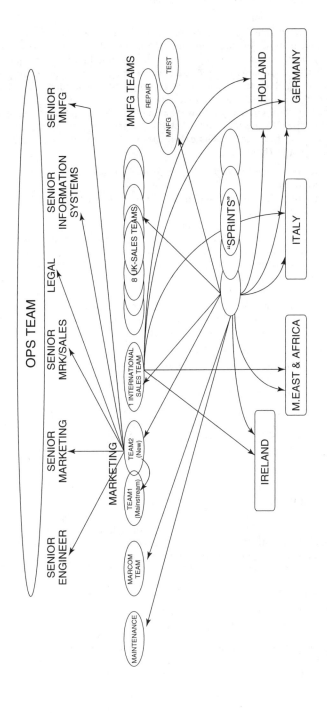

vote. This is called the OPS team. The OPS team is available for consultation by any member of staff. Their offices, previously accessible with difficulty, have been transferred to open space in the middle of the company's site. This OPS team consists of 1 specialist in engineering, 1 marketing, 1 sales/marketing, 1 legal, 1 information technologist, 1 manufacturing, 1 human resources manager and 1 finance expert.

- The rest of the company is now structured into teams headed by team leaders. While the OPS specialists overview the respective functions of the teams, the teams and the team leaders can request advice from anyone they consider appropriate. There are:

    - 3 teams in manufacturing (1 responsible for production, 1 for repairs, and 1 for testing).
    - 2 teams in information technology (1 for maintenance, and 1 for development of new systems).
    - 9 sales teams (8 for sales in the UK and 1 for international sales).
    - 2 product management teams. One is responsible for new products until their release. Currently, the members of the new product development team seek the maintenance of a strong communication link with the TMT North American operation. They regularly fly out to United States and Canada (every 4–5 weeks) and stay there for a week spending time with the NPD N. American shop floor engineers. This team transfers product responsibility, within 3 months from product launch, to teams which overview the already launched products. These teams are in 4 areas:

        the 'installed base' (1st area),
        the 'new' domestic UK buyers (2nd area),
        the 'new' international customers (3rd area), and
        new services (4th area).

    - A 'sprint' team is assigned the responsibility of new product rollouts. These 'sprint' teams are formed for a period of about 6–7 months. TMT has an average of 5–6 'sprint' teams at any time (mainly for peripherals). They are given specific product launch responsibility, they are time bound and receive all the resources they require.

RxE Europe Ltd

RxE Europe Ltd (RxE) is the European HQ of RxE Inc, a US company, founded in March 1988 with the specific goal of becoming the industry leader in microcomputer digital signal processing computer telephony (voice processing). RxE offers three computer telephony hardware product groups:

- voice processing platforms;
- telephone network interface cards; and
- companion technologies.

The core applications include voice messaging, inbound and outbound call processing, information services and database access via telephone. An example will be given here. Incoming callers are transferred from a standard telephone to a PC voice card and are given a greeting (...thank you for calling...). After they are asked if they have a touch-tone telephone they are switched to a speech recognition port for provision of information or sent a hard copy. They can also download a fax copy (through a fax port) or be transferred to the operator.

The product

Voice processing platforms are available for use in the US, British and international telephone environments. Products include the top-of-the-line Vantage series, the mid-range RDSP series, and the low-cost Prelude series. The company provides open architecture through compliance to industry-standards [the Multi-Vendor Integration Product (MVIP) and the analogue bus connectors] considered as necessary for compatibility between products from different manufacturers and a wide variety of peripherals.

The project under consideration is the RDP/9400-I Series of high performance voice processing boards for international markets. The company occupies an estimated 25 per cent (£1m) of the European market[1] for this type of product. At the time of its development, it was a truly new product targeted to an emergent market, RxE being among the pioneers in the sector. These are the characteristics of the product:

- It can be used with either 2 or 4 different telephone lines. It supports applications such as voice mail, automated attendant, audiotex, interactive voice response, outbound marketing or dictation.
- It is designed for IBM PC/AT or ISA bus compatible computers and supports multi-tasking operating systems such as OS/2, Unix, Qnx, Solaris, Windows NT as well as MS-DOS.
- It is capable of running on 286, 386, 486 and Pentium class ISA-bus compatible systems in either 8 or 16 bit mode allowing for a large number of applications to operate simultaneously in a single system.
- It uses digital signal processors and complex software algorithms. These algorithms[2] provide all functions [playback speed control, security coding, selectable speech digitisation rates, call progress monitoring (frequency and cadence), pulse or tone detection, volume control and speech detection] for the development of advanced voice processing systems.

Standardisation of the European market

Technology customisation, complexity of such customisation and approvals hardware and approvals

The computer telephony integration market experiences a phenomenal and explosive growth. Strongly linked to the appearance of strong PC microprocessor and robust operating systems (i.e. OS/2, Windows NT), it was a nascent technological area just a few years ago. Nonetheless, the core applications for voice processing have remained relatively constant and even today, most are sold into the following markets:

- voice messaging;
- inbound and outbound call processing;

- information services;
- database access via telephone.

There is a substantial heterogeneity between hardware technologies in different countries regarding both digital and analogue applications. Many of the digital products available today are developed for use on North American T1 circuits. Unfortunately, European and North American digital networks are technically very different. The variation in digitisation and incompatibility between digital line interfaces is due, among others, to differences in data rates, coding of speech and signalling. At present, the digital line interface specifications in some European countries are 'hybrids', other countries having their own fully digital protocols with a variety of interfaces and proprietary PBX switches. The analogue communication products have an even greater heterogeneity because of the multitude of individual country protocols.

There is a need to undergo long, complex and laborious approval procedures, regarding safety, harness and electromagnetic/radio frequency interferences in most countries. The products are tested in specific laboratories on a country-by-country basis, something difficult for smaller companies because of long waiting lists and the need to test-retest in case of product non-compliance to the standards.

Software and software platforms

Voice processing has been characterised by:

- Multiple operational systems despite similarity of performed functions by the applications. It is only very recently that there is a shift towards common interoperability (via the TAPI and API standards) for telephony and call control.
- An increasing use of common software development tools and incorporation of multi-vendor integration (MVIP) programs for greater compatibility and interconnectivity between uses.[3]

RxE supplies common software development tools to its clients with the first order. They include an MS-DOS driver, utilities, demo system and programming manual for use with multiple versions of the most commonly used C programming language (development tools, software algorithms, utilities, libraries and operating system drivers).

Market

The company develops voice processing hardware and the software directly associated with the operation of the boards. It focuses its sales upon voice system developers. Buyers of RxE products are falling into the following 5 groups:

- large companies with in-house engineers;
- system resellers who can provide software development (VARs);
- switch manufacturers with own software engineers;
- system integrators; and
- independent developers, or distributors and engineers with no software development support.

These segments require different types and extent of customer support. Big multinationals with own in-house personnel need lower support than smaller independent distributors or engineers. Furthermore, each client uses different software platforms and develops or sells different applications.

In terms of countries, RxE has 4 key country-markets: UK (40 per cent of European sales), Germany (20 per cent), Italy (5 per cent), Spain (5 per cent) and 15 secondary country-markets (30 per cent). The company has some 200 customers spread across Europe. Only a few among them are repeat-purchase-major-clients (a mere 10 per cent of total clients), but they account for 60 per cent of company turnover.

Availability of adequate quality engineering and marketing resources

Engineering

There are substantial synergies between this product and other company products regarding hardware and software, but the tightness of approval requirements has not permitted the company to capitalise on these synergies. These synergies are:

- *Core hardware architecture*: Synergies in hardware design architecture are rooted back to the time of incorporation of the company. RxE had an excellent hardware engineer who developed the original core hardware architecture. This core architecture has evolved without substantial changes and became a standard in the sector;
- *RxE expertise in hardware customisation*: One RxE engineer is expert in circuitry design. He spends an estimated 3 months/year in the US-based RxE HQ and he communicates daily with the US-based 3-people-strong hardware development team. The UK-based laboratories have excellent testing facilities, obtained all European technical specifications, and developed emulators for different country specifications;
- *Software standardisation and compatibility with older applications*: Most of the software is common for all products independently of target country or segment. Advanced digital signal processing software algorithms are also robust and well proven. These have resulted in stability of software and compatibility between older and new applications, a substantial competitive advantage for the company. It is noticeable that applications written by third developers 4 years ago, are still running on today's boards, in an industry where 6 months is a long time. Unfortunately though, the company still has a limited number of engineers able to write advanced digital signal processing software algorithms and buying-in is expensive;
- *Synergies in manufacturing*: Reasons include:
  - circuitry does not require expensive state-of-the-art manufacturing lines (i.e. narrow width circuitry printing facilities),
  - there is a multitude of circuitry printers who work on a sub-contracting basis and can supply an unlimited number of boards in days.
- Printing of such boards is cheap (i.e. the actual cost of the board is in the range of $20).

These have not played an important role though, because of:

- the need to adapt the product to different country requirements;
- all the necessary preparation to acquire government approvals in the different European markets; and
- the need to provide strong technical support to many smaller clients.

Marketing

Information about new products rapidly transcends national boundaries and attendance to computer shows like CeBIT (in Germany) draws visitors from all countries. The company tries to be in close contact with its smaller and repeat-purchase-major clients. Smaller independent developers and engineers are a major force in the field because of their innovativeness. RxE supplies up-to-date technical information and elaborate engineering support when necessary. These are hindered, however, by:

- RxE's lack of language ability despite the extensive use of English in the sector;
- the actual number of RxE's available engineers;
- the actual number of technical support personnel; and
- financial and resource constraints of RxE at the time (early 90s) of intended launch of the RDP/9400-I Series in Europe. RxE was an one-man company;
- the view adopted by the corporate executives regarding the scope of the US market. Given the sheer size, technological homogeneity and explosion of the US market in terms of growth for voice processing and computer telephony integration products, much of RxE's attention was directed to their domestic US market, leaving RxE on its own to solve problems regarding the European market.

These had an adverse impact upon the rollout of the specific new product.

Synergies in product handling by the sales force and in use by customer

The product complexity as perceived by the final customer, and the amount of training the various developers need to handle the product, is quite extensive. This happens because the product area is very rapidly evolving in technological terms and several of the developers active in the sector are engineers working from home in their spare time. They need substantial technical support.

Co-ordination of relationships with subsidiaries/agents

RxE sells direct to all its five different client groups. RxE has handled sales from the UK, even though the company is moving now into the appointment of engineers as agents in major markets (Italy, Germany). It has also been imperative for RxE to keep close contact with most its clients. Reasons include:

- the computer telephony is a new technological area and there are few engineers across Europe familiar with the technology;
- the smaller clients need continuous support. In addition to sending programming code and a library of utilities with every sale, RxE uses its own

personnel to support client applications and deal with testing procedures for local country approvals of its own products. The company invites all its 200 clients to product shows in its different country markets[4] and provides them with technical information and transfer of know-how.

At the same time, RxE tries to keep a close contact with its US parent company. As mentioned earlier, RxE's expert in circuit design spends an estimated 3 months/ year in the US. The company also sends its new recruits to the USA for training and familiarisation with the US engineers. The Managing Director also visits the US HQ 3–4 times a year.

New product development process

Shortly after the incorporation of the company, RxE initiated the development of the RDP/9400-I Series with the intention of product availability in the USA 6 months later, and in the UK and Europe in 1991 (a total of 2 years). Severe delays in new product development happened. The time taken to complete the final prototype was $2^1/_2$ years for the original US product and 5 years (end of 1993) for completion of versions for the European market (Holland, Belgium, Norway, Poland, Denmark and Sweden). Reasons include the following:

- The product was primarily developed in the US for the US market. At the time of the development of the RDP/9400-I Series, the European market was playing a minor role, so the product primarily targeted the US market. Final customers in Europe have not been involved and they have not provided feedback to the project engineers. Neither the technical, nor the marketing US-based engineers had access to information regarding approval procedures.
- Technical problems and continuous re-design. The forthcoming new EU requirements for electromagnetic compatibility were much tighter than foreseen. The company increased the processor speed; engineers had not enough experience of circuit design; and RxE was attempting to design the full product on a single board using few layers of copper. No less than 12 reworkings of the board were then carried out and the design eventually failed regarding the number of required layers of copper.

The company also failed to meet its 6-month rollout plan regarding its key, and the 14-month regarding its secondary, European target country markets. The company has still not (end 1995) acquired government approvals in all its intended target country markets.

These development and rollout delays are so important that the RDP/9400-I Series is to be replaced soon by a second generation product (the Vant VPS Series), whose development is now complete. The VPS Series also faced delays. The VPS Series was announced in March 1993 for immediate availability, yet the company only succeeded having the final prototype pass the tests in January 1996.

ITS Holdings Ltd

ITS Holdings Ltd is a subsidiary of a US company, established some 50 years ago. The total corporate turnover reached $122,827,000 and profitability reached $2,485,000 in 1993. ITS manufactures testing equipment. Manufacturing is performed in Massachusetts, US and High Wycombe, UK. Operations in North and South America, Japan and Asia are controlled from the US based corporate HQ. Sales to Europe, Middle East and Arab countries are managed from the UK HQ. The company has replaced all its products in the last 3 years. ITS is currently manufacturing the following dynamometer testing equipment:

- Series 4400 & 5500 (low-end products). A reduction in the number of product versions took place in this recent NPD programme regarding the number of products. ITS used to have 3 products within the Series 4300 and two products within the Series 4500 (the older replaced products);
- Series 8500; and customised testing systems (called 'structures').

The investigated product here is the Series 4400 and 5500.

Product and its characteristics

The differences between the product lines lie in the physical dynamic capacity (e.g. load to be exercised) and sophistication of controls. For instance, the model 8580 is a digital system used to control multiple servohydraulic actuators for simulation testing (multi-axial structural testing) or to simultaneously control a number of independent single-channel testing systems. The Series 4400/5500 is equipment designed for simpler applications. In terms of difference in prices, '*structures*' may cost £0.5 m compared to a mere £30,000 for a Series 4400 machine.

There are several available models for each product. The Series 4400/5500 consists of 20 models. The Series 8500 consists of 6 models. They regard different physical dimensions of load frames, dynamic capacities (e.g. kgs of applicable load) and number of column frames (2–4). There is a wide range of accessories for the different products (cameras, etc.). The Series 4400/5500 type of products compared to its predecessor incorporated:

- a major change in electronics (introduction of product-control through Windows-based software); and
- a minor change in testing frames. Multiple frames were replaced by a single one of higher specifications.

The rollout of the Series 4400 and 5500 has failed and the company has since experienced a drop of between 40 per cent and 50 per cent in sales (see Tables 1 and 2).

Table 1   ITS products, turnover and number of units sold (1993)

Products	Turnover (%)	ITS UK sales
Series 4400 & 5500	60	500 units
Series 8500	20	200 units
Structures	20	40 units

Table 2 Number of units sold of Series 4400 versus 4300 and 5500 versus 4500 (units)

Product	1993 (Jan.–June)	1993 (July–Dec.)	1994 (Jan.–May)
Series 4300	220		
Series 4400		120	60
Series 4500	100		
Series 5500		60	20

Standardisation of the European market

Technological customisation of markets, complexity of such customisation and approvals

The products are standardised across both US and UK but customised across the main European countries. This customisation was easier to accomplish when the products were manually controlled. The incorporation of the Windows based software has rendered product customisation more difficult.

The company does not possess precise quantitative information about the size of the individual segments in the countries where it operates, this partly due to the character of the products and applications. Clients (industrial laboratories, educational and training institutions, to support, maintenance and calibration services) greatly vary (see Table 3).

The company's products target different industrial sectors and can be used in a wide range of different applications (see Table 3). This renders the product hardware less functional and more expensive than competition. There are

Table 3 Sales of ITS per industrial sector and type of applications

Industry	Sales (%)	Applications
Metals	31.9	Strength, stress and strain from bolts and rivets through sheet metal and castings
Plastics	20.2	Hairdryers, compact disks, power tools, automotive
Composites	10.0	Material selection and product design in aircraft, aerospace, automotive, sporting goods
Textiles	7.6	Evaluation of wear and tear of fabrics, strength of cord and yarn from clothing to furniture and commercial carpeting.
Ceramics	7.1	Testing from high temperature structures to electronic substrates (mounting of computer chips)
Rubber	5.5	Shock and vibration mountings in components such as hoses, belts, tires.
Biomedical	5.2	Testing endurance life for products like orthopaedic implants, dental restoration, sutures and sterile packaging.

Table 4   Sales of ITS per country
(Series 4400 & 5500)

Country	%
Italy	20
France	15
Germany	10
Spain	5
UK	15
Eastern Europe	15
Others	20

enormous differences in the requirements between applications. Software is also generic. It is available in a single software programme and takes a lot of computer memory and drive space. Many of the software components are not necessary in individual applications. In contrast, competition is application-specific and sells at lower prices. Due to the above problems, 50 per cent of current engineering time goes into cost reduction. There is no need for special approvals for the product, but the product needs to conform to individual country specifications.

Market

The company targets a variety of industrial sectors, each one having individual needs (see Table 3). In terms of importance of individual countries, Italy, France, Germany and the UK account for 60 per cent of total European turnover (see Table 4).

Availability of adequate quality resources

Manufacturing, design, R&D and NPD is performed in both the USA and the UK in close co-operation. The company acquired two smaller companies (in the US and Germany) in materials testing, something which increased the company's engineering expertise and technological leadership in the dynamometers' sector. ITS faced though, substantial delays in the adaptation and rollout of its Series 4400/5500 to the European countries. These were due to problems which will be developed below:

Synergies in product handling and use by customers

European sales force and customers were used to manually-handled-equipment. The adoption of the Windows interface rendered the Series 4400/5500 a sophisticated testing equipment, and has resulted in difficulties of handling by the sales force and use by the final customer. The new product required extensive training and an important investment in buyers' technical personnel time to learn how to control it. Many technicians were confused with how to use it.

Co-ordination of relationships with agents/distributors

The company owns 11 subsidiaries and 18 sales offices in different countries, among which are the principal European markets. The company employs a handful of salesmen in its major European countries (France, Italy, Spain, Germany). Contacts are infrequent and there is lack of detailed feedback to the European HQ from these subsidiaries. Limited communication also takes place between the subsidiaries themselves, each one focusing in its respective domestic market.

It has been reported that this organisational structure is unsatisfactory and currently under change. The company plans to reorganise its distribution channels across Europe. Alternatives under consideration are the organisation of the subsidiaries into business units or into application areas across individual country borders.

New product development process

It took two years to develop the new Series. The initial decision was to develop the Series 5500, a Windows based software controlled testing equipment with a generic interface for many applications. The software was going to be designed in English and then translated into other foreign languages. Such an equipment:

- requires lengthy familiarisation by the technician;
- comprises unnecessary software components; and
- is expensive to build.

Six months within the Series 5500 project, the company understood that they may face problems with the launching of the Series 5500 and decided to develop a manual version of it (the Series 4400). Launching of the Series 5500 took place simultaneously in the UK and the USA in March 1993 (the new product would be available in June 1993). The product launch in the US market was successful for the following reasons:

- The product was a great improvement over the previous versions.
- It was fully compatible with other machinery and software.
- It was fully compatible with existing standards in the US.
- It permitted the integration of dynamometer testing with all other Windows software available in the US market in a single operational platform.

Launching of the Series 5500 in European countries was planned to take place 3 months after product launch in the British and American markets (September 1993). This eventually faced delays for the following reasons:

- The instability of the system and difficulties to customise the software to the measurement requirements and standards of the company's main European markets. Rolling out to Germany was characteristic of the company's difficulties. The DIN system is different to the UK/US system of standards and the Windows environment had not penetrated the German market to the same extent as in the US and the UK at the time of the rollout of the new product.

- Language difficulties in operating the machine as well as training and support resources. The size of the company did not permit rapid translation of the software into 6 different languages (among them German, French, Italian and Spanish). Finding software developers for Windows environment products was also very difficult. ITS's technicians were unfamiliar with the Windows software and there are few software developers who also possess specific technical knowledge in dynamometer engineering.
- Lack of specific market focus. The focus and requirements of individual applications varied greatly from country to country in Europe. The Series 5500 was inferior to tailored products offered by competitors. ITS did not focus its product development on specific industries or applications. Its generic approach to target markets resulted in high prices compared to competition.
- The company drive to make available a substantial number of accessories (e.g. cameras) and software features to its potential buyers. These accessories were not on schedule by the time of the development of the core equipment. Important software features were also not available.

Faced with problems of high prices, generic application of the software, competitors marketing a more customised product to the particular needs of every industry, windows acceptance across Europe and problems of translation, ITS's sales force in the different European countries rapidly abandoned sales of the more sophisticated Series 5500 for sales of the manual controlled Series 4400. The sales right up to the time of the interview were seriously biased in favour of the Series 4400 and in an overall decline for the entire product line (Series 4400 and 5500).

LxL International

LxL International (Lxl) is a British company which specialises in the manufacture and supply of laminated ID cards. Its products fall into two distinct categories:

- plastic/paper lamination products, consisting of roll-fed and desktop laminators, film and laminated ID cards;
- two PC-based ID-card data base, handling and lamination systems. The first product is a DOS software driven card reader/personnel database system (PMS). The second one is a Windows software driven system which acquires video images/photographs and prints laminated ID cards/badges on a laser printer.

The two PC-based systems are new products for the company and constitute a major shift from the company's core activity. The product under investigation here is Lxl's video imaging photo-ID handling Windows software driven system (henceforth VI-ID system). The company has faced increased competition in its traditional laminated products' domestic market with many Far East and European companies entering the British market. The company has decided to expand its European operations with the VI-ID system, but has failed in the rollout of the new product. The company has sold some 30–40 VI-ID systems in the two years since initiation of sales in the UK, and none in its European markets. This figure is unsatisfactory compared to US sales (200 systems).

The product

The VI-ID system is a versatile system which basically captures (through camera or scanner) the card-holder's portrait as a video image, processes it through a database management facility and prints on laserjet, inkjet, PVC card printer or laser printer a laminated badge or ID card. This badge/card can be magnetically encoded. There are only a few competitors in the laminated ID card business. Big multinational competitors like Kodak or 3M are focusing on the wider image capturing/processing or security access business.

Customisation of the European market

Technology customisation, complexity of such customisation and approvals

The domestic UK market is the major focus of the company's activities. Exports account for a small percentage of company business. They target Holland (70 per cent of exports), France (20 per cent of exports) and Germany (5 per cent of exports). The remaining 5 per cent is spread across Spain, Austria and Switzerland.

The new product basically targets corporate clients (blue chip organisations, government establishments, exhibitions centres, hospitals) needing the rapid production of a personalised security access ID card. A base system can handle, for instance, at least 3,500 individual records. The basic configuration of Lxl's VI-ID system costs £8,000. More advanced configurations, including video capturing, scanner and alternative printing options or LAN connection, can reach £30,000. The technology of the new product does not require customisation across countries, but customers require a tailored product offering. Reasons include:

- the market is highly segmented. There is a variation of target customers and specifications because of user differences regarding security and restrictions of access. The type of badge/ID-cards design, installation and operator's training vary too;
- the potential use of multiple image capturing means, including digital still camera, flatbed or hand scanner, video camera, Polaroid instant camera, photo-CD, CCTV camera or VCR;
- the multitude of data entry means, including typing, bar code reader, magnetic stripe reader, while other options comprise magnetic stripe encoding, remote viewing stations via LAN; and
- a multitude of report-generating software modules, including audit trail reports and multiple user data bases.

Availability of adequate quality engineering and marketing resources

The company has first launched the product in the UK with the intention to subsequently launch it across Europe. It has faced though, severe delays in the rollout of the new product. Reasons include the following:

Engineering

- Configuration of the system to the requirements of each individual customer is complex despite the easiness of purchasing the individual hardware components (i.e. a 486-PC, laser printers and image capturing equipment).
- There is lack of software skills in Lxl. It is US-LxL Inc that has developed the software of the system and Lxl has not actively participated in the design and development of the new product. The VI-ID system is bought from LxL Inc by Lxl on a royalty base. Even though Lxl closely co-operates with a small independent UK software company (Euclid), such access provides minimal synergies. Euclid has not sufficient knowledge of the Windows operating platform. It specialises in DOS-based software products which is substantially different from Windows-based software products.
- Lxl has not easy access to, and lacks communication with, the US-based NPD team. LxL US and Lxl are two completely independent companies.
- Product deficiencies (software instability) have not been solved by the US-based NPD team. This has resulted in many customer complaints in the UK.

In view of these, Lxl has decided to hold back the sales of the VI-ID system in Europe.

Marketing

Severe lack of appropriate marketing resources and skills is evident in Lxl:

- The company's UK sales force are not in a position to handle sales of both paper/plastic badges/ID cards and the VI-ID system. The lamination industry has undergone a major technology shift. Security ID activity has moved from a plastic/paper base to electronics in only few years. Lxl's sales force, used to selling plastic/paper laminated ID cards, have found it difficult to comprehend the software and hardware details necessary to handle sales to communication and security officers of sophisticated corporate customers. The company has decided to hire marketing personnel from the internet, but is further delaying this until Euclid develops the new mid-range Windows based VI-ID system.
- The same difficulties in handling of the product were experienced by Lxl's traditional distribution channels across Europe. The company's distributors and agents, used to handling paper products, are not in a position to handle the VI-ID products' sale.
- Lxl has been lacking marketing information regarding potential distribution channels for the product in Europe.

Co-ordination with subsidiaries/agents

The company's European country markets are served through agents:

- Holland is served by an ID card specialist agent who also sells laminating machines.
- France is served by one exclusive agent covering the business equipment, printing and binding markets, and a second one concerning the consumer market.

- Germany is served by two agents/distributors active in binding and document presentation materials and a third one active in laminating film.
- Sales to the rest of the countries take place through other independent distributors in an infrequent manner.

There is basically no co-ordination of the company's European agents. The company used to employ two salesmen for export sales across Europe. Both of them have left, however, at the period of introduction of the VI-ID system to the UK market. Since their departure, only export order processing is taking place (by one single employee). Also, none in the company possesses information regarding either the company's existing export sales or prospect segments for the new product. These are attributed to the currently low contribution of exports to the company's total turnover.

New product development process

The actual product development started in 1991 with a 12-month completion period target. It eventually took 24 months to complete the new product, the product being eventually available in 1993. The problems faced during 1993–95 have eventually resulted in the company's decision to indefinitely withhold the sales of the VI-ID system to Europe. Reasons include the following:

- LxL Inc. didn't know from the beginning of the process the final features required by the UK or European markets. This product was Lxl's first product in the electronic higher-end laminated badge/ID cards markets and Lxl had limited prior knowledge of the sector.
- Integration between Lxl and the NPD team in the USA was not particularly strong and communication was difficult for the following reasons:
  - Non proficient execution of market screening activities for the UK and European markets. The focus of the US team was the US market. Also, there was limited availability of marketing information about European markets.
  - Communication obstacles between LxL Inc. and Lxl during the development of the product, despite travelling of the Technical Director (once/month) to US. The Managing Director complained of myopia of the US team and their limited understanding of the differences between the US/UK markets. He has further complained about the time differences. The UK operation used to transmit its demands at 03:00–04:00 pm British time corresponding to 09:00 am Eastern US time. By the time US required more information or feedback, it was late night in the UK. This was seen as an American intrusion to British privacy and relaxation.
- Problems of product instability and difficulty of communication with the US-based NPD team to satisfy customisation requirements of UK customers.

Lxl recently decided to invest in the acquisition of a 10-people strong UK-based software development company (Euclid). Lxl is expecting Euclid to develop a mid-range Windows VI-ID software product to be sold through established software retail distribution channels. This software product will be sold for use with common laser printer printable multiple badge A4-size pages.

Notes

1. For comparative purposes, the prices for a small typical 6 port voice system start at $400 while a combined voice/fax can start at $600. A move to 8–12 ports will increase the cost to $2000.
2. One of them for instance is the AccuEleTalk which provides high fidelity audio compression and reproduction with automatic gain control, record cue, voice-activated record and dual-channel record. Another algorithm (the RxE AccuEleDigit) provides reliable DTMF detection with talk-off rejection. Another one (AccuEleCall) provides precise programmable call progress monitoring with quick disconnection and PBX integration capabilities. A fourth one (RxE AccuEleRate) provides a linear speed control option for voice, control of speed-up or slow-down of recorded messages. A fifth one (RxE AccuElePulse) provides on-board rotary pulse detection.
3. The use of MVIP products indeed allows higher capacity and a common interface for different manufacturers' products permitting integrated switching and resource sharing, bridge for audio and video conferencing, interface for digital and analogue telephone lines, multi-channel fax and speech recognition between users.
4. For information purposes, RxE carried out 9 different shows in the last 6 months in France, Germany, UK (1 day), Switzerland (12 days), the Czech Republic (1 weekend) and Italy (1 weekend).

Appendix II: Timely Cases

BtH International Europe Ltd

BtH International Europe Ltd is the European HQ for BtH Industries, a Japanese manufacturing company active in two business areas: 'fashion' and 'image'. The 'image' business (office equipment and computer peripherals) accounts for some 70 per cent of the total corporate turnover. Europe represents 50 per cent of BtH activities outside Japan (the other 50 per cent is in the US) in the 'image' industry. Printers represent 30 per cent of the European sales in revenue terms. BtH manufactures two printer product ranges: one destined to the domestic/small office market and another one targeted to the high-end laser printer segment (banks, insurance companies). BtH's second product range consists of one single model (BTH-1260), the focus of the present discussion (see figure).

The product and its characteristics

The BTH-1260 is a product that possesses the features which are usually required by the typical user. It is an energy-saver 600/1200 dpi laser printer at 12 ppm. The machine has enhanced memory management, a RISC-based high speed controller, network suitability and the option of an additional feeder (see picture). The BTH-1260 replaced a previous generation of laser printers (the BTH-10V and BTH-10H). The product emulates all the major software drivers in the market, making it appropriate for use with all major software. In addition, the product has all the characteristics available in Hewlett Packard printers and other leading products in the laser printer market.

Standardisation of the European market

Technology customisation, complexity of such customisation and approvals

European markets are homogeneous in terms of product specifications, features, and technology. Some minor differences across countries concern:

- cable type and electric currency fluctuation; and
- printer software drivers in local language. This is not a substantial product customisation issue since the major software platforms (Windows 3.1 or Windows 95) are the same across the world.

The company's subsidiaries across Europe have developed an expertise in acquiring safety and electromagnetic inference approvals because they carry multiple product lines (fax machines, typewriters, etc.) in each country market and these approvals are not complex.

Market

The company is present in almost all European markets either through its own subsidiaries or through agents. BtH's *key* European markets represent some 80 per cent of total European printer sales. The biggest country markets are Germany (22 per cent), UK (18 per cent), Switzerland (18 per cent), France (14 per cent) and Belgium (7 per cent). Holland, Norway, Sweden follow with Italy and Spain being the least important countries for the company in terms of sales of the BTH-1260 printer. Some 60 per cent of sales of the product take place between September and December with a second peak in March–May. These peaks correspond to the end of budgeting semesters. The product is targeted to corporate clients. Size of order depends, orders ranging from a few to several hundred machines.

Availability of adequate quality engineering and marketing resources

Engineering

- Substantial R&D and technology resources exist. Back in the 80s BtH used Canon engines in its laser printers. However, the cost of purchasing Canon engines was high and BtH investigated the possibility of developing their own engines. BtH continues to use Canon consumables, but they now produce on their own some 200,000 laser engines and printers a year, a figure that corresponds to some 10 per cent of the European market. This positions the company among the most important world laser printer manufacturers.
- The BTH-1260 and its predecessors (BTH-10H and BTH-10V) use the same print method (electrophotography by semiconductor laser beam scanning).
- Plain paper fax machines and laser printers share similar technologies and BtH is an important global player in fax machines.
- BtH also had adequate software drivers for the European market. The printer drivers were already available since the BTH-10V and BTH-10H products used them. The product also emulates all other major laser printers in the market (i.e. HP LaserJet III and LaserJet 4, BR-Script, Diablo 630, IBM Proprinter XL, Epson 850). Such simulation technology is widely available.

Marketing

- The BTH-1260 laser replaced the older BTH-10V and BTH-10H laser printers and targeted the same segments as its predecessors.
- The company has faced resource limitations in secondary markets, where it is lagging behind its competitors, but it possesses very strong direct sales capabilities in its key target markets (Germany, the UK, Belgium, Switzerland and France). Direct sales is the best method of promoting the BTH-1260. BtH employs some 1500 employees across its European subsidiaries and agents, with a strong sales monitoring and product management team being located in the UK HQ.
- The decision of the European HQ to centralise translations of the user guides in the UK also permitted the company to closely monitor production of product brochures and documents.

- The company's marketers and engineers remain with the company for many years. This life long type of employment permits accumulation of marketing and engineering expertise and capabilities.
- If the company ever faces delays in product availability because of delays in its actual development process, they air freight stock for one month of sales. By the end of this period, sufficient stock has arrived by sea (shipment from Japan takes 30 days).

Synergies in product handling by the sales force or use by the customer

The new product is not complex and the final user does not experience problems with it. It is a typical laser printer, similar in its features to Hewlett Packard's products (the market leader). Installation and functioning are relatively easy for any computer literate person, and corporate clients have their internal engineering personnel for staff assistance.

Co-ordination of relationships with subsidiaries/agents

BtH International Europe is organised in 4 sections, one of which is responsible for the computer peripherals business. Seven people are working exclusively for the printers' business. Their activities are divided between sales monitoring, order processing, shipment checking, forecasting, sales leaflets and pricing negotiations with Japan. Marketing support and product management is carried out by the business development group consisting of five people and the technical support is carried out by the technical support group consisting of some fifteen more people.

As BtH's operations are grouped in 4 sections (fax machines, printers, labelling products and typewriters/wordprocessors), the company runs separate discussion groups. Technical or sales sessions of one or more days are arranged regularly (every 1–2 months), with a core of senior staff from all European subsidiaries/ agents attending both. Ideas about future products, updates upon new products and information about launches are exchanged during these meetings. Some of the meetings are devoted to decisions regarding pricing, delivery dates and quantities required. Others are devoted to transfer of technical knowledge and specifications for the new products.

European HQ staff fly frequently to Japan. The European operations are also headed by Japanese personnel which keeps its links with the corporate Japanese HQ. There is also a constant flow of fax messages and control. One of the respondents characteristically said: 'We continuously check every single detail. We check, we check, we check.'

New product development process

Two R&D facilities are located in Japan and a third one in the US. The first facility focuses upon development of new technologies and products in completely new product areas. The second facility focuses on improving manufacturing processes and existing products for printers and fax products. The third one focuses on fax or labelling products for the American market. The company practice for the development of the BTH-1260 was to bring initially the new product idea for discussion in one of the frequent meetings between the new product development team (in Japan) and sales personnel (from Japan, Europe and the US). Then a deci-sion was made regarding 'SPQD' (Specifications, Price, Quantity, and Delivery) for the product. This helps BtH's engineers because they knew since the start of the new product development process the final characteristics of the product.

Strong interaction between Japanese and European HQ and UK-managers across European countries permitted to incorporate agents' and subsidiary per-sonnel's views on the features and other characteristics of the new product. Communication and feedback on prototypes and progress of the project were also extensive. The company hasn't consulted the final customers though. Managers in the European HQ would wish to do that, but it becomes extremely difficult to co-ordinate customer/final user feedback for their entire range of prod-ucts. They trust though, the opinion of attendants of the discussion sessions. Also, there was a strong and continuous flow of information from Japan to Europe and the European country managers through the regular technical and sales sessions as explained in the previous section.

The product was planned and eventually rolled out simultaneously across all but one European markets for the product as follows: Germany (December 1994), Switzerland (December 1994), Belgium (December 1994), France (December 1994/January 1995), UK (January/February 1995).

OEL Europe Ltd

OEL Data Corporation is part of OEL Electric Industries Co. Ltd, a major player in telecommunications, information processing systems and electronic devices. OEL Data Corporation (henceforth OEL) develops and markets 5 different printer product groups (dot matrix printers, non-impact printers, low-end printers, ink-jet printers and facsimiles/multi-functional products (i.e. desktop document processing systems). The company's non-impact printer range comprises 4-, 6-, 8- and 12-ppm (pages per minute) laser printers.

The product and product superiority

The focus of the present discussion is the 6-ppm laser printer called OEL 610ex, designed for personal/small business use. This product replaced the OEL 410ex (4-ppm) as part of OEL's regular upgrading of product lines. The OEL 610ex offers a series of clearly visible benefits and value for money to the user. More precisely:

- The product enables the use of separate toner and drum consumables within the printer (unlike the combined units of most other printer manufacturers) leading to cost advantages for the user.
- The characteristics of the product are also in line with competing products. They include density of resolution (600 dpi), use of industry standard inter-faces (emulation of the HP Laserjet 4 through a PCL5e compatible emulation), a standard 100 sheet paper tray, compliance with energy saving standards, lit-tle weight (7.7 Kg), short time to first page print (17 seconds), use of different letter and envelope sizes.

- The product is equipped with a powerful R3000 RISC processor (at 25 Mhz clock speed using 16 bit bus width), possesses a sufficient number (45) of scaleable fonts and uses an adequate 2MB of memory (for comparable purposes HP's LaserJet 4 printing 12 ppm offers similar memory).
- The product has an Apple talk interface on an optional Adobe Postscript Board for the printing of intensive graphic applications and desktop publishing.
- The product is backed up by a 5 year warranty for the printer head and a minimum life of 180,000 pages corresponding to at least 5 years of intensive use (calculated at 270 pages/day).

Standardisation of the European market

Technology customisation, complexity of such customisation and approvals

European markets are homogeneous in terms of product specifications, features, and technology. Some minor differences across countries concern:

- cable type and electric currency fluctuation; and
- printer software drivers in local language. This is not a substantial product customisation issue since the major software platforms (Windows 3.1 or Windows 95) are the same across the world.

The company's subsidiaries/agents across Europe have developed an expertise in acquiring safety and electromagnetic interference approvals because they carry multiple printer and fax product lines in each country market and these approvals are not complex.

Marketing

There is a great variation in the type of target market segments and channels across Europe. Printer speed is a major criterion for segmentation of markets by OEL, yet the boundaries between sub-segments remain hazy. While there is a clear distinction between buyers of the low and high-end printers (4- and 12-ppm), it is difficult to distinguish the type of customers for the middle 6-ppm printers (both consumer and business buyers). Users are spread across all economic and social groups, but it is not a major problem in marketing the product. OEL Europe is active in 20 European country markets. The most important key markets are Germany (35 per cent), UK (15 per cent), France (10 per cent) and Scandinavia (30 per cent).

Availability of adequate quality engineering and marketing resources

Technology

The company had sufficiency of engineering resources for the OEL 610ex product:

- There is sufficient technical personnel and R&D funds to develop laser printers, the entire company being primarily focused upon development and marketing of printer products.
- The OEL 610ex has benefited from synergies with its predecessor and the company's other printers. The product is part of a much wider laser printer

range, it uses technology that is fully compatible with technology and shares components with other products. The print technology (OEL's microfine spherical toner technology) and microprocessor (R3000 RISC) are, for instance, the same as in the OEL 810ex and the OEL 1200ex printers.

Marketing

OEL Europe has a skilled and substantial resource base for the OEL 610ex:

- The product targets existing markets, something that increases accuracy of prediction of sales, and costs.
- OEL dominates the European market in the business and professional segment in the dot matrix printers and they are currently at the third place regarding non-impact printers.
- The company opened its first European sales offices more than 20 years ago, and Europe is now one of OEL's largest markets for non-impact printers (1/3 of total corporate sales).
- OEL Europe is active in 20 different European countries. It has 10 subsidiaries in the UK, Denmark, Germany, Spain, France, Holland, Ireland, Italy, Norway, and Sweden and agents in ten more European country markets.
- OEL's staff have considerable skills and knowledge of the European market. Existing sales and marketing devote all their time and efforts to marketing and sales of printers and related products because printers are the company's main business. The company has adequate marketing channels and a sufficient number of quality local repair centres.
- The European HQ co-ordinate promotion and advertising across all European countries.
- The company launches multiple similar product lines and has accumulated experience regarding the potential of each product.

Synergies in product handling by the sales force or use by the customer

No special setup directions are required for the use of the product. The printer is a fairly standard laser printer for straight-from-the-box use. OEL's sales force do not also need any specific training and service/maintenance requirements remain the same as for most laser printers. The handling or 'feeling' of the product has not changed for the customer compared to its predecessor or other products and the way the user is informed, by the product about its function, is similar to most laser products.

Co-ordination of relationships with subsidiaries/agents

OEL Data Corporation is organised in terms of its 5 main product groups (dot matrix printers, non-impact printers, low-end printers, ink-jet printers and fac-similes/multi-functional products) at corporate level.

- One Japanese Vice President (called 'Process Owner') is in charge of each one of these 5 corporate activities. The 'process owners' regularly initiate global meetings. These global meetings are attended by marketing and technical staff from Europe, the USA and Asia and staff from the Japan-based manufacturing, R&D, finance and procurement.

- OEL Europe is also organised around the same 5 product groups. There are 5 European product managers. These European product managers visit extensively every European country (at least twice a year) and constantly communicate with their individual European country counterparts.
- Each local European market also employees, in turn, 5 country product groups corresponding to the same 5 corporate product groups. They handle promotion, advertising methods, segments to serve in each country, channels to use and pricing.

In addition to the 5 product groups at corporate, European and country level, there also exist:

- Product Line Teams (PLTs). The 5 most competent people for each individual product line (drawn from any European country), marketing and technical staff from the European HQ form PLTs at European level. There are also PLTs at individual country level. The PLTs meet at regular intervals to clarify and consolidate the European position for each specific product line. Their role is central regarding technology, specifications and time to launch. The PLTs prevent problems of product acceptability through early identification of the common requirements of all European countries. They negotiate differences at the initial phases of the new product development process both before and after the PPT (see below) world-level meetings.
- Product Planning Teams (PPTs). A PPT world-level meeting is attended by at least 50 different people who provide engineering advice. These meetings typically take place 4 times a year and last 3–4 days. All products are discussed in their respective corporate product groups. Video conferencing is used between world meetings for communication and discussions.
- A Strategic Planning Group (SPG) at world level. The SPG considers plans for the development of new products.

At the same time OEL controls very tightly its European subsidiaries through intensive formalisation. The company uses cost and profit centres, comprehensive management information systems, formal performance appraisals, written marketing strategies, written procedures and master marketing plans.

New product development process

OEL Data Corporation has spread its manufacturing, R&D and sales across the world. Manufacturing facilities are in Japan, Thailand, the US and the UK. R&D facilities are in the US and Japan. Sales are managed from OEL Data in the US, OEL Europe Ltd (in the UK) and OEL Electric Industry Co. Ltd (in Japan).

OEL extensively co-ordinates its new product development activities. Decisions are taken in a participative mode, conflicts are resolved at the initial stages of the development process and flow of information is frequent. Subsidiaries and agents are strongly involved. They provide inputs and receive continuous feedback by OEL. The new product development process followed by OEL for the OEL 610ex is presented in turn:

- An individual country PLT first met to discuss the market opportunity identified for a product similar to the OEL 610ex. They quantified opportunity, price and expected market share for the product.
- The new product idea was communicated to the European Marketing and Strategic Planning Manager who agreed for it to be discussed at the next meeting of the European-level PLT.
- After the European-level PLT considered the new product idea at face value, individuals from the proposing country communicated the idea to other European countries asking for comments and opinions for the development of a European Review and Business Plan.
- This was followed by a recommendation to the Strategic Planning Group (SPG) at world level. The SPG considered the plan for the new product and gave permission to proceed into a Formal Product Review which consists of four design reviews (DR1, DR2, DR3, DR4). Specifications and a business plan for the entire world and a time schedule of some 12–15 months were set during the first design review.
- A PPT world-level meeting considered the business plan and endorsed the development of the new product.
- European marketing managers initiated at this point a 14-point list of activities (this expands to 32 points if the product is a new instead of replacement product). It comprises activities, responsibilities, scheduled start, scheduled finish, actual finish and remarks for pending issues. This 32-point (or 14-point) list also plays the role of the master schedule for the rollout of the new product across Europe.

The product development process for the OEL 610ex was similar to most other OEL products. OEL planned to have developed the product over 15 months from initiation of the development process to first sales. It eventually took 18 months for technical reasons. A potential delay was incorporated, though, in the schedule and has not affected the launch. Product was available on time in all countries in order to benefit from seasonal higher sales (October–December). The product was announced in the CeBit Fair in March 1995 and was made available in October 1995.

Alme Tel International Ltd

The company is active in all three main trade blocs (North America, Europe and Japan). Each one of these trade areas accounts for one-third of its sales. The global HQ are in the West Coast of the US and the company's manufacturing base is in Singapore. It is a production-volume led manufacturer targeting the wide and established segments of the computer network market. Its five divisions are:

- unmanaged network products;
- managed network switches and products;
- network adapter cards;
- ATM; and
- network management software.

The company does not develop products that need customisation across the US and Europe, it avoids pioneering technology and it does not target emerging markets. The focus of the present discussion is the ATS-2560TX 10/100 Fast Ethernet Adapter Card for PCI-bus motherboards.

Product and product superiority

The ATS-2560TX is an upgrade generation over existing company products. It marks the company's transition from the 10BASE-T standard to the emerging 100BASE-T standard. The product offers unique attributes and clearly visible and useful benefits to the user as well as superior quality, performance and value for money. The product targets those users who want to buy equipment which will not need replacement when the new 100 Mbps technology becomes widespread. These are the major characteristics of the product:

- The product uses the TX standard which:
  - is a faster version of ordinary Ethernet, it has technological and pricing advantages for demanding network applications and permits access to 100BASE-X technologies;
  - permits quicker transfers and facilitates handling of video, audio and data all in one full-duplex bundle (especially helpful in a server connection, where the need for two-way traffic often arises);
  - is fully compatible with ATM and ATI access switches. The ATM is the future standard for data transfer. It is still very expensive but in use by big users (banks etc.). The ATI is in use by ISA-bus motherboards which is another widely adapted type of bus in workstations;
  - permits access to other standard technologies including the Media Access Control, the CSMA/CD, the Fiber Distributed Data Interface, and the Physical Layer (see *Byte*, October 1994).
- The product uses the PCI-bus which offers a number of advantages including independence from the CPU (Central Processing Unit). This frees the CPU for additional processing and increases the performance of data-intensive peripherals. Testing results show a higher throughput than competition and low CPU utilisation.
- The product uses a connector to an external transceiver that provides conversion between wiring schemes.
- The product is a 'plug-and-play' card and has full European Community Safety and Electromagnetic approvals.
- The card has received approvals from the main operating systems developers (Microsoft and Novel) for compliance with Windows NT, Windows 95 and 3.1 and Novel Netware and supports Banyan Vines, DEC Pathworks, IBM LAN Server and other operating systems in an attempt to appeal to the mass of network users.
- The product's software drivers automatically sense the hub's speed and set the adapter accordingly. It can also perform auto-negotiation. Switching from 10 to 100 Mbps can be done by simple reset of the network (automatic determination of speed by both the card and the hub). There are external speed indicators, too.

- The card is backed with a Lifetime Warranty and free technical support. New and enhanced software drivers and features are available 24h/day via BBS or Compuserve.

Standardisation of the European market

Technology customisation, complexity of such customisation and approvals

The 10BASE-T LAN is a standardised technology, but the move to 100BASE-T technology has been accompanied by disagreement between major manufacturers. Thus, there were in February 1996 four 100 Mbps Ethernet standards: three media standards for 100BASE-T (part of the so called 802.3 standard) and an additional one for 100VG-AnyLan, which are explained in turn:

- The TX standard which uses only two pairs of Category 5 wiring just like the 10BASE-T which is the actual current de-facto Ethernet standard. This is followed by Intel, SMC, 3COM and Digital Semiconductor.
- The T4 which uses unshielded twisted pairs (i.e. 8 wires total) has no duplex option and is promoted by Broadcom (a company that manufactures T4 transceiver components).
- The proposed T2 standard which supports a different type of signalling but it is not in production yet.
- The 100VG-AnyLan which uses a separate protocol and is not an 802.3 standard.

The TX standard is fully compatible with existing LANs though, and appeals to the largest section of the LAN market across countries, estimated at 30+ million Ethernet nodes. No product customisation is required from market to market, with the exception of the electrical input. This is not considered to be an important product adaptation.

Market

Most of the segments resemble across countries because of common technology requirements across Europe and the US. European customers (LAN network managers in organisations) closely follow developments in the USA. The United States serves as the technology leader and the setter of market trends. There are no specific government regulations with the exception of minor electromagnetic interference and safety. Approvals by Microsoft, Novell and other network Operating Systems developers are necessary. This is not difficult however, since the ATS-2560TX like most competitive products is designed in accordance with widely disseminated specifications by these developers.

European sales are split between the UK (15 per cent of sales), Germany (20 per cent), France (18 per cent), Italy (14 per cent), Scandinavia and Denmark (15 per cent), Eastern Europe (15 per cent), Benelux and other European countries (the rest). The UK is also responsible for sales to Scandinavia (Finland, Denmark, Sweden and Norway). The German office is responsible for sales to East Europe (The Czech Republic and Russia) and Switzerland. The French office is responsible for sales to Benelux, and the Italian office for North Africa, Greece, Spain, Turkey and Israel.

Availability of adequate quality resources

Engineering

- The ATS-2560TX is an upgrade to existing technology and fully compatible with existing LANs. It appeals to the largest section of the LAN market across countries. The market for Ethernet is large and the move towards the 100BASE-T is spreading throughout the world. A proportion of the 100BASE-T installations are already in the market.
- No product customisation is required from market to market with the exception of the electrical input. Multilingual user guides may also be needed. The company insists on providing US cabling only in a conscious effort to avoid any customisation.
- All tools created for the standard 10BASE-T Ethernet may be used with minor modifications in the 100BASE-T environment.

Marketing

- Target segments remain the same as for the previous generation products. Also, the company markets a wide range of products to these segments.
- The company has insufficient availability of marketing and technical support personnel for all countries, but this is of no importance. Ninety per cent of sales is absorbed by distributors, OEMs accounting for the rest (10 per cent). The company has appointed 4 main distributors in the four main European countries to supply dealers, system integrators (SIs) and value added resellers (VARs) (see figure below). These vary from 200 to 1000 per country. SIs, VARs and dealers have substantial own technical support personnel and Alme Tel's ATS-2560TX uses technology the business community is familiar with. Among the dealers, SIs and VARs only a small number (circa 20 per country) are the most important and most regular clients. They are considered to compete successfully in their respective markets.
- This small number (20 main clients per country) permits extensive communication and makes easier direct mail of product information. Alme Tel also dispatches – prior to product launch – samples of its new products to country managers, press release agents and main clients' engineers.

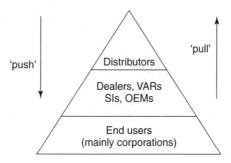

- The European marketing staff create the internal and external product documentation ahead of the USA. This leaves enough time to proceed with translations.
- Alme Tel has its own sales and technical support offices in its main European countries including the UK, Germany, France and Italy.

Synergies in product handling by sales force and use by customers

Complexity of use and handling by the sales force and end users are higher than for the current 10BASE-T products. Nonetheless, dealers, SIs, VARs and final users are familiar with most of the technical solutions and requirements.

Co-ordination of relationships with subsidiaries/agents

There is a 'cut-throat competition' culture within the company which creates difficulties. Communication, though, is extensive and informal. The company makes limited use of cost and profit centres or formal appraisal and no use of written marketing strategy, procedures and fixed rules. While there are some master marketing plans and schedules, operations are left with the individuals who are expected to perform through their own initiatives. Any under-achievement usually results in redundancy. There is:

- one European Business Manager (EBMr) responsible for all European operations who is located in Seattle, US. From a French–US origin, he is fully familiar with circumstances and developments in the European market. The EBMr operated 3 years from France and has been instrumental in initiating and developing business in Europe. The EBMr visits the four offices once a year and holds additional meetings during the company's Global Strategic Planning Conference (once a year in the US) and during the major trade shows.
- There are four Managing Directors responsible for the four European offices (UK, Germany, France and Italy). While these four MDs report direct to the US-based EBMr (continuous lines in the figure on p. 221), the UK MD serves as a privileged liaison with the US. The UK MD meets his three counterparts at a monthly meeting at Heathrow Airport prior or after his monthly visits to the US.
- Under the UK MD there is 1 European Marketing Director (E-Mrk-D), 4 European Product Marketing Managers (E-PMrk-M) and a Marketing Communications team (translations, advertising material, press releases, dispatch of product information to resellers and co-ordination of European trade shows). The E-Mrk-D keeps flying out to the US once per month and spends at least one week in both the East and West Coast sites of the company in order to influence business developments.
- There is in each of the main European countries:
  - 1 person acting as 'Distribution' Manager exclusively dealing with logistics and flow of products to the 3–4 major distributors of Alme Tel products per country; and
  - 1 person acting as 'Liaison' Manager between the European HQ and the local market. The remaining sales personnel are responsible for 'talking' to dealers, VARs and SIs. Total sales and technical support personnel totals 27 people in the UK, 30 in Germany, 15 in France and 8 in Italy.

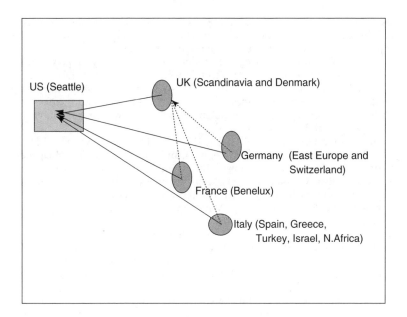

The E-PMrk-M and the E-Mrk-D fly out to the main European countries on a regular basis (every 1–2 months), and the E-PMrk-M is in direct and frequent fax, e-mail and telephone contact with both the 'Distribution' and the 'Liaison' Managers in each country. This takes place on top of the regular monthly meetings between:

- MDs at Heathrow Airport;
- the visits by the EBMr;
- the meetings during the international and local trade shows; and
- the company's Global Strategic Planning Conference where some 50 people attend. Although such a number of people make difficult a genuine planning exercise, the 4-day conference and the streams of parallel meetings permit a strong interaction between the EBMr and the personnel in the UK, Germany, France and Italy.

Salesmen also travel extensively. They frequently visit local buyers in the remaining European countries.

New product development process

New Product Development is separate from Product Management (henceforth NPD and PM respectively). The responsibility of marketing people in each division of 5 existing divisions (unmanaged network products, managed network switches and products, network adapter cards, ATM and network management software) is to liaise with sales, manufacturing and feedback to NPD teams, track the market developments and produce internal and external documentation including technical data and newsletters. The PM Divisions have no control over actual new product development undertaken by the NPD teams.

Three of the most knowledgeable people of the company (1 person from Germany and 2 from the UK) decide upon what features and characteristics of new products to suggest to the US-based PM Divisions. The country offices have limited input in technology, specifications for new products and their pricing, but wider freedom in choice of segments served and how to serve their clients with the new product.

The decision to develop the ATS-2560TX was taken back in October 1995 in consultation between the PM division, NPD, and the US, European and Japanese Business Managers. This is followed by the initiation of a formal procedure applied to all new products. A 'market requirement document' was generated in the US and sent to Europe. The European Marketing Manager in consultation with the European Product Marketing Manager and the 'Liaison' and 'Distribution' Managers in Germany, France and Italy commented upon the document within a week. Changes were debated and a product development plan with expected completion and availability date were established.

This was the only official information that the UK received from the US for its new product for the ATS-2560TX. It has been commented as representative of the one-way flow of information from European offices to the US-based PM Divisions of the company. European HQ staff complain that the US-based NPD team is not aware of European requirements and have difficulty in understanding the differences between the US and European market. This is a main reason for the regular monthly trips of the E-Mrk-D to East and West Coast sites of the company.

The project completion date for the ATS-2560TX project was set for December 1995. This date would be 3 months after initiation of the development of the new product and in line with competitive launches of major manufacturers such as 3Com's Etherlink 3C595-TX (December 1995). The project has not evolved though as expected. The NPD teams did not consider the PM Adapter Card Division marketers to be in a position to understand technology, be good at suggesting new products and prompted the replacement of the PM Divisional Manager in November 1995. Following this, 4 new marketing people were brought into the company and 1 more was promoted.

These changes resulted in a delay in the actual target day for product availability from the Singapore manufacturing facility. In a fire-fighting exercise, Alme Tel decided to outsource the product sub-contracting production to third parties and a new launch date was established for February 1996. This was easy because the company is a technology follower and know-how was available in the industry.

Samples of the ATS-2560TX were eventually dispatched to country managers, press and technical support people across Europe on 20 January, 1996. A product information sheet was also sent to Alme Tel's 20 major clients per country (SIs, VARs and dealers). The product was eventually simultaneously rolled out across all Europe at the beginning of February 1996.

Final customers were not involved in the development process of the ATS-2560TX and they did not provide any feedback. This was not important however, since the trends are set by a few technology leaders and there is rapid dissemination of the characteristics and features of emerging technology across the globe.

HnCC UK

HnCC (UK) Ltd (henceforth HN/UK) and HnCC (Europa) GmbH (henceforth HN/D) are the European HQ for HnCC (HN) industrial and professional (i.e. reporter recording) cameras. HN is also active in North America (USA and Canada), South East Asia and China.

The European operations are split between the UK and German office. HN/UK is responsible for sales to France, Holland, Belgium, UK, and Iceland, and HN/D is responsible for the rest of Europe. Even though the two offices are separate, they share the same Managing Director. The focus of the present is a series of small tubular black and white cameras designed to capture moving objects in the factory automation and machine vision industrial areas.

The product and product superiority

The PP-M1 Series accounts for some 40 per cent of HN/UK sales. The Series consists of several models developed on the basis of the older PP-M1 Type camera of the company. The products are small, light weight black and white cameras with maximum shutter speed of about 10,000 frames/second. The Series was launched in July 1993 and more models added into it in July 1994. It has replaced the first generation single product launched in 1992. Compared to the previous single product generation, each model in the current multiple product range has the ability to perform different functions. For instance, the PP-MB1 model offers an extremely compact and lightweight camera head, by separating, by a distance of up to 1m, the lens and CCD assembly from the camera electronics, making it ideal for optical uses. In the PP-MC1 model, the lens/CCD assembly is rotated around the normal position for reducing the front-to-back depth of the camera. This camera is appropriate for machine vision applications, where little depth is available for camera mounting. The PP-MD1 camera offers high precision mounting. The CCD inclination and position with respect to the centre of the optical axis is set with micron accuracy. This precision makes the camera ideal for critical image input applications and object positioning.

The PP-M1 Series has some characteristics that differentiate it from competition. Some of the models are available in right-angle versions, something rare, and image is captured through square instead of rectangular pixels. This makes computation of distances between objects very accurate. Moreover, the characteristics and functionality make them flexible in several situations, an advantage over competition.

Standardisation of the European market

Technology customisation, complexity of such customisation and approvals – marketing customisation

The cameras are used for the recording of the movement of machine objects, mechanical parts, or positioning of parts in factory automation tasks. Clients for this type of product require substantial customisation related to the task at sight. The diversity of applications in factory automation is extreme, making the market for these products highly heterogeneous. The company follows, however, a standardised approach, where some 85 per cent of total cameras sold are supplied without any customisation. This is harmful for the sales of the European offices since some customers are diverted to competition. Nonetheless, the range of products offers some flexibility since they can cover a number of different applications.

With some 10,000 units sold per year, sales to the UK, France, Belgium, Holland and Iceland account for an estimated 7.5 per cent of HD world sales for the specific product range. Some 80 per cent of HN/UK's sales are directed to the UK itself. The rest is split between the rest of the company's European country markets as follows: France (8 per cent), Holland (8 per cent), Belgium and Iceland (4 per cent of sales).

Availability of adequate quality engineering and marketing resources

Engineering

- Corporate HnCC has established an independent heavily funded corporate R&D unit focus upon basic research. New technologies regularly come out of its laboratories, and they are diffused or transmitted throughout the corporation. Because these new technologies are so diverse, it is up to the R&D teams in each unit of the corporation (such as HD) to identify which ones to use in their own products.
- HnCC pursues a policy of product standardisation in order to minimise heterogeneity of operations and increase synergies. Only 15 per cent of cameras sold by HN/UK are modified locally after consultation with the Japanese R&D department.

Marketing

- HN/UK and HN/D target SIs (20 per cent of turnover) and OEMs (60 per cent) which incorporate the cameras into their own automated machinery. These are estimated to be 100, in total, across all Europe. The number of actual major buyers for the PP-M1 Series is about 10 across HN/UK's region of responsibility.
- The German office is a separate entity but organisationally close to its sister British subsidiary. They share the same Managing Director and the two subsidiaries exchange information, interact between themselves and source components or inventory items from each other.
- The PPM1 Series has benefited from existing resources. The company had successfully marketed its predecessor. Target market segments and sales force were the same and buyers were familiar with the product.

Synergies in product handling by the sales force or use by the customer

The new product remained the same regarding its complexity compared to the older generation product. The HN/UK engineers were able to handle support to buyers. The use of intermediaries (OEMs and SIs) who were well knowledgeable regarding their own activities also permitted the minimisation of support to final users. This is undertaken by the OEMs or SIs.

Co-ordination of relationships with subsidiaries/agents

HN/UK and HN/D avoid selling directly to end users. They primarily sell to SIs and OEMs for the following reasons:

- OEMs buy in large quantities. This minimises the need for interaction with the final user.
- The company through a policy of exclusive sales to intermediaries (OEMs, and SIs) and avoidance of sales to end users also benefited from good reputation. SIs and OEMs cease sourcing from suppliers, if they sell direct to final users. This has happened to HD's own competitors.
- Purchase of factory automation machinery is a capital investment project, rendering individual purchases infrequent. The final users are not repeat buyers.

Co-ordination of marketing is easy because of the small number (10) of actual major product buyers. The company employs one single salesman for the OEM buyers. The French distributor has its own local agents across the country and transmits back to London requirements and information. Due to its long co-operation with the company and product/market familiarity, the quality of transmitted information has increased. There is some room for improvement according to HN/UK personnel though. This became apparent in a recent exhibition when HN/UK realised that some salesmen were not fully aware of some of the features of the company's PP-M1 Series. The company intends to educate 2–3 salesmen in each buyer for improvement of communication and sales.

New product development process

Personnel from Japan visit in their world tour, the regional Head offices twice a year. The Japanese team usually consists of the international sales representative based in Tokyo, and the Japanese Head Engineer. The European location for the meeting rotates between the UK and Germany (once in the UK and once in Germany). The European personnel explain their product preferences and required features and the Japanese mission present their own ideas, targets and world market trends. While US and Asian market preferences prevail most of the times regarding the type of products and features developed, HN/UK personnel are confident that justification of sufficient sales finds support in Tokyo by both the design and marketing teams.

HD often faces delays in the development of its new products. Judging from the overall company presence in its European markets over the years though, the HN/UK personnel have come to the conclusion that the company may lag sometimes behind competition, but other times is ahead of it. Technology incorporation derived from developments at the corporate HnCC R&D unit is helping HD to compete head-on-head.

HN/UK finds it easy to identify market trends across Europe. Re-transmission of customer requirements by OEMs or SIs increases company market knowledge despite limited communication between the company and the final users. The very nature of factory automated products requires extensive interaction between engineers from both HD and the buyer (OEM or System Integrator) side.

The first generation PP-M1 product was initially launched in 1992. Some of the replacing models (e.g. PP-MB1; PP-MC1; PP-MD1; PP-ME1) were launched a year later (July 1993). Additional models were made available two years later in July 1994 (the PP-M1Z model). All models were made simultaneously available to all customers across all European markets. This has happened for the following reasons:

- The company was aware of the development and the time of availability of the forthcoming products long before the actual launch. Also, pre-sales information was sent to the company's customers by mail some 1–3 months prior to availability.
- HN/UK and HN/D engineers provided technical details and information to all those they were contacting during the company's regular activities.
- The company sent samples to its major clients for trial-tests.

Bibliography

Aaby, Nils-Eddy and S. F. Slater (1989) 'Management Influences on Export Performance – a Review of the Empirical Literature', *International Marketing Review*, 6, 7–26.

Abell, D. F. (1980) *Defining the Business: the Starting Point of Strategic Planning*. Englewood Cliffs, NJ: Prentice-Hall.

Adler, P. (1989) 'Technology Strategy: a Guide to the Literatures', in *Research on Technological Innovation, Management and Policy*, Vol. 4, R. Rosenbloom and R. Burgelman, eds. Greenwich, CT: JAI Press, 25–151.

Alexander, R. S. (1964) 'The Death and Burial of "Sick" Products', *Journal of Marketing*, 1–9.

Ali, Abdul (1994) 'Pioneering Versus Incremental Innovation: Review and Research Propositions', *Journal of Product Innovation Management*, 11, 46–61.

Ali, Abdul, Robert Krapfel and Douglas Labahn (1995) 'Product Innovativeness and Entry Strategy: Impact on Cycle Time and Break-Even Time', *Journal of Product Innovation Management*, 12, 54–69.

Allen, T. J. (1971) 'Communications, Technology Transfer, and the Role of Technical Gatekeeper', *R and D Management*, 1, 14–21.

Allen, T. J. (1977) *Managing the Flow of Technology*. Cambridge, MA: MIT Press.

Amine, Lyn S. (1993) 'Linking Consumer Behavior Constructs to International Marketing Strategy: a Comment on Wills, Samli, and Jacobs and an Extension', *Journal of the Academy of Marketing Science*, 21, 71–7.

Ancona, D. G. and D. F. Galdwell (1990) 'Beyond Boundary Spanning: Managing External Dependence in Product Development Teams', *Journal of High Technology Management Research*, 1, 119–35.

Ancona, D. G. and D. F. Galdwell (1992a) 'Bridging the Boundary: External Process and Performance in Organizational Teams', *Administrative Science Quarterly*, 37, 634–65.

Ancona, D. G. and D. F. Galdwell (1992b) 'Demography and Design: Predictors of New Product Team Performance', *Organization Science*, 3, 321–41.

Andersen, Otto (1993) 'On the Internationalisation Process of Firms – a Critical Analysis', *Journal of International Business Studies*, 24, 2, 209–31.

Anderson, Erin and Hubert Gatignon (1986) 'Modes of Foreign Entry: a Transaction Cost Analysis and Propositions', *Journal of International Business Studies*, 17, 1–26.

Andrews, K. R. (1971) *The Concept of Corporate Strategy*. Homewood, IL: Irwin.

Ansoff, Igor H. (1958) 'A Model of Diversification', *Management Science*.

Ansoff, Igor H. (1965) *Corporate Strategy*. London: Penguin.

Ansoff, Igor H. and Edward McDonnell (1990) *Implanting Strategic Management*, 2nd edn. Hemel Hempstead: Prentice-Hall.

Argyris, C. (1952) 'Human Problems with Budgets', Controlship Foundation.

Asher, Herbert B. (1983) *Causal Modeling: Quantitative Applications in the Social Sciences*, 1st edn., Vol. 3. Beverly Hills and London: Sage Publications.

Avlonitis, George J. (1980) 'An Exploratory Investigation of the Product Elimination Decision-Making Process in the UK Engineering Industry', unpublished PhD dissertation, University of Strathclyde, Glasgow.

Avlonitis, George J. (1983a) 'Improving Product Elimination in Engineering Companies', *Journal of General Management*, 9, 42–56.

Avlonitis, George J. (1983b) 'The Product Elimination Decision and Strategies', *Industrial Marketing Management*, 12, 31–43.

Avlonitis, George J. (1984) 'Industrial Product Elimination: Major Factors to Consider', *Industrial Marketing Management*, 13, 77–85.

Avlonitis, George J. (1985) 'Advisors and Decision-Makers in Product Eliminations', *Industrial Marketing Management*, 14, 17–26.

Avlonitis, George J. (1985) 'Product Elimination Decision Making: Does Formality Matter?', *Journal of Marketing*, 49, 41–52.

Avlonitis, George J. (1985) 'Revitilizing Weak Industrial Products', *Industrial Marketing Management*, 14, 93–105.

Avlonitis, George J. (1985) 'The Techno-Economic Ecology of the Product Elimination Process', *International Journal of Research in Marketing*, 2, 175–84.

Avlonitis, George J. (1986) 'The Identification of Weak Industrial Products', *European Journal of Marketing*, 20, 24–42.

Avlonitis, George J. (1986) 'The Management of the Product Elimination Function: Theoretical and Empirical Analysis', in *Advances in Business Marketing: a Research Annual*, Vol. 1, Arch G. Woodside, ed. Greenwich, Conn.: JAI Press, 1–66.

Avlonitis, George J. (1987) 'Linking Different Types of Product Elimination Decisions to Their Performance Outcome: "Project Dropstrat"', *International Journal of Research in Marketing*, 4, 43–57.

Avlonitis, George J. (1990) '"Project Dropstrat": Product Elimination and the Product Life Cycle Concept', *European Journal of Marketing*, 24, 55–67.

Avlonitis, George J. (1993) 'Project Dropstrat: What Factors Do Managers Consider in Deciding Whether to Drop a Project?', *European Journal of Marketing*, 27, 35–57.

Avlonitis, George J. and Bert G. S. James (1982) 'Some Dangerous Axioms of Product Elimination Decision-Making', *European Journal of Marketing*, 16, 36–48.

Ayal, Igal and Jehiel Zif (1978) 'Competitive Market Choice Strategies in Multinational Marketing', *Columbia Journal of World Business*, 72–81.

Ayal, Igal and Jehiel Zif (1979) 'Market Expansion Strategies in Multinational Marketing', *Journal of Marketing*, 43, 84–94.

Aylmer, R. J. (1970) 'Who Makes Marketing Decisions in the Multinational Firm?', *Journal of Marketing*, 34, 25–30.

Baccour, A. (1971) 'Product Deletion Decisions: a Systematic Approach and an Empirical Analysis', unpublished PhD dissertation, University of Illinois at Urbana Champaign.

Banville, G. R. and B. Pletcher (1974) 'The Product Elimination Function', *Journal of the Academy of Marketing Science*.

Bartlett, Christopher, A. (1986) 'Building and Managing the Transnational – the New Organizational Challenge', in *Competition in Global Industries*, Michael E. Porter, ed. Boston, Mass.: Harvard Business School Press, 367–401.

Bartlett, Christopher, A. and Sumantra Ghoshal (1987a) 'Managing Across Border – New Strategic Requirements', *Sloan Management Review*, 7–17.

Bartlett, Christopher, A. and Sumantra Ghoshal (1987b) 'Managing Across Borders – New Organizational Responses', *Sloan Management Review*, 43–53.

Bass, Frank M. (1969) 'A New Product Growth Model for Consumer Durables', *Management Science*, 15, 215–27.

Baumol, W. J. (1965) *Economic Theory and Operations Analysis*. Englewood Cliffs, NJ: Prentice Hall.

Bentler, P. M. (1994) *EQS: Structural Equations Program Manual*. Los Angeles: BMDP Statistical Software.

Berenson, C. (1963) 'Product Abandonment: a Forgotten Step in Innovation', in *Innovation – Key to Marketing Progress*, American Marketing Association.

Bilkey, Warren J. (1982) 'An Attempted Integration of the Literature on the Export Behaviour of Firms', *Journal of International Business Studies*, 33–46.

Bilkey, Warren, J. and G. Tesar (1977) 'The Export Behavior of Small-Sized Wisconsin Manufacturing Firms', *Journal of International Business Studies*, 8, 93–8.

Bollen, K. A. (1989) *Structural Equations with Latent Variables*. New York: John Wiley.

Bonoma, T. V. (1985) 'Case Research in Marketing-Opportunities, Problems and a Process', *Journal of Marketing Research*, XXII, 199–208.

Booz, Allen, and Hamilton (1982) *New Product Management for the 1980s*. New York: Booz Allen and Hamilton.

Borden, Neil, H. (1963) 'The Growing Problems of Product Line Planning', in *Readings in Marketing*, C. Dirksen J, A. Kroger, and L. Lockley C., eds. Homewood, IL: Irwin.

Borden, Neil, H. (1964) 'The Concept of Marketing-Mix', *Journal of Advertising Research*, 2–7.

Bowman, Douglas and Hubert Gatignon (1995) 'Determinants of Competitor Response Time to a New Product Introduction', *Journal of Marketing Research*, XXXII, 42–53.

Brems, H. (1951) *Product Equilibrium Under Monopolistic Competition*. Cambridge, Mass: Harvard University Press.

Brown, Shona L. and Kathleen M. Eisenhardt (1995) 'Product Development: Past Research, Present Findings, and Future Directions', *Academy of Management Review*, 20, 343–78.

Browne, W. G. and P. S. Kemp (1976) 'A Three-Stage Product Review Process', *Industrial Marketing Management*, 5, 333–42.

Brownlie, D., Michael Saren, R. Whittington and J. R. C. Wensley (1994) 'The New Marketing Myopia: Critical Perspectives on Theory and Research in Marketing – an Introduction', *European Journal of Marketing*, 28, 6–12.

Buckley, Peter J. (1990) 'Barriers to Internationalisation Process of the Firm', paper presented at the conference of strategic change, University of Venice, Italy.

Buckley, Peter J. and Pervez Ghauri (1993) 'Introduction and Overview', in *The Internationalisation of the Firm – a Reader*, Peter J. Buckley and Pervez Ghauri, eds. London: The Dryden Press.

Buckley, Peter, J. and M. Casson (1976) *The Future of the Multinational Enterprise*. London: Macmillan – now Palgrave Macmillan.

Buckley, Peter J., G. D. Newbould, and J. C. Thurwell (1979) *Foreign Direct Investment by Smaller UK Firms – the Success and Failure of First-Time Investors*. London: Macmillan – now Palgrave Macmillan.

Business Week (1992), 'Inside Intel', 1 June, 86–90, 92, 94.

Buskirk, R. H. (1966) *Principles of Marketing: the Management View*, rev. edn. New York: Rinehart and Winston.

Buzzell, Robert D. (1968) 'Can You Standardize Multinational Marketing?', *Harvard Business Review*, 102–13.

Byrne, Barbara M. (1994) *Structural Equation Modeling with EQS and EQS/Windows – Basic Concepts, Applications and Programming*. California: Sage.

Calantone, Roger J. and Robert G. Cooper (1979) 'A Discriminant Model for Identifying Scenarios of Industrial New Product Failure', *Journal of the Academy of Marketing Science*, 7, 163–83.

Calantone, Roger J. and Robert G. Cooper (1981) 'New Product Scenarios: Prospects for Success', *Journal of Marketing*, 45, 48–60.

Carpenter, G. S. and K. Nakamoto (1989) 'Consumer Preference Formation and Pioneering Advantage', *Journal of Marketing Research*, 26, 285–98.

Carpenter, Gregory S. and Kent Nakamoto (1994) 'Reflections on "Consumer Preference Formation and Pioneering Advantage"', *Journal of Marketing Research*, XXXI, 570–3.

Caves, R. E. (1982) *Multinational Enterprise and Economic Analysis*. London: Cambridge University Press.

Caves, Richard E. and Pankaj Ghemawat (1992) 'Identifying Mobility Barriers', *Strategic Management Journal*, 13, 1–12.

Cavusgil, S. Tamer (1980) 'On the Internationalisation Process of Firms', *European Research*, 273–81.

Cavusgil, S. Tamer and Shaoming Zou (1994) 'Marketing Strategy – Performance Relationship: an Investigation of the Empirical Link in Export Market Ventures', *Journal of Marketing*, 58, 1–21.

Chamberlin, E. H. (1933) *The Theory of Monopolistic Competition*. Cambridge, Mass.: Harvard University Press.

Chamberlin, E. H. (1957) *Towards a More General Theory of Value*. Oxford: Oxford University Press.

Chandler, A. D. (1962) *Strategy and Structure: Chapters in the History of the American Industrial Enterprise*. Cambridge, Mass.: MIT Press.

Chen, Ming-Jer, Ken G. Smith and Curtis M. Grimm (1992) 'Action Characteristics as Predictors of Competitive Responses', *Management Science*, 38, 439–55.

Chetty, Sylvie K. and R. T. Hamilton (1993) 'Firm-Level Determinants of Export Performance: A Meta-Analysis', *International Marketing Review*, 10, 26–34.

Chryssochoidis, George (2000) 'Repercussions of Consumer Confusion for Late Introduced Differentiated Products', in *European Journal of Marketing*, 34, 5/6, 705–22.

Chryssochoidis, George and Veronica Wong (1998a) 'Rolling Out New Products Across Country Markets: an Empirical Study of Causes of Delays', *Journal of Product Innovation Management*, 15, 1, 16–41.

Chryssochoidis, George and Veronica Wong (1998b) 'Modeling the Interactions between the Causes of Delays in Rolling Out New High-Tech Electronic Products Across Country Markets – a Refinement', in Christer Karlsson, Emilio Bartezzaghi, Harry Boer, Koenraad Debackere, Mike Gregory, Marco Iansiti and Jim Utterback (eds), *Proceedings of the 5th International Product Development Management Conference*, Como, EIASM and Politechnico di Milano, 25–26 May, 219–37.

Chryssochoidis, George and Veronica Wong (2000a) 'Customization of Product Technology and International New Product Success: Mediating Effects of New Product Development and Rollout Timeliness', in *Journal of Product Innovation Management*, 17, 4, 268–85.

Chryssochoidis, George and Veronica Wong (2000b) 'Service Innovation Multi-Country Launch: Causes of Delays', *European Journal of Innovation Management*, 3, 1, 35–44.

Chryssochoidis, George and Vasilis Theoharakis (in press) 'Attainment of Competitive Advantage by the Exporter–Importer Dyad: the Role of Export Offering and Import Objectives', in *Journal of Business Research*.

Churchill, Gilbert A. Jr and J. Paul Peter (1984) 'Research Design Effects on the Reliability of Rating Scales: a Meta-Analysis', *Journal of Marketing Research*, XXI, 360–75.

Clark, J. M. (1954) 'Competition and the Objectives of Government Policy', in *Monopoly and Competition and Their Regulation*, E. H. Chamberlin, ed. New York: Macmillan and Co.

Clark, Kim B. and T. Fujimoto (1991) *Product Development Performance*. Boston, Mass.: Harvard Business School.

Clark, Kim B., W. B. Chew and T. Fujimoto (1987) 'Product Development in the World Auto Industry', *Brookings Papers on Economic Activity*, 3, 729–81.

Clayton H. L. (1966) 'The Pruning of Sick Products', *Management Accounting* (USA), 17–8.

Cohen, Jacob and Patricia Cohen (1983) *Applied Multiple Regression/Correlation Analysis for the Behavioural Sciences*, 2nd edn. Hillsdale, NJ and London: Lawrence Erlbaum Associates.

Cook, T. D. and Campbell, D. T. (1979) *Quasi Experimentation: Design and Analysis for Field Settings*. Chicago: Rand McNally.

Cooper, Robert G. (1975) 'Why New Industrial Products Fail', *Industrial Marketing Management*, 4, 315–26.

Cooper, Robert G. (1979) 'The Dimensions of Industrial New Product Success and Failure', *Journal of Marketing*, 43, 93–103.

Cooper, Robert G. (1983a) 'The Impact of New Product Strategies', *Industrial Marketing Management*, 12, 243–56.

Cooper, Robert G. (1983b) 'The New Product Process: an Empirically-Based Classification Scheme', *R and D Management*, 13, 1–13.

Cooper, Robert G. (1984) 'The Performance Impact of Product Innovation Strategies', *European Journal of Marketing*, 18, 5–54.

Cooper, Robert G. (1985a) 'Industrial Firms' New Product Strategies', *Journal of Business Research*, 13, 107–21.

Cooper, Robert G. (1985b) 'Overall Corporate Strategies for New Product Programs', *Industrial Marketing Management*, 14, 179–93.

Cooper, Robert G. (1988) 'The New Product Process: a Decision Guide for Management', *Journal of Marketing Management*, 3, 238–55.

Cooper, Robert G. (1992) 'The Newprod System: the Industry Experience', *Journal of Product Innovation Management*, 9, 113–27.

Cooper, Robert G. (1994) 'New Products: the Factors that Drive Success', *International Marketing Review*, 11, 60–76.

Cooper, Robert G. and Elko J. Kleinschmidt (1987) 'Successful Factors in Product Innovation', *Industrial Marketing Management*, 16, 215–23.

Cooper, Robert G. and Elko J. Kleinschmidt (1991) 'New Product Processes at Leading Industrial Firms', *Industrial Marketing Management*, 20, 137–47.

Cooper, Robert G. and Elko J. Kleinschmidt (1993a) 'Major New Products: what Distinguishes the Winners in the Chemical Industry?', *Journal of Product Innovation Management*, 10, 90–111.

Cooper, Robert G. and Elko J. Kleinschmidt (1993b) 'New Product Success in the Chemical Industry', *Industrial Marketing Management*, 22, 85–99.

Cooper, Robert G. and Elko J. Kleinschmidt (1994) 'Determinants of Timeliness in Product Development', *Journal of Product Innovation Management*, 11, 381–96.

Cooper, Robert G. and Elko J. Kleinschmidt (1995a) 'New Product Performance: Keys to Success, Profitability and Cycle Time Reduction', *Journal of Marketing Management*, 11, 315–37.

Cooper, Robert G. and Elko J. Kleinschmidt (1995b) 'Performance Typologies of New Product Projects', *Industrial Marketing Management*, 24, 439–56.

Cordero, Rene (1991) 'Managing for Speed to Avoid Product Obsolescence: a Survey of Techniques', *Journal of Product Innovation Management*, 8, 283–94.

Craig, A. and S. J. Hart (1992) 'Where to Now in New Product Development Research?', *European Journal of Marketing*, 26, 3–49.

Cvar, M. (1984) 'Competitive Strategies in Global Industries', Harvard Business School, unpublished DBA dissertation.

Das, T. K. and Teng, B. S. (2000) 'A Resource-Based Theory of Strategic Alliances', *Journal of Management*, 26, 31–61.

David, P. (1985) 'Clio and the Economics of QWERTY', *American Economic Review*, 75, 332–7.

Davidson, W. H. and R. Harrigan (1977) 'Key Decisions in International Marketing: Introducing New Products Abroad', *Columbia Journal of World Business*, 15–23.

Davidson, W. H. and P. Haspeslagh (1982) 'Shaping a Global Product Organization', *Harvard Business Review*, 125–32.

Day, George S. (1977) 'Diagnosing the Product Portfolio', *Journal of Marketing*, 29–38.

De Brentani, Ulrike (1991) 'Success Factors in Developing New Business Services', *European Journal of Marketing*, 25, 33–59.

De Brentani, Ulrike and Emmanuel Ragot (1995), 'New Industrial Services: a Classical and Structural Model of the Factors that Determine Success', in *EMAC Proceedings*, Michelle Bergadaa, ed. Cergy-Pontoise: ESSEC, 177–96.

Debruyne, Marion, R. Moenaert, A. Griffin, S. Hart, E. J. Hultink and H. Robben (2002) 'The Impact of New Product Launch Strategies on Competitive Reaction in Industrial Markets', *Journal of Product Innovation Management*, 19, 2, 159–70.

Desphande, R. (1983) 'Paradigms Lost – on the Theory and Method in Research in Marketing', *Journal of Marketing*, 47, 101–10.

Dhebar, Anirudh (1995) 'Complementarity, Compatibility, and Product Change: Breaking with the Past?', *Journal of Product Innovation Management*, 12, 136–52.

Dosi, G. (1988) 'Sources, Procedures, and Microeconomic Effects of Innovation', *Journal of Economic Literature*, 26, 1120–71.

Dougherty, Deborah (1990) 'Understanding New Markets for New Products', *Strategic Management Journal*, 11, 59–78.

Dougherty, Deborah (1992a) 'A Practice-Centered Model of Organizational Renewal Through Product Innovation', *Strategic Management Journal*, 13, 77–92.

Dougherty, Deborah (1992b) 'Interpretive Barriers to Successful Product Innovation in Large Firms', *Organization Science*, 3, 179–202.

Douglas, S. P. and C. S. Craig (1989) 'Evolution of Global Marketing Strategy: Scale, Scope and Synergy', *Columbia Journal of World Business*, 24, 47–59.

Douglas, S. P. and C. S. Craig (1992) 'Advances in International Marketing', *International Journal of Research in Marketing*, 9, 291–318.

Douglas, S. P. and Rhee, D. K. (1989) 'Examining Generic Competitive Strategy Types in U.S. and European Markets', *Journal of International Business Studies*, 20, 437–63.

Doyle, Peter (1994) *Marketing Management and Strategy*. London: Prentice-Hall.

Doz, Yves L. and C. K. Prahalad (1991) 'Managing Dmncs – a Search for a New Paradigm', *Strategic Management Journal*, 12, 145–64.

Drucker, P. (1963) 'Managing for Business Performance', *Harvard Business Review*, 53–60.

Dumaine, B. (1989) 'How Managers Can Succeed Through Speed', *Fortune*, February, 13.

Dumaine, B. (1991) 'Closing the Innovation Gap', *Fortune*, 56–9, 62.

Dunning, John, H. (1980) 'Towards an Eclectic Theory of International Production: Some Empirical Tests', *Journal of International Business Studies*, 11, 9–31.

Dunning, John, H. (1988) 'The Eclectic Paradigm of International Production: a Restatement and Some Possible Extensions', *Journal of International Business Studies*, 1–31.

Dutton, J. E. and R. B. Duncan (1987) 'The Creation of Momentum for Change Through the Process of Strategic Diagnosis', *Strategic Management Journal*, 8, 279–95.

Dwyer, L. and R. Mellor (1991) 'Organizational Environment, New Product Process Activities, and Project Outcomes', *Journal of Product Innovation Management*, 8, 39–48.

Eckles, R. W. (1971) 'The Product Deletion System', unpublished DBA thesis, Washington University.

Edström, A. and J. R. Galbraith (1977) 'Transfer of Managers as a Coordination and Control Strategy in Multinational Organizations', *Administrative Science Quarterly*, 22, 248–63.

Egelhoff, William G. (1988) 'Strategy and Structure in Multinational Corporations: a Revision of the Stopford and Wells Model', *Strategic Management Journal*, 9, 1–14.

Eisenhardt, Kathleen M. (1989) 'Building Theories from Case Study Research', *Academy of Management Review*, 14, 532–50.

Eisenhardt, Kathleen M. (1989) 'Making Fast Decisions in High-Velocity Environments', *Academy of Management Journal*.

Eisenhardt, Kathleen M. and B. Tabrizi (1995) 'Accelerating Adaptive Processes: Product Innovation in the Global Computer Industry', *Administrative Science Quarterly*, 40, 84–110.

Elinder, Eric (1964) 'How International Can Advertising Be?', in *International Handbook of Advertising*, Watson S. Dunn, ed. New York: McGraw-Hill, 59–71.

Erez, M., P. C. Earley, and C. L. Hulin (1985), 'The Impact of Participation on Goal Acceptance and Performance: a Two-step Model', *Academy of Management Journal*, 28, 1, 50–65.

Evans, R. H. (1977) 'Adding Soft Data to Product Elimination Decisions', *Industrial Marketing Management*, 6.

Farrell, J. and G. Saloner (1985) 'Standardization, Compatibility, and Innovation', *Rand Journal of Economics*, 16, 70–83.

Fatt, Arthur C. (1967) 'The Danger of "Local" International Marketing', *Journal of Marketing*, 31, 60–2.

Fiske, Susan and Shelley Taylor E. (1984) *Social Cognition*. New York: Random House.

Fluitman, L. P. (1973) 'The Necessity of an Industrial Product-Mix Analysis', *Industrial Marketing Management*, 2, 345–52.

Ford, David Igor and Leonidas Leonidou (1991) 'Research Developments in International Marketing – a European Perspective', in *New Perspectives on International Marketing*, Stanley Paliwoda, ed. London: Routledge, 3–32.

Forrester, Jay W. (1958) 'Industrial Dynamics: a Major Breakthrough for Decision Makers', *Harvard Business Review*, 26.

Forrester, Jay W. and Peter M. Senge (1980) 'Tests for Building Confidence in System Dynamics Models', in *System Dynamics*, Vol. 14, A. A. Legasto Jr, Jay W. Forrester and J. M. Lyneis, eds, [Studies in the Management Sciences]. Amsterdam, New York, Oxford: North-Holland Publishing, 209–28.

Franko, L. G. (1976) *The European Multinationals: a Renewed Challenge to American and British Big Business*. Stamford, Conn.: Greylock.

Gabowski, H. and D. Mueller (1972) 'Managerial and Stockholder Welfare Model of Firm Expenditures', *Review of Economics and Statistics*, 52, 9–24.

Galbraith, J. R. (1973) *Designing Complex Organizations*. Reading, Mass.: Addison-Wesley.

Galbraith, J. R. and R. K. Kazanjian (1986) *Strategy Implementation: Structure, Systems and Process*. St Paul, Minn.: West Publishing.

Gatignon, Hubert and Erin Anderson (1988) 'The Multinational Corporations's Degree of Control Over Foreign Subsidiaries: an Empirical Test of a Transaction Cost Explanation', *Journal of Law, Economics, and Organization*, 4, 305–36.

Gatignon, Hubert and Thomas S. Robertson (1985) 'A Propositional Inventory for New Diffusion Research', *Journal of Consumer Research*, 11, 849–67.

Gatignon, H. and J. M. Xuereb (1997) 'Strategic orientation of the firm and new product performance', *Journal of Marketing Research*, 34, 77–90.

Gatignon, Hubert, Erin Anderson and Kristiaan Helsen (1989) 'Competitive Reactions to Market Entry: Explaining Interfirm Differences', *Journal of Marketing Research*, XXVI, 44–55.

Gatignon, H. A., J. Eliashberg and T. S. Robertson (1989) 'Modeling Multi-national Diffusion Patterns: an Efficient Methodology', *Marketing Science*, 8, 231–47.

Gauthier J. P. (1985) 'The Product Elimination Process in French Manufacturing Companies: a Theoretical and Empirical Analysis', unpublished MSc thesis, Department of Marketing, University of Strathclyde, Glasgow.

Geertz C. A. (1973) *The Interpretation of Cultures*. New York: Basic Books.

Gerstenfeld, A. (1976) 'A Study of Successful Projects, Unsuccessful Projects and Projects in Process in West Germany', *IEEE Transactions in Engineering Management*, 23, 116–23.

Ghemawat, Pankaj (1979) 'Sustainable Advantage', in *Strategy: Seeking and Securing Competitive Advantage*, Cynthia A. Montgomery and Michael E. Porter, eds. Boston, Mass.: Harvard Business School Publishing Division, 27–38.

Ghoshal, Sumantra (1987) 'Global Strategy: an Organizing Framework', *Strategic Management Journal*, 8, 425–40.

Ghoshal, Sumantra and Christopher A. Bartlett (1988) 'Creation, Adoption, and Diffusion of Innovations by Subsidiaries of Multinational Corporations', *Journal of International Business Studies*, 365–88.

Ghoshal, Sumantra and Nitin Nohria (1989) 'Internal Differentiation Within Multinational Corporations', *Strategic Management Journal*, 10, 323–37.

Ghoshal, Sumantra and Nitin Nohria (1993) 'Horses for Courses: Organizational Forms for Multinational Corporations', *Sloan Management Review*, 23–35.

Ghoshal, Sumantra, Harry Korine, and Gabriel Szulanski (1994) 'Interunit Communication in Multinational Corporations', *Management Science*, 40, 96–110.

Ginsberg, A. (1988) 'Measuring and Modelling Changes in Strategy: Theoretical Foundations and Empirical Directions', *Strategic Management Journal*, 9, 559–75.

Glaser, B. and A. L. Strauss (1967) *The Discovery of Grounded Theory*. Archive Publishing.

Golder, Peter N. (2000) 'Insights from Senior Executives about Innovation in International Markets', *Journal of Product Innovation Management*, 17, 326–40.

Griffin, Abbie and Albert L. Page (1993) 'An Interim Report on Measuring Product Development Success and Failure', *Journal of Product Innovation Management*, 10, 291–308.

Gupta, Ashok K. and David L. Wilemon (1990) 'Accelerating the Development of Technology-Based New Products', *California Management Review*, 32, 24–44.

Gupta, Ashok K. and David Wilemon (1991) 'Improving R&D/Marketing Relations in Technology-Based Companies: Marketing's Perspective', *Journal of Marketing Management*, 7, 25–45.

Gupta, Ashok K. and V. Govindarajan (1991) 'Knowledge Flows and the Structure of Control Within Multinational Corporations', *Academy of Management Review*, 16, 768–92.

Gupta, Ashok K., S. P. Raj and David Wilemon (1986) 'A Model for Studying R&D – Marketing Interface in the Product Innovation Process', *Journal of Marketing*, 50, 7–17.

Hair, Joseph F., Rolph E. Anderson, Ronald L. Tatham and William C. Black (1995) *Multivariate Data Analysis*, 4th edn., Englewood Cliffs, NJ: Prentice Hall.

Hallaq, John H. (1976) 'Optimal Product Replacement: a Computer Model', *Journal of the Academy of Marketing Science*, 4, 407–17.

Hambrick, D. C. (1980) 'Operationalising the Concept of Business-Level Strategy in Research', *Academy of Management Review*, 5, 567–75.

Hamelman, P. H. and E. M. Mazze (1972) 'Improving Product Abandonment', *Journal of Marketing*, 20–6.

Harrigan, Kathryn Rudie (1983) 'Research Methodologies for Contingency Approaches to Business Strategy', *Academy of Management Review*, 8, 398–405.

Hart, Susan J. (1988) 'The Causes of Product Deletion in British Manufacturing Companies', *Journal of Marketing Management*, 3, 328–43.

Hart, Susan J. (1989) 'Product Deletion and the Effects of Strategy', *European Journal of Marketing*, 23, 6–17.

Hart, Susan J. (1990) 'The Managerial Setting of the Product Deletion Decision', *Irish Marketing Review*, 5, 41–56.

Hart, Susan J. (1996) 'Introduction and Overview', in *New Product Development – a Reader*. London: The Dryden Press.

Hart, Susan J. and Michael J. Baker (1994) 'The Multiple Convergent Model of New Product Development', *International Marketing Review*, 11, 77–92.

Hayes, R. H., Steven C. Wheelwright, and Kim B. Clark (1988) *Dynamic Manufacturing*. New York: The Free Press.

Heckscher, Eli (1919) 'The Effect of Foreign Trade on the Distribution of Income', reprinted in 1949 as Ch. 13, in *Readings in the Theory of International Trade*, American Economic Association. Philadelphia: Blakiston.

Hedlund, G. (1986) 'The Hypermodern MNC – a Heterarchy?', *Human Resource Management*, 9–35.

Heil, O. P. and R. G. Walters (1993) 'Explaining Competitive Reactions to New Products: an Empirical Signalling Study', *Journal of Product Innovation Management*, 10, 53–65.

Heil, Oliver and Robertson Thomas, S. (1991) 'Toward a Theory of Competitive Market Signalling: a Research Aganda', *Strategic Management Journal*, 12, 403–18.

Hennart, Jean-François (1982) *A Theory of the Multinational Enterprise*. Ann Arbor: University of Michigan Press.

Hill, J. S. and W. L. James (1991) 'Product and Promotion Transfers in Consumer Goods Multinationals', *International Marketing Review*, 8, 6–17.

Hill, J. S. and R. R. Still (1984) 'Adapting Products to LDC Tastes', *Harvard Business Review*, 92–101.

Hill, J. S. and Upknown (1992) 'Product Mixes in US Multinationals', *Journal of Global Marketing*, 6, 55–73.

Hise, R. T. and McGinnis, M. A. (1975) 'Product Elimination: Practices, Policies and Ethics', *Business Horizons*, 25–32.

Hise, R. T., A. Parasuraman and R. Viswanathan (1984) 'Product Elimination: a Neglected Management Responsibility', *Journal of Business Strategy*.

Hise, R. T., L. O'Neal, A. Parasuraman and J. U. McNeal (1990) 'Marketing/R&D Interaction in New Product Development: Implications for New Product Success Rates', *Journal of Product Innovation Management*, 7, 142–55.

Hisrich, Robert D. and Michael P. Peters (1991) *Marketing Decisions for New and Mature Products*, 2nd edn. New York: Macmillan.

Houfek, L. J. (1952) 'How Do You Decide Which Products to Junk', *Printers Ink*, 21–3.

Hout, Thomas, Michael E. Porter and Eileen Rudden (1982) 'How Global Companies Win Out', *Harvard Business Review*, 98–108.

Hultink, E. J. and Atuahene-Gima, Kwuaku (2000) 'The Effect of Sales Force Adoption on New Product Selling Performance', *Journal of Product Innovation Management*, 17, 435–450.

Hultink, Erik, J., Griffin, A., Hart, S. and Robben, H. S. J. (1997) 'Industrial New Product Launch Strategies and Product Development Performance', *Journal of Product Innovation Management*, 14(4), 243–57.

Hultink. E. J and S. Hart (1998) 'The World's Path to the Better Mousetrap – Myth or Reality', *European Journal of Innovation Management*, 3, 106–122.

Hultink, E. J. and Fred Langerak (2002) 'Launch Decisions and Competitive Reactions: an Exploratory Market Signaling Study', *Journal of Product innovation Management*, 19, 3, 199–212.

Hultink, E. J. and H. S. J. Robben (1999) 'Launch Strategy and New Product Performance: an Empirical Examination in The Netherlands', *Journal of Product Innovation Management*, 16, 6, 545–56.

Iansiti, M. (1992), 'Science-Based Product Development: an Empirical Study of the Mainframe Computer Industry', working paper, Harvard Business School, Cambridge, Mass.

Iansiti, M. (1993) 'Real-World R&D: Jumping the Product Generation Gap', *Harvard Business Review*, 71, 138–47.

Imai, K., N. Ikujiro and H. Takeutchi (1985) 'Managing the New Product Development Process – How Japanese Companies Learn and Unlearn', in *The Uneasy Alliance: Managing the Productivity – Technology Dilemma*, R. Hayes, H. K. Clark and Lorenz, eds. Boston, Mass.: Harvard Business School Press.

Jacobson, R. (1988) 'Distinguishing among Competing Theories of the Market Share Effect', *Journal of Marketing*, 52, 68–80.

Jain, S. C. (1989) 'Standardization of International Marketing Strategy', *Journal of Marketing*, 53, 70–9.

James, W. L. and J. S. Hill (1993) 'MNC Product and Promotion Transfers: a Cluster Analysis of Executive Perceptions and Linkages to Environmental Conditions and Subsidiary Strategies', *Journal of Global Marketing*, 7, 51–74.

Jarillo, J. C. and J. I. Martinez (1990) 'Different Roles for Subsidiaries: the Case of Multinational Corporations in Spain', *Strategic Management Journal*, 11, 501–12.

Jauch, Lawrence R., Richard N. Osborn and Thomas N. Martin (1980) 'Structured Content Analysis of Cases: a Complementary Method for Organisational Research', *Academy of Management Review*, 5.

Johanson, J. and J.-E. Vahlne (1977) 'The Internationalisation Process of the Firm: a Model of Knowledge Development and Increasing Foreign Market Commitment', *Journal of International Business Studies*, 8, 23–32.

Johanson, J. and J.-E. Vahlne (1990) 'The Mechanism of Internationalisation', *International Marketing Review*, 7, 11–24.

Johanson, J. and Wiederscheim-Paul (1975) 'The Internationalisation Process of the Firm – Four Swedish Case Studies', *Journal of Management Studies*, 305–22.

Johansson, Johny K. and George S. Yip (1994) 'Exploiting Globalization Potential: US and Japanese Strategies', *Strategic Management Journal*, 15, 579–601.

Johne, F. A. (1984) 'The Organisation of High-Technology Product Innovation', *European Journal of Marketing*, 18, 55–71.

Johne, F. A. and P. A. Snelson (1989) 'Product Development Approaches in Established Firms', *Industrial Marketing Management*, 18, 113–24.

Kahneman, D., J. L. Knetsch and R. Thaler (1986a) 'Fairness and the Assumptions of Economics', *Journal of Business*, 59, 285–354.

Kahneman, D., J. L. Knetsch and R. Thaler (1986b) 'Fairness as a Constrain on Profit Seeking', *American Economic Review*, 76, 728–41.

Kalish, Shlomo, Mahajan, Vijay and Muller, Eitan (1995) 'Waterfall and Sprinkler – New Product Strategies in Competitive Global Markets', *International Journal of Research in Marketing*, July, 105–19.

Karakaya, Fahri (1993) 'Barriers to Entry in International Markets', *Journal of Global Marketing*, 7, 7–24.

Kardes, Frank R. and Gurumurthy Kalyanaram (1992) 'Order-of-Entry Effects on Consumer Memory and Judgment: an Information Integration Perspective', *Journal of Marketing Research*, XXIX, 343–57.

Katz, R. (1982) 'The Effects of Group Longevity on Project Communication and Performance', *Administrative Science Quarterly*, 27, 81–104.

Katz, R. and Tushman, M. L. (1981) 'An Investigation into the Managerial Roles and Career Paths of Gatekeepers and Project Supervisors in a Major R&D Facility', *R and D Management*, 11, 103–10.

Keegan, Warren J. (1969) 'Multinational Product Planning – Strategic Alternatives', *Journal of Marketing*, 33, 58–62.

Keller, R. T. (1986) 'Predictors of the Performance of Project Groups in R&D Organizations', *Academy of Management Journal*, 29, 715–26.

Kent, R. (1984) 'Marketing Faith and Marketing Practice: a Study of Product Range in the Scottish Food Processing Industry', unpublished MSc thesis, Department of Marketing, University of Strathclyde, Glasgow.

Kerin, R. A., P. R. Varadarajan and R. A. Peterson (1992) 'First-Mover Advantage: a Synthesis, Conceptual Framework, and Research Propositions', *Journal of Marketing*, 56, 33–52.

Kerin, Roger A., Vijay Mahajan and Rajan P. Varadarajan (1990) *Contemporary Perspectives on Strategic Market Planning*. Needham Heights, Mass.: Allyn and Bacon.

Kerlinger, F. (1973) *Foundations of Behaviour Research*, 2nd edn.: Holt, Rinehart and Winston.

Kim, Chan W., P. Hwang and W. P. Burgers (1989) 'Global Diversification Strategy and Corporate Profit Performance', *Strategic Management Journal*, 10, 45–57.

Kirpalani, W. H. and Macintosh, N. B. (1980) 'International Effectiveness of Technology-Oriented Small Firms', *Journal of International Business Studies*, 81–90.

Kobrin, Stephen J. (1991) 'An Empirical Analysis of the Determinants of Global Integration', *Strategic Management Journal*, 12, 17–31.

Kogut, Bruce (1985a) 'Designing Global Strategies: Comparative and Competitive Value-Added Chains', *Sloan Management Review*, 26, 34–43.

Kogut, Bruce (1985b) 'Designing Global Strategies: Profiting from Operational Flexibility', *Sloan Management Review*, 26, 27–37.

Kogut, Bruce (1989) 'A Note on Global Strategies', *Strategic Management Journal*, 10, 383–9.

Kotabe, Masaaki (1990) 'Corporate Product Policy and Innovative Behavior of European and Japanese Multinationals: an Empirical Investigation', *Journal of Marketing*, 43, 19–33.

Kotler, Philip (1965) 'Phasing-Out Weak Products', *Harvard Business Review*, 108–18.

Kotler, Philip (1974) 'Marketing During Periods of Shortages', *Journal of Marketing*, 20–9.

Kotter, J. (1982) *The General Managers*. New York: The Free Press.

Kratchman, S. H., R. T. Hise and T. A. Ulrich (1975) 'Management's Decision to Discontinue a Product', *The Journal of Accountancy*, 50–4.

Kreutzer, R. T. (1988) 'Marketing-Mix Standardisation: an Integrated Approach in Global Marketing', *European Journal of Marketing*, 22, 19–30.

Kriger, M. P. and E. E. Solomon (1992) 'Strategic Mindsets and Decision-Making Autonomy in US and Japanese MNCs', *Management International Review*, 32, 327–43.

Kulvik, H. (1977) *Factors Underlying the Success and Failure of New Products*, Report No 29. Helsinki, Finland: University of Technology.

Lambkin, Mary (1988) 'Order of Entry and Performance in New Markets', *Strategic Management Journal*, 9, 127–40.

Langley, Ann and Jean Truax (1994) 'A Process Study of New Technology Adoption in Smaller Manufacturing Firms', *Journal of Management Studies*, 31, 619–52.

Lawrence, Paul R. and Jay W. Lorsch (1967) 'Organization and Environment', Boston: Harvard Graduate School of Business Administration.

Learned, E. P., C. Christensen, K. R. Andrews and E. Guth (1965) *Business Policy*. Homewood, IL: Irwin.

Legasto, Augusto A. Jr, Jay W. Forrester and James M. Lyneis (eds) (1980) *System Dynamics: Studies in the Management Sciences*, Vol. 14. Amsterdam, New York, Oxford: North-Holland Publishing.

Lemak, David J. and Jeffrey S. Bracker (1988) 'A Strategy Contingency Model of Multinational Corporate Structure', *Strategic Management Journal*, 9, 521–6.

Leontief, W. W. (1954) 'Domestic Production and Foreign Trade: the American Capital Position Re-Examined', *Economia Internazionale*, 7, 3–32, reprinted in *Readings in International Economics*, American Economic Association, 1968. Homewood, Ill.: Richard D. Irwin.

Levitt, T. (1983) 'The Globalisation of Markets', *Harvard Business Review*, 92–102.

Lilien, Gary L. and Eunsang Yoon (1989) 'Determinants of New Industrial Product Performance: a Strategic Reexamination of the Empirical Literature', *IEEE Transactions in Engineering Management*, 36, 3–10.

Lilien, Gary L. and Eunsang Yoon (1990) 'The Timing of Competitive Market Entry: an Exploratory Study of New Industrial Products', *Management Science*, 36, 568–85.

Linder, Staffan (1961) *An Essay on Trade and Transformation*. New York: John Wiley.

Littler, Dale (1994) 'Marketing and Innovation', in *The Handbook of Industrial Innovation*, Mark Dodgson and Roy Rothwell, eds. Aldershot: Edward Elgar, 293–300.

Lutz, James M. and Robert T. Green (1983) 'The Product Life Cycle and the Export Position of the United States', *Journal of International Business Studies*, 14, 77–93.

Mabert, Vincent A., John F. Muth, and Roger W. Schmenner (1992) 'Collapsing New Product Development Times: Six Case Studies', *Journal of Product Innovation Management*, 9, 200–12.

Macmillan, I. C., M. McCaffery L., and G. Vanwijk (1985) 'Competitors' Responses to Easily Imitated New Products – Exploring Commercial Banking Product Introductions', *Strategic Management Journal*, 6, 75–86.

Madsen, T. K. (1987) 'Expirical Export Performance Studies – a Review of Conceptualizations', in *Advances in International Marketing – A Research Annual*, Vol. 2, S. Tamer Cavusgil, ed. Conn.: JAI Press, 177–98.

Mahajan, Vijay, Subhash Sharma and Yoram Wind (1984) 'Parameter Estimation in Marketing Models in the Presence of Influencial Response Data: Robust Regression and Applications', *Journal of Marketing Research*, XXI, 268–77.

Mahajan, Vijay and Robert A. Peterson (1985) *Models for Innovation Diffusion*. Beverly Hills, CA: Sage.

Mahajan, Vijay and Jerry Wind (1992) 'New Product Models: Practice, Shortcomings and Desired Improvements', *Journal of Product Innovation Management*, 9, 128–39.

Mahajan, Vijay, Eitan Muller and Frank M. Bass (1990) 'New Product Diffusion Models in Marketing: a Review and Directions for Research', *Journal of Marketing*, 54, 1–26.

Mahajan, Vijay, Eitan Muller and Frank M. Bass (1993) 'New-Product Diffusion Models', in *Handbooks in OR and MS*, Vol. 5, J. Eliashberg and G. L. Lilien, eds New York: Elsevier Science Publishers.

Mahajan, Vijay, Eitan Muller and Frank M. Bass (1995) 'Diffusion of New Products: Empirical Generalizations and Managerial Uses', *Marketing Science*, 14, G79–88.

Maidique, Modesto A. and Billie Jo Zirger (1984) 'A Study of Success and Failure in Product Innovation: the Case of the U.S. Electronics Industry', *IEEE Transactions in Engineering Management*, 4, 192–203.

Maidique, Modesto A. and Billie Jo Zirger (1985) 'The New Product Learning Cycle', *Research Policy*, 14, 299–313.

Mansfield, Edwin (1982) *Technology Transfer, Productivity, and Economic Policy*. New York: Norton.

Mansfield, Edwin *et al.*, (1972) *Research and Innovation in the Modern Corporation*. London: Macmillan – now Palgrave Macmillan.

Manu, Franklyn, A. (1992) 'Innovation, Orientation, Environment and Performance: A Comparison of U.S. and European Markets', *Journal of International Business Studies*, 23, 333–59.

Marshall, Alfred (1930) *Pure Theory of Foreign Trade*. London: London School of Economics and Political Science. (First published in 1879.)

Martinez, J. I. and J. C. Jarillo (1989) 'The Evolution of Research on Coordination Mechanisms in Multinational Corporations', *Journal of International Business Studies*, 489–514.

Martinez, J. I. and J. C. Jarillo (1991) 'Coordination Demands of International Strategies', *Journal of International Business Studies*, 429–44.

Mascarenhas, B. (1992a) 'First Mover Effects in Multiple Dynamic Markets', *Strategic Management Journal*, 13, 237–43.

Mascarenhas, B. (1992b) 'Order of Entry and Performance in International Markets', *Strategic Management Journal*, 13, 499–510.

McClintock, Charles C., Diane Brannon and Maynard Steven Moody (1979) 'Applying the Logic of Sample Surveys to Qualitative Case Studies: the Case Cluster Method', *Administrative Science Quarterly*, 24.

McGee, John and Howard Thomas (1988) 'Making Sense of Complex Industries', in *Strategies in Global Competition*, Neil Hood and Jan-Erik Vahlne, eds. London: Croom Helm.

McSurely, H. B. and David L. Wilemon (1973) 'A Product Evaluation, Improvement and Removal Model', *Industrial Marketing Management*, 2.

Meadows, Donella, H. (1980) 'The Unavoidable a Priori', in *Elements of the System Dynamics Method*, Jorgen Randers, ed. Cambridge, Mass, and London: The MIT Press.

Michael, G. C. (1971) 'Product Petrification – a New Stage in the Life Cycle Theory', *California Management Review*, 38–41.

Miesenbock, K., J. (1988) 'Small Business and Exporting – a Literature Review', *International Small Business Journal*, 6, 42–61.

Miles, Matthew B. (1979) 'Qualitative Data as an Attractive Nuisance – the Problem of Analysis', *Administrative Science Quarterly*, 24, 590–601.

Miles, M. B. and A. M. Huberman (1984) *Qualitative Data Analysis: a Sourcebook of New Methods*. Beverly Hills, CA: Sage.

Miles, R. E. and C. Snow (1978) *Organisational Strategy, Structure, and Process*. New York: McGraw-Hill.

Miller, Danny and Cornelia Dröge (1986) 'Psychological and Traditional Determinants of Structure', *Administrative Science Quarterly*, 31, 539–60.

Millson, Murray R., S. P. Raj and David Wilemon (1992) 'A Survey of Major Approaches for Accelerating New Product Development', *Journal of Product Innovation Management*, 9, 53–69.

Mintzberg, Henry (1978) 'Patterns in Strategy Formation', *Management Science*, 24, 934–48.

Mintzberg, Henry (1983) *Power in and Around Organizations*. Englewood Cliffs, NJ: Prentice-Hall.

Montoya-Weiss, Mitzi M. and Roger J. Calantone (1994) 'Determinants of New Product Performance: a Review and Meta-Analysis', *Journal of Product Innovation Management*, 11, 397–417.

Moon, Junyean and Haksik Lee (1990) 'On the Internal Correlates of Export Stage Development: an Empirical Investigation in the Korean Electronics Industry', *International Marketing Review*, 7, 16–26.

Morrison, A. J. and Kendall Roth (1992) 'A Taxonomy of Business-Level Strategies in Global Industries', *Strategic Management Journal*, 13, 399–418.

Mullor-Sebastian, Alice (1983) 'The Product-Life Cycle Theory', *Journal of International Business Studies*, 14, 95–105.

Myers, S. and D. G. Marquis (1969) *'Successful Industrial Innovations'*, NSF 69–17. Washington, DC: National Science Foundation.

Nelson, R. and S. Winter (1977) *An Evolutionary Theory of Economic Change*. Cambridge: Belknap Press.

Nicholson, W. (1978) *Microeconomic Theory*, 2nd edn. New York: The Dryden Press.

Nunnally, Jum C. (1978) *Psychometric Theory*, 2nd edn. New York: McGraw-Hill.

Oackley, Paul (1996) 'High-Tech NPD Success Through Faster Overseas Launch', *European Journal of Marketing*, 30, 8.

Ohlin, Bertil (1933) *Interregional and International Trade*. Cambridge, Mass.: Harvard University Press.

Ohmae, Kenichi (1991) 'Managing in a Borderless World', in *Strategy: Seeking and Securing Competitive Advantage*, Cynthia A. Montgomery and Michael E. Porter, eds. Boston, Mass.: Harvard Business School Publishing Division, 205–21.

Olson, Eric M., Orville C. Jr Walker and Robert W. Ruekert (1995) 'Organizing for Effective New Product Development: The Moderating Role of Product Innovativeness', *Journal of Marketing*, 59, 48–62.

Olugosa, S. A. (1993) 'Market Concentration Versus Market Diversification and Internationalization: Implications for MNE Performance', *International Marketing Review*, 10, 40–59.

Onkvisit, Sak and John J. Shaw (1983) 'An Examination of the International Product Life Cycle and Its Application within Marketing', *Columbia Journal of World Business*, 73–9.

Papandreou, A. G. (1952) 'Some Basic Problems in the Theory of the Firm', in *A Survey of Contemporary Economics*, B. F. Haley, Ed. Englewood Cliffs, NJ: Prentice Hall, 183–222.

Parry, Mark and Frank M. Bass (1990) 'When to Lead Or Follow? It Depends', *Marketing Letters*, 1, 187–98.

Parry, Mark E. and Michael X. Song (1993) 'Determinants of R&D-Marketing Integration in High-Tech Japanese Firms', *Journal of Product Innovation Management*, 10, 4–22.

Patterson, M. L. (1990) 'Accelerating Innovation: a Dip Into the Mem Pool', *National Productivity Review*, 9, 409–18.

Pennings, Enrico and Lint, Otto (2000) 'Market Entry, phased Rollout or Abandonment? a Real Option Approach', *European Journal of Operational Research*, 124, 125–138.

Penrose, E. T. (1959) *The Theory of the Growth of the Firm*. New York: John Wiley.

Perlmutter, Howard V. (1969) 'The Tortuous Evolution of the Multinational Corporation', *Columbia Journal of World Business*, 4, 9–18.

Peter, J. Paul (1979) 'Reliability – a Review of Psychometric Basics and Recent Marketing Practices', *Journal of Marketing Research*, 16, 6–17.

Peterson, Robert A. (1994) 'A Meta-Analysis of Cronbach's Coefficient Alpha', *Journal of Consumer Research*, 21, 381–91.

Pettigrew, Andrew (1993) 'Contextualist Research', Speech at the Annual Conference of the British Academy of Management, Milton Keynes.

Pfeffer, J. (1982) *Organizations and Organization Theory*. Marshfield, MA: Pitman.

Porter, Michael E. (1980) *Competitive Strategy*. New York: The Free Press.

Porter, Michael E. (1985) *Competitive Advantage – Creating and Sustaining Superior Performance*. New York: The Free Press.

Porter, Michael E. ed. (1986) *Competition in Global Industries*. Boston, Mass.: Harvard Business School Press.

Prahalad, C. K. (1975) 'The Strategic Process in a Multinational Corporation', doctoral dissertation, Boston: Harvard Business School.

Prescott, J. E. (1983) 'Competitive Environments, Strategic Types and Business Performance: an Empirical Analysis', unpublished PhD Dissertation, Pennsylvania State University.

Quinn, J. B. (1985) 'Managing Innovation: Controlled Chaos', *Harvard Business Review*, 63, 73–84.

Rackham, Neil (1998) 'From Experience: Why Bad Things Happen to Good New Products' *Journal of Product Innovation Management*, 15, 3, 201–7.

Randers, Jorgen (ed.) (1980) 'Guidelines for Model Conceptualization', in *Elements of the System Dynamics Method*, Jorgen Randers, ed. Cambridge, Mass. and London: The MIT Press, 117–39.

Rao, T. R. and G. M. Naidu (1992) 'Are the Stages of Internationalization Empirically Supportable?', *Journal of Global Marketing*, 6, 147–70.

Reid, Stanley D. (1981) 'The Decision-Maker and Export Entry and Expansion', *Journal of International Business Studies*, 101–12.

Reid, Stanley D. (1984) 'Market Expansion and Firm Internationalisation', in *International Marketing Management*, Erdener Kaynak, ed. New York: Praeger.

Ricardo, David (1817) '*The Principles of Political Economy and Taxation*'. (A recent edition is published by Cambridge: Cambridge University Press, 1981.)

Robertson, Thomas S. and Hubert Gatignon (1986) 'Competitive Effects on Technology Diffusion', *Journal of Marketing*, 50, July, 1–12.

Robinson, William T. and C. Fornell (1985) 'Sources of Market Pioneer Advantages in Consumer Goods Industries', *Journal of Marketing Research*, XXII, 305–17.

Rogers, Everett M. (1983) *Diffusion of Innovations*, 3rd edn. New York: The Free Press.

Ronkainen, Ilkka A. (1983) 'Product Development in the Multinational Firm', *International Marketing Review*, 1, Winter, 24–30.

Rosenzweig, P. M. and J. V. Singh (1991) 'Organizational Environments and the Multinational Enterprise', *Academy of Management Review*, 16, 340–61.

Roth, Kendall (1992) 'International Configuration and Coordination Archetypes for Medium-Sized Firms in Global Industries', *Journal of International Business Studies*, 533–49.

Roth, Kendall, D. M. Schweiger and A. J. Morrison (1991) 'Global Strategy Implementation at the Business Unit Level: Operational Capabilities and Administrative Mechanisms', *Journal of International Business Studies*, 369–402.

Rothe, J. T. (1970) 'The Product Elimination Decision', *MSU Business Topics*, 45–52.

Rothwell, Roy (1972) *Factors for Success in Industrial Innovations from Project SAPPHO – a Comparative Study of Success and Failure in Industrial Innovation*. Brighton: SPRU.

Rothwell, Roy, C. Freeman, A. Horsley, V. Jervis, T. A. Robertson and J. Townsend (1974) 'SAPPHO Updated-Research Sappho Phase II', *Research Policy*, 3, 258–91.

Salerno, F. (1983) 'Processus et Comportements D'abandon de Produit: analyse et Implications', unpublished Thèse De Doctorat D'Etat Es Sciences De Gestion, Universite De Lille.

Samiee, Saeed (1994) 'Customer Evaluation of Products in a Global Market', *Journal of International Business Studies*, 579–604.

Samiee, Saeed and Kendall Roth (1992) 'The Influence of Global Marketing Standardisation on Performance', *Journal of Marketing*, 56, 1–17.

Samli, Coskun A., James R. Wills and Laurence Jacobs (1993) 'Developing Global Products and Marketing Strategies: a Rejointer', *Journal of the Academy of Marketing Science*, 21, 79–83.

Saunders, John and David Jobber (1988) 'An Exploratory Study of the Management of Product Replacement', *Journal of Marketing Management*, 3, 344–51.

Saunders, John and David Jobber (1994) 'Product Replacement: Strategies for Simultaneous Product Deletion and Launch', *Journal of Product Innovation Management*, 11, 433–50.

Schender, B. R. (1992) 'How Sony Keeps the Magic Going', *Fortune*, 76–9, 82, 84.

Scherer, F. M. and D. Ross (1990) *Industrial Market Structure and Economic Performance*. Boston, Mass.: Houghton Mifflin.

Schmalensee, R. (1982) 'Product Differentiation Advantages of Pioneering Brands', *American Economic Review*, 72, 350–71.

Selltiz, C. L., S. Wrightsman and S. W. Cook (1976) *Research Methods in Social Relations*, 3rd edn. New York: Holt, Rinehart and Winston.

Selznick, P. (1957) *Leadership in Administration – a Sociological Interpretation*. New York: Harper and Row.

Simmods, K. (1968) 'Removing the Chains from Product Strategy', *Journal of Management Studies*.

Simon, H. A. (1976) *Administrative Behaviour*, 3rd edn. New York: The Free Press.

Song, X. M. and M. E. Parry (1996) 'What Separates Japanese New Product Winners from Losers?', *Journal of Product Innovation Management*, 13, 5, 422–39.

Song, X. M. and M. E. Parry (1997) 'The Determinants of Japanese New Product Success', *Journal of Marketing Research*, 34, 64–76.

Sonnecken, E. H. and D. O. Hurst (1960) 'How to Audit Your Existing Products for Profit', *Management Methods*.

Spital, Francis C. (1983) 'Gaining Market Share Advantage in the Semiconductor Industry by Lead Time in Innovation', in *Research on Technological Innovation, Management and Policy*, R. Rosenbloom, ed. Greenwich, Conn.: JAI Press, 55–67.

Stalk, George Jr (1988) 'Time – the Next Source of Competitive Advantage', in *Strategy: Seeking and Securing Competitive Advantage*, Cunthia A. Montgomery and Michael E. Porter, eds. Cambridge, Mass.: Harvard Business Press, 39–60.

Stalk, George Jr and Thomas M. Hout (1990) *Competing Against Time*. New York: The Free Press.

Still, Richard R. and John S. Hill (1985) 'Multinational Product Planning: a Meta-Market Analysis', *International Marketing Review*, 2.

Stopford, J. M. and L. T. Wells (1972) *Managing the Multinational Enterprise*. New York: Basic Books.

Sullivan, D. (1992) 'Organization in American MNCs: the Perspective of the European Regional Headquarters', *Management International Review*, 32, 237–50.

Sullivan, D. and A. Bauerschmidt (1991) 'The "Basic Concepts" of International Business Strategy: a Review and Reconsideration', *Management International Review*, 31, 111–24.

Sultan, Fareena, Farley, John U. and Lehmann, Donald R. (1990) 'A Meta-Analysis of Applications of Diffusion Models', *Journal of Marketing Research*, XXVII, 70–7.

Szakasits, G. G. (1974) 'The Adoption of the SAPPHO Method in the Hungarian Electronics Industry', *Research Policy*, 64, 18–28.

Szymanski, David M., Sundar G. Bharadwaj and P. R. Varadarajan (1993) 'Standardisation versus Adaptation of International Marketing Strategy: an Empirical Investigation', *Journal of Marketing*, 57, 1–17.

Szymanski, David M., Lisa C. Troy and Sundar G. Bharadwaj (1995) 'Order of Entry and Business Performance: an Empirical Synthesis and Reexamination', *Journal of Marketing*, 59, 17–33.

Takeutchi, H. and I. Nonaka (1986) 'The New Product Development Game', *Harvard Business Review*, 64, 137–46.

Takeutchi, H. and Michael E. Porter (1986) 'Three Roles of International Marketing in Global Competition', in *Competition in Global Industries*, Michael E. Porter, ed. Boston: Harvard Business School Press, 111–46.

Tavlaridis, Ioannis (1989) 'A Product Deletion in Greek Manufacturing Industry', unpublished MPhil. thesis, University of Strathclyde, Glasgow.

Teece, D. J. (1977) 'Technology Transfer by Multinational Firms: the Resource Cost of Transferring Technical Knowhow', *Economic Journal*, 87, June, 242–261.

Thölke, Jurg M., E. J, Hultink and H. S. J. Robben (2001) 'Launching New Product Features: a Multiple Case Examination', *Journal of Product Innovation Management*, 18, 3–14.

Thomas, H. and D. Gardner (eds) (1985) *Strategic Marketing and Management*. Chichester: John Wiley.

Thompson, J. D. (1967) *Organizations in Action*. New York: McGraw-Hill.

Ting, W. (1982) 'The Product Development Process in NIC Multinationals', *Columbia Journal of World Business*, 76–81.

Turnbull, P. W. (1987) 'A Challenge to the Stages Theory of the Internationalisation Process', in *Managing Export Market and Expansion: Concepts and Practice*, Philip Rosson and D. Stanley Reid, eds. New York: Praeger.

Turnbull, P. W. (1987) 'Interaction and International Marketing: an Investment Process', *International Marketing Review*, 7–19.

Turnbull, P. W. and Jean-Paul Valla (1986) *Strategies for International Industrial Marketing*. London: Croom Helm.

Ughanwa, D. and Michael J. Baker (1989) *The Role of Design in International Competitiveness*. London: Routledge.

Urban, Glen L., Theresa Carter, Steven Gaskin and Zofia Mucha (1986) 'Market Share Rewards to Pioneering Brands – an Empirical Analysis and Strategic Implications', *Management Science*, 32, 645–59.

Van Maanen, J. (1979) 'The Fact of Fiction in Organizational Ethnography', *Administrative Science Quarterly*, 24, 539–51.

Varadarajan, Rajan P. (1990) 'Product Portfolio Analysis and Market Share Objectives: an Exposition of Certain Underlying Relationships', *Journal of the Academy of Marketing Science*, 18, 17–29.

Vázquez, Margarita, M.Liz and J. Aracil (1996) 'Knowledge and Reality: Some Conceptual Issues in System Dynamics Modeling', *System Dynamics Review*, 12, 1, 21–37.

Vernon, Raymond (1966) 'International Trade and International Investment in the Product Life Cycle', *Quarterly Journal of Economics*, 80, 190–207.

Vessey, Joseph T. (1991) 'The New Competitors: They Think in Terms of Speed-to-Market', *The Executive*, 5, 2 (May) 23–33.

Walters, Peter G. P. and Brian Toyne (1989) 'Product Modification and Standardization in International Markets: Strategic Options and Facilitating Policies', *Columbia Journal of World Business*, 37–44.

Wells, Louis T. (1968) 'A Product Life Cycle for International Trade?', *Journal of Marketing*, 32, 1–6.

Wells, Louis T. (1969) 'Test of a Product Life Cycle Model of International Trade', *Quarterly Journal of Economics*, 152–62.

Wentz, W. B., G. I. Eyrich and D. K. Stevenson (1973) 'Marketing of Products', in *Marketing Manager's Handbook*, H. Britt, ed. Darnell Corp.

Wernerfelt, B. (1984) 'A Resource Based View of the Firm', *Strategic Management Journal*, 5, 171–80.

Whitten, Ira T. (1979) *'Brand Performance in the Cigarette Industry and the Advantage to Early Entry'*, Washington, DC: Staff Report, US Federal Trade Commission.

Williamson, O. (1963) *The Economics of Discretionary Behaviour*. Englewood Cliffs, NJ: Prentice-Hall.

Wills, James, Coskun A. Samli and Laurence Jacobs (1991) 'Developing Global Products and Marketing Strategies: a Construct and A Research Agenda', *Journal of the Academy of Marketing Science*, 19, 1–10.

Wind, Jerry and Clayclamp, H. J. (1976) 'Planning Product Line Strategy: a Matrix Approach', *Journal of Marketing*, 40.

Wind, Yoram Jerry and Gary L. Lilien (1993) 'Marketing Strategy Models', in *Handbooks in OR and MS*, Vol. 5, J. Eliashberg and Gary L. Lilien, eds. New York: Elsevier Science Publishers, 773–826.

Winkler, J. (1972) *Winkler on Marketing Planning*, Cassell Associated Business Programmes.

Womack, J. P., D. T. Jones and D. Roos (1990) *The Machine that Changed the World*. New York: Harper Collins.

Wong, Veronica (2002) 'Antecedents of International New Product Rollout Timeliness', *International Marketing Review*, 19, 2, 120–132.

Worsley, Peter *et al.* (1970) *Introducing Sociology*. Harmondsworth: Penguin.

Worthing, P. M. (1971) 'The Assessment of Product Deletion Decision Indicators', in *Fortran Applications in Business Administration*, T. Schriber J. and L. Madeo A. eds. Ann Harbor: The University of Michigan.

Wortzel, L. H. and H. V. Wortzel (1981) 'Export Marketing Strategies for NIC and LDC-Based Firms', *Columbia Journal of World Business*, 51–60.

Wotruba, T. R. and Rochford, L. (1995) The Impact of New Product Introductions on Sales Management Strategy', *Journal of Personnel Selling and Sales Management*, 15, 35–51.

Wright, S. (1921) 'The Relative Importance of Heredity and Environment in Determining the Piebald Pattern of Guinea-Pigs', *Proceedings of the National Academy of Sciences*, 6, 320–32.

Yaremko, R., M., Herbert Harari, Robert C. Harrison and Elizabeth Lynn (1982) *Reference Book of Research and Statistical Methods in Psychology: for Students and Professionals*. New York: Harper and Row.

Yeoh, Poh-Lin (1994) 'Speed to Global Markets: an Empirical Prediction of New Product Success in the Ethical Pharmaceutical Industry', *European Journal of Marketing*, 28, 11, 29–49.

Yin, Robert, K. (1984) *Case Study Research Design and Methods*. Beverly Hills, CA: Sage.

Young, Stephen (1990), Editorial, *International Marketing Review*, No 4.

Young, Stephen and Neil Hood (1976) 'Perspectives on the European Marketing Strategy of US Multinationals', *European Journal of Marketing*, 10, 240–56.

Zirger, Billie Jo and Modesto A. Maidique (1990) 'A Model of New Product Development: an Empirical Test', *Management Science*, 36, 867–83.

Index